PENGUIN

THESE MY WORDS

EUNICE DE SOUZA taught English literature at St Xavier's College, Mumbai, for over thirty years and retired as head of department. She is a poet and novelist, and editor of anthologies of nineteenth- and early-twentieth century writing in English in India, among others. She has also written for children.

MELANIE SILGARDO was born and educated in Mumbai. Her involvement in the poetry scene in Mumbai in the 1980s resulted in the founding of the Newground publishing venture. She has worked in publishing both in India and in the UK where she was an editor at Virago Press for many years. She has edited anthologies of poetry and short fiction. She lives in London.

THESE MY WORDS

THE PENGUIN BOOK OF INDIAN POETRY

Edited by
EUNICE DE SOUZA
& MELANIE SILGARDO

PENGUIN BOOKS
Published by the Penguin Group
Penguin Books India Pvt. Ltd, 11 Community Centre, Panchsheel Park, New Delhi 110 017, India
Penguin Group (USA) Inc., 375 Hudson Street, New York, New York 10014, USA
Penguin Group (Canada), 90 Eglinton Avenue East, Suite 700, Toronto, Ontario, M4P 2Y3, Canada (a division of Pearson Penguin Canada Inc.)
Penguin Books Ltd, 80 Strand, London WC2R 0RL, England
Penguin Ireland, 25 St Stephen's Green, Dublin 2, Ireland (a division of Penguin Books Ltd)
Penguin Group (Australia), 707 Collins Street, Melbourne, Victoria 3008, Australia (a division of Pearson Australia Group Pty Ltd)
Penguin Group (NZ), 67 Apollo Drive, Rosedale, Auckland 0632, New Zealand (a division of Pearson New Zealand Ltd)
Penguin Group (South Africa) (Pty) Ltd, 24 Sturdee Avenue, Rosebank, Johannesburg 2196, South Africa

Penguin Books Ltd, Registered Offices: 80 Strand, London WC2R 0RL, England

First published by Penguin Books India 2012

Anthology copyright © Penguin Books India 2012
Introduction copyright © Eunice de Souza and Melanie Silgardo 2012

Pages 420–46 are an extension of the copyright page

The copyright for individual poems vests with the poets, translators or their estates

All rights reserved

10 9 8 7 6 5 4 3 2 1

While every effort has been made to trace copyright holders and obtain permission, this has not been possible in all cases; any omissions brought to our attention will be remedied in future editions.

ISBN 9780143414537

Typeset in Adobe Jenson Pro by Eleven Arts, Delhi
Printed at HT Media Ltd, Noida

This book is sold subject to the condition that it shall not, by way of trade or otherwise, be lent, resold, hired out, or otherwise circulated without the publisher's prior written consent in any form of binding or cover other than that in which it is published and without a similar condition including this condition being imposed on the subsequent purchaser and without limiting the rights under copyright reserved above. No part of this publication may be reproduced, stored in or introduced into a retrieval system, or transmitted in any form or by any means (electronic, mechanical, photocopying, recording or otherwise), without the prior written permission of both the copyright owner and the above-mentioned publisher of this book.

ALWAYS LEARNING   **PEARSON**

Contents

Introduction xxi

'WHAT THEN SHALL POETRY BE ABOUT?' 1
Arun Kamble/Which Language Should I Speak?/Marathi 3
Kalidasa/Is Poetry Always Worthy When It's Old?/Sanskrit 3
Ezhuthacchan/*From* Adhyatma Ramayana/Malayalam 4
Nissim Ezekiel/Poet, Lover, Birdwatcher/English 4
Michael Madhusudan Dutt/Banglabhasha/Bangla 5
Agha Shahid Ali/In Arabic/English 6
Chandrasekhar Kambar/The Character I Created/Kannada 7
Hemant Divate/The Average Temperature of a Word Required for it to be Used in a Line of Poetry/Marathi 8
Nara (Velcheru Narayana Rao)/White Paper/Telugu 9
K. Satchidanandan/Gandhi and Poetry/Malayalam 10
Debarati Mitra/Alphabet/Bangla 11
Nanne Coda/*From* On Poetry in Telugu/Telugu 13
Bhavabhuti/If Learned Critics Publicly Deride/Sanskrit 15
Meena Kandasamy/Mulligatawny Dreams/English 15
Kunchan Nambiar/*From* Prologue to The Progress to the Palace/Malayalam 16
Chellapilla Venkata Sastri/I Was Born for Poetry/Telugu 17

Mona Zote/What Poetry Means to Ernestina in
Peril/English 17
Hiren Bhattacharya/These My Words/Assamiya 19
J.P. Das/After Gujarat/Oriya 19
Arvind/First Poem/Dogri 21
Govindadas Jha/Homage to Jayadeva/Maithili 22
Kazi Nazrul Islam/*From* My Explanation/Bangla 23
Rituraj/Poets/Hindi 24
Vallathol Narayana Menon/*From* Faith and Erudition/Malayalam 25
Nilmani Phookan/Poetry Is for Those Who Wouldn't Read It/
Assamiya 27
Firaq Gorakhpuri/If There Are No Flowers/Urdu 28
Smita Agarwal/Daywatch in the Scriptorium/English 29
Sunil Gangopadhyay/City of Memories/Bangla 30
Bhartrhari/Her Face Is Not the Moon, Nor Are Her Eyes/Sanskrit 31
Dilip Chitre/Evenings in Iowa City, Iowa/English 31
Thangjam Ibopishak/Poem/Manipuri 32
Mangalesh Dabral/Outside/Hindi 33
Jayavallabha/On Poetry/Prakrit 33
Buddhadeva Bose/For My Forty-Eighth Winter: 2/Bangla 35
B.C. Ramchandra Sharma/An Old Tale from China/Kannada 36
Kedarnath Singh/On Reading a Love Poem/Hindi 37

'IN YOUR GRACIOUS GARDEN' 41

From the Rig Veda/Creation Hymn/Sanskrit 43
From the oral Kannada epic Halumatha Mahakavya/Kannada 44
Akhtar-ul Iman/Creation/Urdu 45
Harihara/*From* Girija Kalyana/Kannada 45

Amiya Chakravarty/Calcutta/Bangla 46
R.V. Pandit/My Goa/Konkani 47
Anon, Gujarati Folk Song/Rain of the World/Gujarati 48
Jyotirmoy Datta/Crabs on the Beach/Bangla 49
Vikram Seth/Flash/English 50
Gajanan Madhav Muktibodh/A Single Shooting Star/Hindi 51
Greece Chunder Dutt/Water Fowl/English 52
Kalidasa/*From* The Loom of Time/Sanskrit 53
Sri Aurobindo/The Tiger and the Deer/English 56
Bana/A Stallion Wakes from His Sleep/Sanskrit 57
Anon, Punjabi Folk Song/Lullaby/Punjabi 58
Anon, Santhal Ritual Song/Erok Sim Bonga/Santhali 58
Sarojini Naidu/The Bird Sanctuary/English 59
Jayavallabha/Summer/Prakrit 60
Sri Jnanadeva/Life of the Opened Self/Marathi 60
Rabindranath Tagore/*From* Gitanjali, 100/Bangla 62
Subramania Bharati/Wind, 9/Tamil 64
A Hymn to Night for Protection and Prosperity/Sanskrit 65
From the Isa Upanishads/Sanskrit 66
Umashankar Joshi/Miles upon Miles/Gujarati 67
Vyasa/*From* the Bhagvad Gita/Sanskrit 68
Eunice de Souza/Learn from the Almond Leaf/English 70
Melanie Silgardo/The Earthworm's Story/English 71
Siddhartha Menon/Beetles/English 71
Santan Rodrigues/The Hang/English 72
Anand Thakore/Tusker Kills Mahout at Religious Ceremony/English 73

'ARE YOU LOOKING FOR A GOD?' 77

Sankaracarya/*From* Sivahandakahari/Sanskrit 79

Rasananda/Many Many Aeons/Oriya 79

Nammalvar/Love's Messengers/Tamil 80

Vidyapati/Imaginary Re-union 2/Maithili 81

Periyazhwar (Vishnuchittan)/*From* Hush-a-bye Baby/Tamil 81

Akkamahadevi/Like an Elephant, Caught/Kannada 82

Arun Kolatkar/Yeshwant Rao/English 83

Arul Cellatturai/Little House (6)/Tamil 85

Muktabai/Open the Wattle-door, O Jnaneshwar!/Marathi 86

Eesar Das Barhat/Let the Pot with Just Water in It/Rajasthani 87

Kanakadasa/Saku Saku/Kannada 88

Allama Prabhu/It's Dark Above the Clutching Hand/Kannada 89

Bahinabhai Chaudhuri/*From* Bahinabai's Life and Thinking/Marathi 89

The Dove of Death/Sanskrit 90

Guru Nanak/Chet (March–April)/Punjabi 91

Basavanna/Like a Monkey on a Tree/Kannada 92

Devadurllabha Das/*From* Rahasya Manjari/Oriya 92

Janabai/God My Darling/Marathi 93

Bullah Shah/Strange Are the Times/Punjabi 93

Amir Khusrau/Ghazal 257: Poverty Is More Pleasant than Majesty/Persian 94

Sheikh Mohamad/So It Is Done by God Gopal/Marathi 95

Namdev/*From* Returning from the Pilgrimage/Marathi 96

Harinath Majumdar/Jaya/Bangla 96

Sheikh Farid/*From* Eight Poems/Punjabi 97

Vipin Parikh/I Want a God.../Gujarati 98

Periyalvar/Who Shall Deliver Me from the Body of This Death?/
Tamil 99

Mohammad Iqbal/Man and God/Urdu 100

Eknath/Wonder of Wonders/Marathi 101

Puspadanta/*From* Sivamahimnahstava/Sanskrit 101

Akha/Vaishnav Struts About Town/Gujarati 102

Ma Basanti Cakrabartti/Ma, If You Wore a Benarasi Sari/Bangla 103

Joaquim Miranda/*From* Jesus Entered the Garden/Konkani 104

Annamayya/Imagine That I Wasn't Here/Tamil 104

Narsinh (Narsi) Mehta/If You Abuse Me with Your Language/
Gujarati 105

Anapiyya/Come So I Can Bedeck, with Anklets and Bells/Tamil 106

Mahadeviyakka/He Bartered My Heart/Kannada 107

Ksetrayya/A Courtesan to Her Lover/Telugu 107

Mirabai/This Pain Has Driven Me Mad/Hindi 108

Palalikkuttar/*From* Tiruccentur Pillaittamil/Tamil 109

Kazi Nazrul Islam/Let's Be Girls, Ma/Bangla 110

Sakalesha Madarasa/Both of Us Are Tired/Kannada 111

Tukaram/God's Own Dog: VI/Marathi 112

Salabega/O Sakhi, the Flute Plays in the Grove/Oriya 112

Ramprasad Sen/What a Joke!/Bangla 113

Tyagaraja/Tell Me Why This Bad Mood Now/Tamil 114

Purandara Dasa/I Swear/Kannada 115

Andal/*From* Tiruppavai/Tamil 116

Subramania Bharati/Krishna the Omnipresent/Tamil 116

S. Joseph/My Sister's Bible/Malayalam 117

Kailash Vajpeyi/Momin/Hindi 118

Minal Sarosh/On the Loft/English 118

'I'M EVER VIGILANT' 119

Ravji Patel/Whirlwind/Gujarati 121

Dhoomil/A City, an Evening, and an Old Man: Me/Hindi 122

Nilakantha Dikshita/*From* Peace/Sanskrit 123

Jayanta Mahapatra/The Abandoned British Cemetery at Balasore, India/English 126

Mahadevi Verma/No Matter the Way Be Unknown/Hindi 128

Nissim Ezekiel/Background, Casually/English 129

Jaya Mehta/When a Stone Is in One's Hands/Gujarati 132

Nirendranath Chakravarti/Old Age/Bangla 133

Firaq Gorakhpuri/Annihilate the Stillness of the Evening/Urdu 134

Narayana/On Hunger/Sanskrit 135

Vinod Kumar Shukla/Those That Will Never Come to My Home/Hindi 135

Mangesh Padgaonkar/Lamp/Marathi 136

Melanie Silgardo/Between/English 137

Basudev Sunani/Satyabhama/Oriya 138

R. Parthasarathy/Taj Mahal/English 140

Shanmuga Subbiah/Salutations/Tamil 141

Dhan Gopal Mukerji/In Bedlam/English 142

Manohar Shetty/Rumour/English 142

Attoor Ravi Varma/Sitting/Malayalam 143

A.K. Ramanujan/Anxiety/English 144

Aziz Bano Darab/Ghazals/Urdu 145

Kunwar Narain/Day by Day/Hindi 145

Bal Sitaram Mardhekar/This Is the Order/Marathi 147

Tishani Doshi/Homecoming/English 148

Padma Sachdev/Sun/Dogri 149

Jerry Pinto/Window/English 150
The Empress Nur Jahan/On the Tomb of Us Poor People/Persian 150
Kutti Revathi/Breasts/Tamil 151
Jyotsna Karmakar/To Grandmother, Long After/Bangla 152
Ranjit Hoskote/Fern/English 152
Adil Mansuri/The City/Gujarati 153
Sitakant Mahapatra/Time Does Not Fly/Oriya 153
Balachandran Chullikkad/A Labourer's Laughter II/Malayalam 155
Jeet Thayil/Spiritus Mundi/English 155
Sitanshu Yashashchandra/Solar/Gujarati 158
Susmita Bhattacharya/Five Acts/Bangla 158
Keki Daruwalla/Map-maker/English 159
Lal Ded/*From* I, Lalla: The Poems of Lal Ded/Kashmiri 162
Pravin Gadhvi/Shadow/Gujarati 162
Mrinal Pande/Two Women Knitting/Hindi 163
Anon, Rajputana Folk Song/A Child-Husband/Rajasthani 164
Gieve Patel/The Ambiguous Fate of Gieve Patel, He Being Neither Muslim Nor Hindu in India/English 165
Gagan Gill/The Girl's Desire Moves among Her Bangles/Hindi 166
Ali Sardar Jafri/A Poem/Urdu 167
Valmiki/Sita's Disgrace/Sanskrit 167
Valmiki/Lanka/Sanskrit 172
Mirza Asadullah Khan Ghalib/On Drinking/Urdu 173

'MY HEART'S OWN LOVE' 175

Punam Nambudiri/The Moon-Rise/Malayalam 177
Habba Khatoon/I Will Seek You Down the Wandering Brooks/Kashmiri 178

Mahe Jabeen/A Love Poem/Telugu 178

Baladev Rath/Oh, Pardon Me/Oriya 179

Amaru/She Neither Turned Away/Sanskrit 181

Palai Patiya Perunkatunko/There Are Good Omens: The House-Lizard Chirps/Tamil 181

Vedanta Deshika/*From* the Prologue of Mission of the Goose/Sanskrit 182

Leela Gandhi/Noun/English 184

Waris Shah/*From* Heer-Ranjha/Punjabi 185

Mustansir Dalvi/Peabody/English 186

Anon, Rajputana Folk Song/The Jewel Knight/Rajasthani 187

Bilhana/*From* Fifty Stanzas of a Thief/Sanskrit 188

Anon, Chhattisgarh Field Song/Complaints/Chhattisgarhi 189

Anon, Punjabi Song/The Ballad of Laila/Punjabi 191

Chandidas/The First Stage of Radha's Love/Bangla 192

Shah 'Madho Lal' Husain/Open the Book, Brother Brahmin/Punjabi 193

Jayadeva/*Fom* Gita Govinda: Song Seven/Sanskrit 194

Habba Khatoon/Let's Go to the Upland Woods, My Friend/Kashmiri 196

Kutti Revathi/I've Brought This Summer Just for You/Tamil 197

Dom Moraes/Asleep/English 198

Harsha/*From* Ratnavali/Sanskrit 199

Anon, Goan Folk Song/On the Banks of a Lake/Konkani 199

Ilanko Atikal/The Song of Praise/Tamil 200

Anon/The Dalliance of the Leopards/Sanskrit 203

Anon/Love Song/Gondi 203

Anon/Distance Destroys Love/Prakrit 204

Anon/The Song of Phatmal/Rajasthani 204
Janna/*From* The Tale of the Glory-Bearer/Kannada 205
Cempulappeyanirar/What He Said/Tamil 208
Allur Nanmullai/What She Said/Tamil 209
Anon/Song/Sanskrit 209
Annamayya/A Woman Talking to Herself/Telugu 210
Shah Abdul Latif/The Wayward Heart/Sindhi 211
Anon/His Infatuates Complain/Tamil 213
Mir Taqi Mir/The Miracle of Wine/Urdu 213

'THE BROOM'S THE LIMIT' 215
Amrita Pritam/Daily Wages/Punjabi 217
Balraj Komal/Saba's Hands Wear a Bridal Henna Tint Now/Urdu 218
Bhanudatta/*From* Bouquet of Rasa/Sanskrit 219
Balaram Das/*From* Lakshmi Purana/Oriya 219
Sutapa Bhattacharya/Draupadi/Bangla 221
Kamala Das/The Stone Age/English 222
Cantirakanti/Wanted: A Broom/Tamil 223
Trilochan/Champa Doesn't Know Her Alphabet/Hindi 224
Arundhathi Subramaniam/Tree/English 225
Sumangala's Mother/'Tis Well with Me/Pali 226
Anon, Gujarati Folk Song/My Husband's Home/Gujarati 226
Soma/The Sceptic Says/Pali 227
Rukmini Bhaya Nair/Paranomasia/English 227
Harindra Dave/The Speck/Gujarati 229
Kadammanitta Ramakrishnan/Tar and Broom/Malayalam 229
Mamta Kalia/Compulsions/English 231

Tukaram/Where Did It Go Wrong?/Marathi 232
Anon, Rajputana Folk Song/There Is No Limit to Desire/Rajasthani 233
Shakunt Mathur/Waiting/Hindi 234
Shobha Bhagwat/Husbands/Marathi 235
Bilqees Zafirul Hasan/Dignity/Urdu 236
Anon/Let Faithful Wives/Prakrit 237
Anon, Gujarati Folk Song/Room Zoom/Gujarati 238
Bihari/What One of Her Companions Said to Another/Hindi 238

'THE SKY BETWEEN US' 239

Manohar Shetty/Personal Effects/English 241
Anuradha Mahapatra/Cow and Grandmother/Bangla 242
Markanda Das/*From* To the Cuckoo/Oriya 243
Shakti Chattopadhyay/A Memory Comes Back/Bangla 244
Srinivas Rayaprol/Married Love/English 244
Dhurjati/My Chest Has Been Worn Away/Telugu 245
G.S. Shivarudrappa/My Pocket/Kannada 246
Natwarlal Pandya 'Ushnas'/I, My Father/Gujarati 246
Anon, Bodo Folk Song/Marriage Song/Bodo 247
Madeshwara/*From* Male Madeshwara/Kannada 248
Gnanakoothan/Son to Mother/Tamil 250
Anjum Hasan/In My Mother's Clothes/English 251
B.S. Mardhekar/Son-in-law/Marathi 252
Narsinh Mehta/Here Is a Palanquin/Gujarati 253
O.N.V. Kurup/Those Who Have Lost the Nectar/Malayalam 255
Nirmal Prabha Bordoloi/In the Smell of Rice Fields in Autumn/Assamiya 256
Daljit Nagra/In a White Town/English 256

S.A. Usha/To Mother/Kannada 257
Anon, Satpura Folk Song/On One Side of the Ganga/Gondi 258
Kampan/Patalam 8; Jatayu Gives Up His Life/Tamil 259
Tulsidas/Childhood of Rama/Hindi 261
Vinda Karandikar/A Stalemate/Marathi 262
Adil Jussawalla/Colour Problems in the Family/English 263
G.J.V. Prasad/Desperately Seeking India/English 264
Imtiaz Dharker/Bombay, Mumbai/English 265
Vinod Kumar Shukla/Dhaulagiri/Hindi 266

'RIVER OF BLOOD' 269

Keshav Malik/In Praise of Guns/English 271
Sri Sri/Really?/Telugu 272
The Bedas of Haligali/Kannada 273
Ajneya/Hiroshima/Hindi 274
Amrita Pritam/Ode to Waris Shah/Punjabi 275
Anon, Songs from the North (Kerala)/*From* Unniyarcha and Aromal Unni/Malayalam 276
Imtiaz Dharker/Gaddi Aa Gayi/English 279
Faiz Ahmad Faiz/The Morning of Freedom, 15th August 1947/Urdu 280
Robin Ngangom/Flight/Manipuri 281
Anon/How Do I Know This Is My Son/Tamil 282
Tenneti Suri/Here Comes God/Telugu 283
K. Ayyappa Paniker/Philistines/Malayalam 284
Auvaiyar/Elegy (for Anci)/Tamil 284
Khadar Mohiuddin/A Certain Fiction Bit Me/Telugu 285
Akbar Ilahabadi/Satirical Verses/Urdu 287
Rangrelo Bithu/Praises Galore to the Land of Dhat/Rajasthani 288
Vanparanar/A Woman and Her Dying Warrior/Tamil 289

Sarala Das/*From* the Mahabharata/Oriya 290
Mirza Mohammad Rafi Sauda/*From* The State of the Realm/Urdu 291
Ajneya/Kalemegdan/Hindi 293
Raghuvir Sahay/Cycle Rickshaw/Hindi 294
Jaysinh Birjepatil/The Secunderabad Club/English 294
Shrikant Varma/Process/Hindi 296
Tabish Khair/Remembering Tiananmen/English 297
Lakhmi Khilani/When That Day Comes/Sindhi 298
Kunwar Narain/Ayodhya/Hindi 299
Vyasa/Bhishma and Parsurama Engage in Combat/Sanskrit 300
Gandhari's Lament for the Slain/Sanskrit 302
Anon, Political Song/This Night Is Endless/Bangla 305
Pash/No, I Am Not Losing My Sleep/Punjabi 306
Narayan Surve/Lifetime/Marathi 307
Sarveshwar Dayal Saxena/Red Bicycle/Hindi 308
Nirala/Breaking Stones/Hindi 309
Chandrashekara Patil/Once Upon a Time/Kannada 310
Purandara Dasa/Where Are the Untouchables/Kannada 311
Gieve Patel/Continuum/English 312
Anon/An Epic of the Dungri Bhils/Gujarati 313

'SLEEP ON YOUR LEFT SIDE' 317
Arvind Krishna Mehrotra/Bhojpuri Descant/English 319
Bhavabhuti/Rama's Last Act/Sanskrit 322
Gopal Honnalgere/How to Tame a Pair of New Chappals/English 323
Dharmakirti/The Tradition/Sanskrit 324

Siddalingaiah/I Must Have a Word/Kannada 325
Vallana/The Oblique Invitation/Sanskrit 326
Ravidas/I've Never Known How to Tan or Sew/Hindi 326
Jibanananda Das/A Strange Darkness/Bangla 327
Kabir/Let's Go/Hindi 327
Vemana/Why Marry?/Telugu 328
Kanaka Ha Ma/Series of Omens/Kannada 329
Anon/*From* The Art of the Courtesan/Malayalam 330
Ravji Patel/That Afternoon/Gujarati 331
Rabindranath Tagore/They Call You Mad/English 331
Jayavallabha/What She Told Her Daughter about Unchaste Women/Prakrit 332
The Dhammapada/*From* The Fool/Pali 333
Namdeo Dhasal/Stone Masons, My Father, and Me/Marathi 334
Kabir/Listen Carefully/Hindi 335
M. Gopalakrishna Adiga/Do Something, Brother/Kannada 336
Asvaghosa/*From* Buddhacarita/Sanskrit 338
Kynpham Sing Nongkynrih/Lines Written to Mothers Who Disagree with Their Sons' Choices of Women/Khasi 342
Siddaramayya/Know How to Tell/Kannada 342
Vijay Nambisan/Madras Central/English 343
Sarangapani/A Wife's Complaint/Telugu 344
Devara Dasimayya/Fire Can Burn/Kannada 346
Hemacandra Suri/O Learned Man/Prakrit 346
Sami/Six Shastras, Eight Puranas, and Four Vedas/Sindhi 347
Vijayalakshmi/What Shall We Sell Next?/Malayalam 347
Anon/A Celibate Monk Shouldn't Fall in Love/Prakrit 348
A.K. Ramanujan/The Guru/English 350

'LIGHT LIKE ASH' 353

Mamang Dai/A Stone Breaks the Sleeping Water/English 355
Joy Goswami/A Mound of Earth, a Heart/Bangla 355
Pranabendu Dasgupta/Man: 1961/Bangla 356
Anon, Kashmiri Song/Nostalgia/Kashmiri 357
B.B. Borkar/Cemetery/Marathi 358
G.S. Sharat Chandra/Facts of Life/English 359
Bhatti/Vibishana's Lament for Ravana/Sanskrit 360
Dursa Adha/On Hearing of Pratap's Passing Away/Rajasthani 361
Adil Jussawalla/Nine Poems on Arrival/English 361
Ramakanta Rath/Reports of Your Passing/Oriya 363
Indira Sant/Absence/Marathi 365
C.P. Surendran/The Colours of the Season's Best Dream/English 366
Kedarnath Singh/Remembering the Year 1947/Hindi 366
Nita Ramaiya/The Year 1979/Gujarati 367
Gagan Gill/I Won't Come and Tell You/Hindi 368
Eunice de Souza/Songs of Innocence/English 370
Anon, Punjabi Song/Life in the Desert/Punjabi 371
Meena Alexander/Looking through Well Water/English 372
The Dhammapada/*From* Old Age/Pali 373
Henry Derozio/The Poet's Grave/English 374
Dom Moraes/Wrong Address/English 375
Balmukund Dave/Moving House/Gujarati 376
B.C. Ramchandra Sharma/On the Death of a Friend/Kannada 376
Anon, Marsiya/Come, O Sisters, Let Us Wail for Our Brothers/Urdu 378
Toru Dutt/Our Casuarina Tree/English 379
Nida Fazli/Prayers for the Dead/Urdu 381

Waris Shah/Ranjha Writes to the Bhabis/Punjabi 381
Kapilar/A Time Was When the Wine Cask/Tamil 382
Manmohan Ghose/Can It Be?/English 383
Mirza Asadullah Khan Ghalib/Lament of Old Age/Urdu 384

Notes on the Poets 385
Notes on the Translators 409
Copyright Acknowledgements 420

Introduction

'An arrow shot by an archer
or a poem made by a poet
should cut through your heart
jolting the head.
If it doesn't, it's no arrow
it's no poem.'

—Nanne Coda, Telugu

'Great translations . . . shoot to kill, and having obliterated the original, transmigrate its soul into another language.'

—Arvind Krishna Mehrotra, *The Absent Traveller*

Our editor's brief was simple—an anthology of Indian poetry from the Vedas to the present day. Of course, the publisher knew, and we knew, that this was a pretty foolhardy brief. (There are more than 300 re-tellings of the Ramayana alone). This anthology comprises almost thirty languages and dialects, all translated into the English, except of course those poems written in English. It includes poems, folk songs, and oral narratives that have now been transcribed. We have sought for a collection which tries to represent the breadth and diversity of Indian poetry—we wanted poems that surprised and delighted, poems that illuminated, and inspired further reading—a book for readers, not scholars and academics. We chose poems that worked in translation, those which crossed the boundary of language, where faithfulness to the original combined with adaptation to produced work that existed on its own merit. We have tried to be as broad and as inclusive as possible, but inevitably we will have made errors of omission. Even as we were closing out the anthology, new translations were being published. There will be other collections but this is ours—a work that has excited us most of the time and exhausted us some of the time.

There's nothing monolithic about Indian poetry, and a number of scholars, of many different nationalities, have provided us with refreshing new perspectives on what we may think of as familiar material. The Tamil Hindu devotional form, the Pillai Tamil, has been used by Muslims and Christians writing in Tamil as well. Men speak in the voices of women. God is addressed in frankly erotic terms. A mother tells a daughter that she may be forced to sleep with her husband if no other men are available in the village.[1] A poet writing in English was the first to enunciate the idea of a nation.[2]

The Mahabharata continues to be recycled in poems, plays, film, in a variety of Indian languages. The Ramayana in turn has also been used again and again to suit the objective of the writer. Paula Richman in her introduction to *Many Ramayanas* says, '[T]he telling of the Ramayana in India has included stories that conflict with one another ... Where Hindu Ramayanas have predominated,

---

[1] Poem 887, *The Absent Traveller*, selected and trans. Arvind Krishna Mehrotra, New Delhi: Ravi Dayal, 1991, p. 66.

[2] 'To India—My Native Land', Henry Derozio, *The Fakeer of Jungheera*, Calcutta: Samuel Smith Co, 1828.

Jain and Buddhist Ramayanas have criticized or questioned those texts by producing their own tellings. Where male dominance has been prescribed in textual traditions women's Ramayana songs have expressed alternative perspectives that are more in keeping with women's own concerns.'[3] In the literary epics, we are told, Rama's birth is described in glorious terms, but the women's songs describe Kausalya in labour, standing upright, holding on to a pair of ropes hung from the ceiling: 'They made Kausalya hold the ropes/Mother, mother, I cannot bear this pain/A minute feels like a hundred years'.[4] And texts such as the *Gita Govinda* marked a transition in literary terms. Krishna's transformation from great warrior as he was in the Mahabharata to great lover here reflects 'the turning away from the traditional heroism and warlike virtues towards virtues of a very different intimate and intense kind'.[5]

John Brough intended to show that Sanskrit literature did not consist exclusively of works like the Upanishads and the Bhagavad Gita and that 'life in India was not universally passed in a haze of theosophical speculation and other-worldly religious preoccupations'.[6] Ingalls chose poems from the *Treasury* of Vidyakara, an anthology of love poetry. Interestingly, Vidyakara was a Buddhist scholar and a monk or priest of high office at the monastery of Jagaddala in Bengal. The anthology begins with

[3] Paula Richman, *Introduction to Many Ramayanas: The Diversity of a Narrative Tradition in South Asia*, p. 9, ed. Paula Richman, Oxford University Press, 1992.

[4] Ibid., Anon, Andhra Pradesh Women's Song, from the *Ramayana*, 'A Description of Kaushalya in Labour', in the essay 'A Ramayana of Their Own' by Velcheru Narayana Rao, p. 119.

[5] Sudipta Kaviraj, Foreword to *Gita Govinda: Love Songs of Radha and Krishna* by Jayadeva, p.xxi, trans. Lee Siegel, Clay Sanskrit Library Series, New York University Press, 2009.

[6] John Brough, *Poems from the Sanskrit*, Penguin UK, 1968, p. 11.

religious poetry from various monasteries but, as Ingalls amusingly remarks, 'One is surprised, and I own I am pleased, by the good abbot's liking for love poetry. By statistical count it considerably outweighs his interest in religion.'[7] We just about thought we'd reached closure after four years of searching and sorting when we discovered the exceptional Clay Sanskrit Library series which breathes fresh life into so many of the Sanskrit classics. We literally had to start over, but the discovery of some freshly translated gems—the wonderful love poems of Amaru and Bhartri-hari, the exquisite new translation of *Gita Govinda* to name a few—made it all worthwhile.

The Interior Landscape: Love Poems from a Classical Tamil Anthology is the first of many invaluable books translated and edited by the poet A.K. Ramanujan, which enriched our understanding of the secular and devotional poetry of the south. He himself wrote in Kannada and in English, and researched material in Tamil, Telugu, Sanskrit and English. In *The Interior Landscape*, Ramanujan explores the exquisite poetry of one of the earliest surviving texts of Tamil poetry, the *Kuruntokai*, an anthology of love lyrics. 'In their antiquity and in their contemporaneity, there is not much else in any Indian literature equal to these quiet dramatic Tamil poems,' Ramanujan writes. 'These poems are not just the earliest evidence of the Tamil genius—the Tamils, in all their 2,000 years of literary effort, wrote nothing better.'[8]

Sanskrit and Tamil both had their conventions of love poetry. In Sanskrit poetry, for instance, jealousy could be expressed by a woman but not by a man. A man expressing jealousy would be

---

[7] Daniel Ingalls, General Introduction, *Sanskrit Poetry: From Vidyakara's 'Treasury'*, trans. Daniel Ingalls, Harvard University Press, 1972, p. 32.

[8] A.K. Ramanujan, *The Interior Landscape*, Oxford India Paperbacks, 1994, p. 11.

comic. In the Tamil poems, certain landscapes, seasons, flowers, birds and animals are always associated with certain states of mind or situations. Lovers' union (before marriage) for instance, is associated with the *kurinci* which flowers once every twelve years, with the landscape of mountains, the cold season and night. Bhanudatta wrote about the conventions that dictated the shape of Sanskrit poetry as he knew it, explaining in his *River of Rasa* the nature of the eight aesthetic emotions or rasas.[9] Bhatti in his *The Death of Ravana* uses the poem form as a vehicle to make more accessible Panini's system of grammar.[10] Other poets worked with what they saw as 'typical' emotions and situations. For example, a young man desiring a beautiful young woman on a moonlit night would be transformed into an erotic rasa. Atypical situations such as an older woman desiring a younger man would have been condemned as 'tasteless'.[11] These were conventions that remained unbroken till modern Indian poetry began to be written in which the very act of violating the expectations of convention became one of its primary attributes.

The great period of Sanskrit poetry spanned around 1500 years roughly from 300 BCE to 1200 CE with the Tamil literary period running almost concurrently with it. Early Tamil poetry from the Sangam period which represented a golden age for Tamil

---

[9] Bhanudatta, *Bouquet of Rasa & River of Rasa*, ed. and trans. Sheldon I. Pollock, Clay Sanskrit Library, New York University Press, 2009, pp. 251–341.

[10] Oliver Fallon, Introduction, p. xx, *Bhatti's Poem, The Death of Ravana* by Bhatti, trans. Oliver Fallon, Clay Sanskrit Library, New York University Press, 2009.

[11] Sheldon I. Pollock, Introduction to *Bouquet of Rasa & River of Rasa* by Bhanudatta, p. xxxiii, Clay Sanskrit Library, New York University Press, 2009

literature was one where grammar was being systematized and human behaviour and emotions classified—the knock-on effect on the poetry of the time was its classification broadly into personal (*akam*) and public (*puram*) categories, the former dealing with love and emotions the latter with war and public affairs. What is interesting is the use of the personal in the interior akam poems, where the emotion is experienced without social milieu. But, to avoid what would then be experience without context, landscapes, animals, birds, seasons were introduced into the settings to evoke mood and meaning.

The medieval pan-Indian Bhakti movement of India has been well served, and continues to be fascinating to translators. And the poems/songs/pilgrimages themselves are very much part of daily life. But even here the reader may find some surprises in some of the forms devotion took or the uses to which such poetry and the poets were put. By its very nature the Bhakti movement transcended social classification. It engaged personal experience in the pursuit of God and encouraged the vernacular to better communicate with God. Guru Nanak's poem 'Chet' uses the season of Spring when nature is bursting with new energy to highlight a crisis of faith and desertion: 'All is seemly—/The humming bumble-bee/And the woodland in flower—/But there is sorrow in my soul/The Lord, my Master is away/If the Husband does not come home, how can a wife/Find peace of mind?'

Tukaram (and many other Bhakti poets) came from a Shudra background, and, as Dilip Chitre says, 'For a Shudra like Tukaram to write poetry on religious themes in colloquial Marathi was a double encroachment on Brahmin monopoly.'[12] Even as far back in the thirteenth century the poet-saint Jnanadev wrote in his native Marathi language despite orthodox opposition. Tukaram

---

[12] Dilip Chitre, *Says Tuka*, Penguin India, 1991, p. viii.

made 'language a form of shared religion and religion a shared language'.[13] It was the Marathi poet-saints who helped mobilize the Marathas against the Mughals 'on the basis not of any ideology but of a territorial cultural identity'.[14] Even in Bengal, devotional writing which falls within the general corpus of bhakti poetry had interesting political connections and ramifications. In *Singing to the Goddess* Rachel Fell McDermott says that in the mid-eighteenth century a large number of wealthy families had adopted Durga and Kali as their clan deities. 'Many scholars,' she says, 'believe that the worship of such powerful, martial goddesses aided the zamindars in their quest for political and social prestige in a rapidly changing and unstable environment, where they had to negotiate between the rising of British ambitions and the threatened system of Mughal governance.'[15] In addition, they sometimes employed poets to write suitable devotional songs, and sometimes wrote them themselves. In the early twentieth century, 'nationalists called for Bengalis to conceive of their motherland as a goddess. Although this goddess was rarely named Kali, Durga or Uma—typically she was Ma (mother) or Bharat Mata (Mother India)—she certainly took over their functions'.[16]

In the work of a few Telugu poets, the god assumes the role of a lover, 'seen, for the most part through the eyes of one of his courtesans, mistresses or wives, whose persona he adopts. These are, then, devotional works of an erotic cast, composed by male poets using feminine voice and performed by women.'[17] In *When God is a Customer: Telugu Courtesan Songs* by Ksetrayya and others,

[13] Ibid., p xvii.
[14] Ibid.
[15] Rachel Fell McDermott, *Singing to the Goddess*, Oxford University Press 2001, p. 8.
[16] Ibid., pp. 9–10.
[17] Oxford India Paperbacks, 1995, p. 2.

edited and translated by A.K. Ramanujan, Velcheru Narayana Rao and David Schulman, the Introduction explains that the courtesan appears as a major figure because '[a]s an expressive vehicle for the manifold relations between devotee and deity, the courtesan offers rich possibilities ... Bodily experience becomes a crucial mode of knowing ... The Tamil devotee worships his deity in a sensually accessible form ... he sees, hears, tastes, smells, and perhaps above all, touches the god. But for the Telugu *padam* poets, the relation has become fully eroticised.'[18] Apologists and reformers have tried to ban some of these 'courtesan poems' as obscene or limit their access only to those with scholarly interests. Some texts have coy ellipses replacing objectionable verses; others explain that the poems were merely allegorical. Perhaps it was reforming zeal or Victorian bashfulness. Whatever the reason, the long history of erotic literature in India is a well-kept secret.

Urdu literature too suffers from stereotyped notions about it. As Mehr Afshan Farooqi says in the introduction to her two-volume Modern Urdu Literature, 'In the mind of the non-Urdu speaker, the image of Urdu literature generally consists of semi-erotic poems addressed to beautiful, cruel women or to boys, and the maker of the poem is believed to be a wandering, socially irresponsible, very nearly mentally deranged lover ...'[19] This image was created partly by Urdu scholars themselves, who blamed poetry for being 'excessively given over to shallow erotic themes,'[20] and other failures. In fact, she says, literature in Urdu began in fifteenth-century Gujarat, and consisted of philosophical–mystical poems.

It was the unsuccessful war of liberation in 1857, which occurred in Ghalib's lifetime, that 'changed the whole world for

---

[18] Ibid., p. 18.
[19] *The Oxford India Anthology of Modern Urdu Literature*, 2008 p. xvii.
[20] Ibid., p. xviii.

the Indian people in general, and for Urdu writers in particular. Old assumptions about the nature of literature and the role of man in society began to be questioned by both writers and non-writers.'[21] New genres and ideas about literature began to emerge, influenced by Western literature, by reformers and those who felt literature should be more socially responsible and progressive. The Progressive Writers Movement, founded in 1936, was pan-Indian, as were the movements they rejected: nationalism, romanticism, mysticism. The Bangla poets after Tagore were fiercely critical of his poetry and felt it had little connection with the world around them. But as always, there were counter-movements in existence at the same time: experimental poetry which produced imagist poems, surrealist and symbolist poems, confessional poems. The influence of Western literature from various countries was widespread, and sometimes led to the charge that Indian writing was, and continues to be, parasitic on Western literary movements. Adil Jussawalla writing in his 1974 Introduction to *New Writing in India* says: 'Such forms and concepts have ... spread all over the world and it would only be fair to call their use in India "parasitic" if all international cross-influences and borrowings went by that name.'[22] In English, Nissim Ezekiel reacted against the lyricism of Sarojini Naidu and the abstract metaphysical poems of Aurobindo. But, as subsequent research has shown, poets writing in English from Henry Derozio onwards were conscious of creating new kinds of poetry. Long before poets in the regional languages, Derozio enunciated a vision of India as a nation, lamenting at the same time its lost glories.

In deciding how to organize the poems in this anthology, we decided against a chronological order. What interested us was the universality and contemporariness of much of the material we

[21] Ibid., xix.
[22] Penguin UK, p. 18.

sought and selected for this book. Most of the poems seemed to fall easily into broad categories such as love, relationships, war and politics, sexual independence, identity and social awareness, religious pursuit, creation and nature, death and loss, and so on. Within these categories we have tried to arrange the poems so that they appear to speak to each other. Languages offset each other, while poets from antiquity sit alongside their modern counterparts, and those writing in English alongside those writing in regional languages.

Where do we go from here? This volume is crying out for a second one, but help us lord if we agree to do it.

Eunice de Souza
Melanie Silgardo

'What then shall poetry be about?'

Arun Kamble (b. 1953)

Which Language Should I Speak?

Chewing trotters in the badlands
my grandpa,
the permanent resident of my body,
the household of tradition heaped on his back,
hollers at me,
'You whore-son, talk like we do.
Talk, I tell you!'

Picking through the Vedas
his top-knot well-oiled with ghee,
my Brahmin teacher tells me,
'You idiot, use the language correctly!'
Now I ask you,
Which language should I speak?

Translated from the Marathi by Priya Adarkar

Kalidasa (c. 5 CE–6 CE)

Is Poetry Always Worthy When It's Old?

Is poetry always worthy when it's old?
And is it worthless, then, because it's new?
Reader, decide yourself if this is true:
Fools suspend judgement, waiting to be told.

Translated from the Sanskrit by John Brough

Ezhuthacchan (16 CE)

From Adhyatma Ramayana

Sreeramayana that runs into a hundred crores
Of books, the one Brahma composed, is not here on earth.
The savage chanting Rama's name turned into a sage,
And Brahma observing this commanded him to write
Ramayana for the deliverance of all beings on earth.
Narada's counsel Valmiki had and the goddess
Of the word dwelt forever on his tongue.
Dwell so on my tongue too: this I long to say
But am too shy so to pray.

Translated from the Malayalam by K. Satchidanandan

Nissim Ezekiel (1924–2004)

Poet, Lover, Birdwatcher

To force the pace and never to be still
Is not the way of those who study birds
Or women. The best poets wait for words.
The hunt is not an exercise of will
But patient love relaxing on a hill
To note the movement of a timid wing;
Until the one who knows that she is loved
No longer waits but risks surrendering—
In this the poet finds his moral proved
Who never spoke before his spirit moved.

The slow movement seems, somehow, to say much more.
To watch the rarer birds, you have to go

Along deserted lanes and where the rivers flow
In silence near the source, or by a shore
Remote and thorny like the heart's dark floor.
And there the women slowly turn around,
Not only flesh and bone but myths of light
With darkness at the core, and sense is found
By poets lost in crooked, restless flight,
The deaf can hear, the blind recover sight.

English

Michael Madhusudan Dutt (1824–73)

Banglabhasha

Oh Bengal, in your treasury lay assorted gemstones—
But I (foolish me!) ignored all that completely.
Maddened by lust for others' riches, I rashly ventured
To a foreign realm, there to beg and grovel.
Profligate, I wasted many a day, forfeiting real satisfaction!
Sleep deprived, my body forced to fast, Mind,
I plunged you into fruitless, worthless austere practices—
I mucked about in algae, unmindful of the lotus blossoms!

Then in a dream, your Goddess-of-the-Family, Lakshmi, spoke
'My child, in your mother's jewellery box are jewels aplenty,
So why today this state of beggary for you?
Go back, benighted one—return home, dearest!'
I happily obeyed her orders and in due time came upon
A mine—my mother tongue—replete with gems untold.

Translated from the Bangla by Clinton B. Seely

Agha Shahid Ali (1949–2001)

In Arabic

A language of loss? I have some business in Arabic.
Love letters: calligraphy pitiless in Arabic.

At an exhibit of miniatures, what Kashmiri hairs!
Each paisley inked into a golden tress in Arabic.

This much fuss about a language I don't know? So one day
perfume from a dress may let you digress in Arabic.

A 'Guide for the Perplexed' was written—believe me—
by Cordoba's jew—Maimonides—in Arabic.

Majnoon, by stopped caravans, rips his collars, cries 'Laila!'
Pain translated is O! much more— not less—in Arabic.

Writes Shammas: Memory, no longer confused, now is a homeland—
his two languages a Hebrew caress in Arabic.

When Lorca died, they left the balconies open and saw:
On the sea his *qasidas* stitched seamless in Arabic.

In the Veiled One's harem, an adultress hanged by eunuchs—
So the rank mirrors revealed to Borges in Arabic.

Ah, bisexual Heaven: wide-eyed houris and immortal youths!
To each desire they say *Yes! O Yes!* in Arabic.

For that excess of sibilance, the last Apocalypse,
so pressing those three forms of S in Arabic.

I, too, O Amichai, saw everything, just like you did—
In Death. In Hebrew. And (please let me stress) in Arabic.

They tell me to tell them what *Shahid* means: Listen, listen:
It means 'The Beloved' in Persian, 'witness' in Arabic.

English

Chandrasekhar Kambar (b. 1937)

The Character I Created

A character in my play
climbed down the stage,
came directly to me,
and took a chair next to me.

I was looking at the play,
he was looking at me.
His looks, like arrows,
pierced my heart.

If I shifted my legs
so that they should not touch his,
his legs wantonly brushed mine.
His hands fell heavily on my shoulder.

When the audience was silent
he burst out in laughter.
When he clapped, it was unnecessary.
All eyes were on him
and his were on me.

It was not just right.
I stood up and walked out.
He followed me.

As I opened the door
he went in before me.

Smiling a familiar smile
he stood—a mirror before me.

Why do these many characters,
educated by me in civility,
behave like this?

Translated from the Kannada by O.L. Nagabhushana Swamy

Hemant Divate (b. 1967)

The Average Temperature of a Word Required for it to be Used in a Line of Poetry

What is the
Average temperature required of a word
To be used in a line of poetry?
I performed this experiment on a poem
I inserted a thermometer in the armpits of words
And
I placed words in lines
Some time later
A stormy condition developed
As the atmosphere in the lines was adversely affected
By the difference between the temperature inside the words and outside them

I was scared
Of the possibility
That while treading the tangle created
By lines containing strong meaning
Exerting pressure on lines containing weak meaning
I might slip and fall tripping
Over the cursives
Or
A whole line whose meaning is backed by no experience may crash
    upon me
From a new poem about to be written
A meaningless word of low pressure
or a deletion
May hit me
Out of fear
Reluctantly I am going to stop this experiment
Of writing a poem
Now
I have closed down this lab itself

Translated from the Marathi by Dilip Chitre

Nara (Velcheru Narayana Rao) (b. 1932)

White Paper

A great man once said to me:
write whatever you want to, but on the condition—
it should be an improvement
on the blank white page.

Blank white paper
is more important

than what I write now.
My poetry
is in the white spaces
between the words.

Like news about the men
who disappeared before dawn,
like seeds buried in the soil,
like the truth that hides
between the heavy headlines,
like a fragrant green flower,
the more I write
the more poetry there is

in the white spaces between the words

Translated from the Telugu by the poet

K. Satchidanandan (b. 1946)

Gandhi and Poetry

One day a lean poem
reached Gandhi's ashram
to have a glimpse of the man.
Gandhi spinning away
His thread towards Ram
Took no notice of the poem
Waiting at his door
Ashamed of not being a bhajan.
The poem now cleared his throat
And Gandhi glanced at him sideways
Through those glasses that had seen hell.
'Ever pulled a scavenger's cart?

Ever stood the smoke of
an early morning kitchen?
Have you ever starved?'

The poem said: 'I was born in the woods,
in a hunter's mouth.
A fisherman brought me up
in a cottage.
Yet I know no work, I only sing.
First I sang in the courts:
then I was plump and handsome
but am on the streets now,
half-starved.'

'That's better,' Gandhi said
with a sly smile, 'But you must give up this habit
of speaking in Sanskrit at times.
Go to the fields. Listen to
the peasant's speech.'
The poem turned into a grain
and lay waiting in the fields
for the tiller to come
and upturn the virgin soil
moist with new rain.

Translated from the Malayalam by the poet

Debarati Mitra (b. 1946)

Alphabet

Nobody introduced the alphabet to me,
nobody taught me to read;

in this cemetery by the sea
so many days went spinning by.
The evening's flock of birds are enclosed in a blue book jacket
the unsmelled book's pages are opened every day.

Roaming around, I learn—
Leslie Louis's, Robert Louis's weeping—
Paul Louis, born 1867—died 1870
'Child, your soul is a shining white flower
may it blossom for ever in heaven's garden.'
Thus I hear aspirates.

'For Agatha at seventeen
my sky remained incomplete,
the wind had no flow, life was lacking,'
wrote Willy Sandhurst at twenty-three.
I learned long vowels by this method.

'Eighty-three-year old Mariam, my mother,
to you I pour out whatever I have
of virtue, of truth, of light
on this writing table of white stone:
may your temple stand'
—the poet Augustus's dedication.
Gradually I understand semi-vowels.

I go to the tomb—
I see the alphabet's mouth seize the stone fruit
the alphabet's soul blossoms
there are no pictures, no books.
Formless clouds make background shadow
birds come and perch on the endless causeway's breast.

I pull and tear so much of the sky's blue
the tender dawn, dyed like startled wisdom
shock nearly blind eyes.
Nobody ever taught me to read
nobody ever introduced the alphabet to me
roaming around alone
I read and write in this solitary tomb.

Translated from the Bangla by Marian Maddern

Nanne Coda (12 CE)

From On Poetry in Telugu

You can only learn about poetry
from one who knows. There's nothing to be gained
from one who doesn't. You need a touchstone,
not a limestone to test gold.

But when ideas come together in good Tenungu
without any slack, and description achieves a style,
and there are layers of meaning, and the syllables
are soft and alive with sweetness, and the words
sing to the ear and gently delight the mind,
and what is finest brings joy, and certain flashes
dazzle the eye while the poem glows like moonlight,
and the images are the very image of perfection,
and there is a brilliant flow of flavour,
and both *magra* and *desi* become the native idiom,
and figures truly transfigure, so that people of taste
love to listen and are enriched
by the fullness of meaning—

that is how poetry works, when crafted
by all real poets.

Good colour, build, apparent softness:
they're all there in a poor image, but if you look inside
it's dead. That's what a bad poet makes.
Good colour, build, softness,
inside and out: you find them
in a living woman, and in good poems.

If you look for good lines in a real poem,
they're everywhere, in dense profusion.
That is poetry. But if one goes on chattering
and, by chance, a few lines
come out well, like a blind man
stepping on a quail,
would you call that a poem?

Skilled words, charming movements,
ornaments, luminous feelings, elevated thoughts,
the taste of life—connoisseurs find all these
in poetry, as in women.

An arrow shot by an archer
or a poem made by a poet
should cut through your heart,
jolting the head.
If it doesn't, it's no arrow,
it's no poem.

Translated from the Telugu by Velcheru Narayana Rao and David Shulman

Bhavabhuti (725 CE)
If Learned Critics Publicly Deride

If learned critics publicly deride
My verse, well, let them. Not for them I wrought.
One day a man shall live to share my thought:
For time is endless and the world is wide.

Translated from the Sanskrit by John Brough

Meena Kandasamy (b. 1984)
Mulligatawny Dreams

anaconda. candy. cash. catamaran.
cheroot. coolie. corundum. curry.
ginger. mango. mulligatawny.
patchouli. poppadom. rice.
tatty. teak. vetiver.

i dream of an english
full of the words of my languages.

an english in small letters
an english that shall tire a white man's tongue
an english where small children practice with smooth round
    pebbles in their mouth to the spell the right zha
an english where a pregnant woman is simply
                             stomach-child-lady
an english where the magic of black eyes and brown bodies
    replaces the glamour of eyes in dishwater blue shades and
      the airbrush romance of pink white cherry blossom skins
an english where love means only the strange frenzy between
    a man and his beloved, not between him and his car

an english without the privacy of its many rooms
an english with suffixes for respect
an english with more than thirty-six words to call the sea
an english that doesn't belittle the brown and black men
                                                    and women
an english of tasting with five fingers
an english of talking love with eyes alone

and i dream of an english

where men
of that spiky, crunchy tongue
buy flower-garlands of jasmine
to take home to their coy wives
for the silent demand of a night of wordless whispered love . . .

English

Kunchan Nambiar (1700–70)

From Prologue to The Progress to the Palace

Men of culture would like to listen to Sanskrit verse;
but the vulgar can find no delight in it.
Before an audience of the common people
who are out to see some vibrant folk show,
only the lovely, shapely language of Kerala is proper.
If we present the sound and fury
of pedantic Sanskrit verse,
the common man won't make head or tail
of such odd and obscure concoctions
and he will just get up and leave the place.

Translated from the Malayalam by G. Kumara Pillai

Chellapilla Venkata Sastri (1870–1950)

I Was Born for Poetry

I was born for poetry.
Making good poems is my business.
That's how I'll cross to the other shore.
All my fortune comes from poetry.
I've conquered death, and I'll defeat old age.

If anyone faults my poetry, even my teacher,
even God himself, I'll fight back
and win.

Translated from the Telugu by Velcheru Narayana Rao

Mona Zote (b. 1973)

What Poetry Means to Ernestina in Peril

What should poetry mean to a woman in the hills
as she sits one long sloping summer evening
in Patria, Aizawl, her head crammed with contrary winds,
pistolling the clever stars that seem to say:
Ignoring the problem will not make it go away.
So what if Ernestina is not a name at all,
not even a corruption, less than a monument. She will sit
pulling on one thin cigarillo after another, will lift her teacup
in friendly greeting to the hills and loquacious stars
and the music will comb on through her hair,
telling her: *Poetry must be raw like a side of beef,*
should drip blood, remind you of sweat
and dusty slaughter and the epidermal crunch
and the sudden bullet to the head.

The sudden bullet in the head. Thus she sits, calmly gathered.
The lizard in her blinks and thinks. She will answer:
The dog was mad that bit me. Later, they cut out my third eye
and left it in a jar on a hospital shelf. That was when the drums began.
Since then I have met the patron saint of sots and cirrhosis who used to stand
in every corner until the police chased her down. She jumped into a taxi.
Now I have turned into the girl with the black guitar
and it was the dog who died. Such is blood.
The rustle of Ernestina's skirt will not reveal the sinful vine
or the cicada crumbling to a pair of wings at her feet.
She will smile and say: *I like a land where babies*
are ripped out of their graves, where the church
leads to practical results like illegitimate children and bad marriages
quite out of proportion to the current population, and your neighbour
is kidnapped by demons and the young wither without complaint
and pious women know the sexual ecstasy of dance and peace is kept
by short men with a Bible and five big knuckles on their righteous hands.
Religion has made drunks of us all. The old goat bleats.
We are killing ourselves. I like an incestuous land. Stars, be silent.
Let Ernestina speak.
So what if the roses are in disarray? She will rise
with a look of terror too real to be comical.
The conspiracy in the greenhouse the committee of good women
They have marked her down
They are coming   the dead dogs the yellow popes
They are coming   the choristers of stone
We have been bombed silly out of our minds.
Waiter, bring me something cold and hard to drink.
Somewhere there is a desert waiting for me
and someday I will walk into it.

English

Hiren Bhattacharya (b. 1932)

These My Words

In these, the words that have caressed
The orchards of my dreams.
In the grace of a lifestyle,
The intimate warmth of time.

I have no inventions of my own.
Like a farmer
I roll words on my tongue,
Tasting every one.
I hold them in my palm
To find how warm they are.

I know words are the lusty offspring
Of man's noble creation.
I am a mere poet;
And in these words that I have relayed
From other shoulders,
Is man's cruel experience
And the maulings of history.

Translated from the Assamiya by D.N. Bezboruah

J.P. Das (b. 1936)

After Gujarat

After Gujarat,
will there be poetry?
Was it possible
to write poetry

after Alexandria was burnt down?
After Auschwitz,
after Hiroshima and Vietnam,
after the Emergency
and Babri Masjid,
after 9/11 and Iraq?

It's not possible
to banish poetry.
Poetry comes back effortless
to Plato's Republic,
to Stalin's Siberia,
to Pokhran and Kalahandi.
Poetry follows
the footprints of violence
as it chronicles
the descent of man.
Like history
poetry has no end.

Poetry is written
despite fatwas and bans.
Poetry laughs at Gulag,
ignores the censor's blue pencil
and the fundamentalist's frown.
Poetry is written
against the backdrop
of bonfire of books.

After Gujarat
there will be poetry
about Gujarat itself.

It will begin
with the shame of Ayodhya,
and track the bloody trail
to Godhra to Gujarat,
on to Mumbai.

When Babri arises again,
poetry will affirm
that temples are built
not with blood-scribed bricks
and stones carved with hatred,
temples are built,
like poetry,
with imagination and faith
in the hearts of men.

After Gujarat,
poems will be written
to affirm the truth
that there is no Ayodhya
outside of the poet's
epic imagination.

Translated from the Oriya by the poet

Arvind (b. 1950)

First Poem

My best poem
Is the one
That I began to write

On a smouldering evening,
In the eighteenth year of my life.
That's the prettiest of my poems.
An unknown feeling stirred in my mind
It was a very tender feeling and I was shy
I couldn't comprehend it
Nor could I articulate it
It couldn't be kept suppressed either.
I picked up a piece of paper and a pen
I had no knowledge of rhyme rhythm or metre
My feeling,
Like a rainy season *nullah*
Gushed from my eyes.
My hand trembled
It scribbled something, rubbed something out.
That wet piece of paper,
Those smudged words,
That was my first poem
The best of all my poems.

Translated from the Dogri by Shivanath

Govindadas Jha (1570–1640)

Homage to Jayadeva

Jayadeva, the paragon of poets,
Is the divine wish-fulfilling tree,
In the shade of whose verdant foliage of songs,
My heart, tormented with the heat of worldly existence
Derives a rare soothing cool, and yearns
To submerge itself into it more and more!

Glory to Jayadeva, blessed with Padmavati's boundless love,
The master supreme among poets inspired to captivate in word
    and rhyme
The divine dalliance of Krishna with Radha!
But low and mean as I am,
I find no means by which to receive and express
The glory and grandeur inherent in Hari's love and life.
But for the shower of grace divine,
The task is all beyond me.
So, with abject surrender at your feet,
With a leaf of grass held between my teeth,
I, Govindadas, the petty poet, beg you, O Radha, O Krishna, to
    inspire me.
And make my ardent desire and dream come true.

Translated from the Maithili by Jagdish Prasad Karna

Kazi Nazrul Islam (1899–1976)

From My Explanation

I am the poet of the present, brother:
No prophet of the future am I.

You may call me a poet or refuse to call me one;
I keep my mouth shut and bear with it all.

Some say: 'Mind, your place in the future will be with
the tribe of stubborn women! Where is the message of
the Eternal such as comes out of the pen of Rabindranath?'

So they all blame me;
yet I am content to sing the morning tune of Bhairabi.

My poet friends read my writings and despair of me.
They sigh for me.

Say they: 'He was useful. But in ministering to politics
he is becoming steadily useless, he has given up studies
and has gone to the dogs.'

Some say: 'He has been devoured by his wife.'
Some say again: 'In jail he used only to play cards, has
got fat and become useless.'

Some others say: 'It was well you were in jail. We
would rather you went to jail.'

Says the guru: 'So you have commenced relieving people
of their beards with your sword!'

I have a lover who in a letter every Saturday abuses me
and says: 'You are the bird with a notoriously coarse voice.'

Translated from the Bangla by Badusha Chakravarty

Rituraj (b. 1940)

Poets

Poets live to an old age
Though they're always getting killed off
they are still around.

Making friends
with fools and lumpens in these selfish times

thrusting poetry books into their hands
poets laugh for days on end
they howl first and then turn silent
but the cursed poems never shut up

Poets find birds in children
and girls in birds
and flowers in girls
collect the seeds of all they've seen
and sow themselves together with the seeds

Poets hide like seeds
only to return in new forms

At least now their breed is in no danger of extinction.

Translated from the Hindi by Manjit Kaur Bhatia, Christi Merrill, Daniel Weissbort and Nalini Taneja

Vallathol Narayana Menon (1878–1958)
From Faith and Erudition

4
Now rises from among those seated just outside,
All wise and erudite, whose prayers never cease,
A man of Kerala. His noble brow is marked
With sandal paste; and as he goes outside to make
His triple journey round the triple-hallowed halls
His lips still tremble with the might of Krishna's names.

5
But now another rises, follows close the first
And lowly in his bearing, low-voiced in his speech:

'A work there is—or call it play—that I have made
Where lurk such lapses—will yourself be pleased to read?
'You cavil at the common tongue—but, Patteri,
I have no comfort else.' It's Bhattathiri then?
Whose thousand flowers wrought of seamless Sanskrit verse
This house of holiness and its great Master praise,
Whose words ensure the good? It is indeed. To him
The Lord has freely given of his choicest gifts.
Who pleads with him to cast his eye of majesty
On screeds which reek of sweat from common peasant hands?
It's Puntanam, whose poems all extol the Lord,
Whose tuneful canticles rival the nightingale.
But Bhattathiri answers in a sharper tone:
'These ditties in Malayalam, show something else!'
Alas! That pride which comes of mastering the texts
Should fasten on this knower of the ultimate.

6
O speech divine, perfected when the gods were young!
This deed of thine is ill, to spurn Kerala's tongue!
Puntanam, crushed beneath the weight of hopes belied,
Soon vanished from that place. But mark the sequel now.

7
That night the sickness fell which long in him had slept
And mightily it seized all Bhattathiri's limbs.
With straining sinews, writhing as if he is aflame,
In vain he struggles, crying, 'O Lord, O Krishna, help!'

And when at last he wins to this near side of sleep
A tender youth appears before his reddened eyes:

O rare is his enchantment! Yellow is his robe,
His hair a cloud of rain where plumes of peacock dance,

A gold chain round his waist, which tinkles as he moves,
He holds a bamboo flute as one may hold a flower.
Now mutely does the Brahmin hear what Krishna says;
In flute-like voice thus speaks the bearer of the flute:

'The Malayalam poet's grief you must relieve;
Your malady can have no other cure but that.
For learning indeed Bhattathiri has a claim;
The burning faith of Puntanam is dearer far.'

Translated from the Malayalam by Vijay Nambisan

Nilmani Phookan (b. 1933)

Poetry Is for Those Who Wouldn't Read It

A poet had stated
poetry is for those who wouldn't read it
for the wounds in their hearts
for their fingers where thorns are embedded
for the anguish and the joy
of the living and the dead
for the outcry that trundles
down the road day and night
for the desert sun
for the meaning of death
and the vacuity of living
for the dark stones cursed by ruins

for the red patch between the lusty lips of maidens
for the yellow butterflies with wings spread on barbed wires
for the insects, the snails and the moss
for the bird flying lonely down the afternoon sky
for the anxiety in fire and water
for the mothers of five hundred million sick and starving children
for the fear of the moon turning red as blood
for each stilled moment
for the world that keeps turning
for one kiss from you
that man of dust will become dust again,
for that old saying.

Translated from the Assamiya by Pradip Acharya

Firaq Gorakhpuri (1896–1982)

If There Are No Flowers

If there are no flowers, I can flirt with nettles
In the heart of autumn, I can flirt with vanished blooms

I can flirt with the vanity of saints
Holding the whole galaxy in their embrace

The poet's vision can scan anything
I can flirt with the entire gamut of despondent scenes

Taking everything in my stride
I can flirt with demure, hidden sparks

A loving look has moved beauty's instruments to speech
I can flirt with the chords of this harp string

If the beloved's goodwill is what life hinges upon
Then I can flirt with the axis of life

I can transform this simple ambience into a conundrum
I can flirt with the eerie suggestion of your eyes

The smile on your lips seems to suggest
That I can flirt with the victims of seductive eyes

Corpses can start breathing afresh
I can so flirt with moving, marching shrines

Fingers that failed to fondle your curls
Are fingers that can surely flirt with the stars

My grief, Firaq, rivals my gaiety
I can flirt with friends even in misery

Translated from the Urdu by Noorul Hasan

Smita Agarwal (b. 1958)

Daywatch in the Scriptorium

The guests have departed.
The raging fever gone.
This blank page beckons me
To give it something of myself.

Oak leaves turn in the wind,
Moss-green on silver. The
Mesh of needles on a coniferous

Branch, flat as a palm, strains
The sunlight. Behind a hill, it
Seems as if an invisible Indian
Chief has hunkered down to puff
Out spreading clouds of peace
A rufous-throated nuthatch
Is disappointed. The apples
are small, hard and green.
It flies away boring through
Haze and rows of hills.

Fair weather, like a leafed twig
Suddenly landing at my feet,
Don't welsh on me. Green lion*
Day in June, live on in memory.

English

Sunil Gangopadhyay (b. 1934)

City of Memories

People at the borders speak prose
In ghettos and factories they speak prose
During the day the city speaks prose
All contemporary miseries speak prose
The parched field and the rough unkempt man speak prose
The entire civilisation of scissors and knives talk prose.

---

*A spirit of great transmuting power supposed to be produced by certain processes in alchemy; sometimes identified with the philosophical mercury (OED).

What then shall poetry be about?

Translated from the Bangla by Kalyan Roy and Bonnie MacDougall

Bhartrhari (c. 400 CE)

Her Face Is Not the Moon, Nor Are Her Eyes

Her face is not the moon, nor are her eyes
Twin lotuses, nor are her arms pure gold:
She's flesh and bone. What lies the poets told!
Ah, but we love her, we believe the lies.

Translated from the Sanskrit by John Brough

Dilip Chitre (b. 1938)

Evenings in Iowa City, Iowa

On top of being a foreigner
I am already an old fart
In this pimple-faced town
Infested with poets and decadent dons
Columbuses on Guggenheims
Magellans on Fulbrights
Vasco da Gamas supported by National Endowments
Set out from this little port to discover
The world we left behind
Statistics show that about the age of forty
Most men go berserk
Even those to whom their women try to be extra kind
Are we already bitter or are we still bewildered
Filling our brown bags with the bounty of America

Wandering through libraries
Boozing and growing long hair or beards
The true exterior of the expatriate
And conversing in exasperated voices
Sometimes even writing poems
While the natives mow their lawns

English

Thangjam Ibopishak (b. 1948)

Poem

Now in this land
One cannot speak aloud
One cannot think openly
So poem,
Like a flower I sport with you.

Before my eyes, incident upon incident,
Awesome, trembling
Walking yet sleeping
Eyes open but dreaming
Standing yet seeing nightmares
in dreams in reality
Only fearsome shivering instances
So around me closing eyes
Palms on ears
Moulding the heart to a mere thing of clay
I write poems about flowers.

Now in this land
One should only think of flowers

Dream of flowers
For my small baby, my wife
For my job
To protect myself from harm.

Translated from the Manipuri by Robin Ngangom

Mangalesh Dabral (b. 1948)

Outside

I closed the door
and sat down to write a poem
There was a light breeze blowing
and a little light
A bicycle stood in the rain
A child was returning home

I wrote a poem
which had no breeze no light
no bicycle no child
and no
door

Translated from the Hindi by the poet

From Jayavallabha's Vajjalagam (c. 8 CE)

On Poetry

The meaning
of a poem

tho' rich in appeal
delights but a few;
indeed, not all trees blossom
at the touch
of a pretty woman's foot.

May Sanskrit poetry
and with it all those poets
who composed it
be burnt down!
The fire crackles
when a house of bamboo burns.

Whoever queries
in Sanskrit,
when a poetic recitation
in Prakrit is on,
is hurling a rock
on a bed of flowers.

Both love and Prakrit poems,
when pressed hard,
perish,
for they're soft and gentle,
and suffer greatly
under love-bites.

Translated from the Prakrit by H.V. Nagaraja Rao and T.R.S. Sharma

Buddhadeva Bose (1908–74)

For My Forty-Eighth Winter: 2

Draw the curtain in that window. In that field there's absolutely
nothing to see.
They only want to seduce you—grass, earth, pond, sky.
Throw away those dolls, flowers, pet birds, pots of precious cacti.
Sink into ennui that's without pique, ever in the same beat, and
doesn't cheat.

There's nothing in that yard. Become deaf if you can.
Who can teach you what's not yours already—what wise man?
Rather, take up on your shoulders Grandad Sindbad's pack,
go search all day for a rime or two, like an ass, like a hack.

Winter drops its anchor. Who needs anything else?
The blank wall wakes up, shows shores, islets, seas.
They all blend—hours, times of the day, change itself.

Casting into darkness its fancy particoloured shawl,
patched with sunlight and moonlight, the earth recedes,
knowing that on the shore of its motion you will re-create all.

Translated from the Bangla by Ketaki Kushari Dyson

B.C. Ramchandra Sharma (1925–2005)

An Old Tale from China

Exquisite, the Emperor exclaimed.
The artist did not raise his head.

> Brush dipped in Nature's essence,
> he had worked for seven years on the wall.
> Forest river and peaks covered in snow—
> Nature seems to have yielded her all.
>
> The moon had sewn a lace of gold
> to the pure black saree of the clouds.
> That is no moon. I want that ball
> Whimpered the queen's little child.

Marvellous, cooed the populace.
There was no smile on the artist's face.

> The stars giggle watching themselves
> in the clear water of the pond.
> Trees plunged to wash their fruits
> as people stood with outstretched hands.
>
> You could hear lovers whisper
> as they made love on the beach.
> The girl opened her eyes. Seeing the silent
> witnesses, a rose bloomed on her cheeks.

Pure magic, the Emperor cried.
Still the artist did not say a word.

> And there was a hill and at its foot
> a half-shut wooden door.
> From beyond the reach of perfect art
> a Mystery called, promising much more.

What is there beyond, asked the Emperor.
The artist turned to look at the door.

> When the Emperor signalled with his eyes,
> he opened the door and vanished in the mist.
> As the ruler took the first step to follow,
> the door banged shut as if in a gust.

Translated from the Kannada by the poet

Kedarnath Singh (b. 1934)

On Reading a Love Poem

When I'd read that long love poem
I closed the book and asked—
Where are the ducks?

I was surprised that they were nowhere
even far into the distance.

It was in the third line of the poem
or perhaps the fifth
that I first felt
there might be ducks here somewhere.

I'd heard the flap flap of their wings
but that may have been my illusion.

I don't know for how long
that woman
had been standing in the twelfth line
waiting for a bus.

The poem was completely silent
about where she wanted to go.
Only a little sunshine
sifted from the seventeenth floor
was falling on her shoulders.

The woman was happy
at least there was nothing in her face to suggest
that by the time she reached the twenty-first line
she'd disappear completely
like every other woman.

There were Sakhu trees
standing where the next line began
the trees were spreading
a strange dread through the poem.

Every line that came next
was a deep disturbing fear and doubt
about every subsequent line.

If only I'd remembered—
it was in the nineteenth line

that the woman was slicing potatoes.
She was slicing
large round brown potatoes
inside the poem
and the poem was becoming
more and more silent,
more solid.

I think it was the smell
of freshly chopped vegetables
that kept the woman alive
for the next several lines.

By the time I got to the twenty-second line
I felt that the poem was changing its location.
like a speeding bullet
the poem had whizzed over the woman's shoulder
towards the Sakhu trees.

There were no lines after that
there were no more words in the poem
there was only the woman
there were only
her shoulders her back
her voice—
there was only the woman
standing whole outside the poem now
and breaking it to pieces.

Translated from the Hindi by Vinay Dharwadker

'In your gracious garden'

From the Rig Veda (c. 17 CE–11 BCE)
Creation Hymn

1. There was neither non-existence nor existence then; there was neither the realm of space nor the sky which is beyond. What stirred? Where? In whose protection? Was there water, bottomlessly deep?
2. There was neither death nor immortality then. There was no distinguishing sign of night nor of day. That one breathed, windless, by its own impulse. Other than that there was nothing beyond.
3. Darkness was hidden by darkness in the beginning; with no distinguishing sign, all this was water. The life force that was covered with emptiness, that one arose through the power of heat.
4. Desire came upon that one in the beginning; that was the first seed of mind. Poets seeking in their heart with wisdom found the bond of existence in non-existence.
5. Their cord was extended across. Was there below? Was there above? There were seed-placers; there were powers. There was impulse beneath; there was giving-forth above.
6. Who really knows? Who will here proclaim it? Whence was it produced? Whence is this creation? The gods came afterwards, with the creation of this universe. Who then knows whence it has arisen?
7. Whence this creation has arisen—perhaps it formed itself, or perhaps it did not—the one who looks down on it, in the highest heaven, only he knows—or perhaps he does not know.

Translated from the Sanskrit by Wendy Doniger

From the oral Kannada epic Halumatha Mahakavya
Creation Myth

Water—water without any form. Earth there was not;
Sky there was not, they say; Earth there was not, they say.
Water—water without any form, wind there was not;
Water—water without any form, waves there were not.
Waves there were none; and then, a bubble arose out of water;
A bubble arose then out of water, and a head out of it.
A head out of it; and then the torso;
To the head were joined three hundred and sixty nerves.
Head first; and then the body, legs and arms were formed.
Hara came into being, Guru came into being;
Sound and music, and then words were created.
Music and word; and then, Hara and Guru came into being.
Eight-colored Jyotirlinga* and the earth were created.
When Jyotirlinga was created, prayers were heard.

Guru makes words then, and Hara watches;
As Hara watches, he hears music.
He hears music, and he listens to the Word.
As speech begins, sacred hymns come into being;
With sacred hymns, fifty-two sounds are created.
Fifty-two sounds become fifty-two letters on their own.
O, Guru! Fifty-two letters are created;
With fifty-two letters speech and chanting begin.
With speech and chants, knowledge and wisdom are seen.

Translated from the Kannada by C.N. Ramachandran and Padma Sharma

* Jyotirlinga: A respectful name for Manteswami, founder and leader of the Neelagaaras, a Shaivite sect.

Akhtar-ul Iman (1915–96)

Creation

I'm sure I could create a world!
A few hamlets, a heart-broken few.
A sun and a moon, and a few shining stars.
Supports forever wavering, and hopes that are never fulfilled.

Let lights be swallowed up in darkness.
Let life forever cry itself to sleep.
And let this tale unfold through all eternity.

Let helplessness be the way of life,
Let death's anguish be the light relief,
And let the desert sand run red with blood.

Let plagues come down from heaven,
Let prayers rise up, quiet and sad,
And let me stay merciless forever.

Translated from the Urdu by Kathleen Grant Jaeger and Baidar Bakht

Harihara (c. 12 ce–13 ce)

From Girija Kalyana

The Summer Sun

The summer sun
Dark in the shade of trees
Fiery inside the forests
Stunning on the hill slopes

Severe in the open plains
And total under the sky.

Translated from the Kannada by K. Narasimha Murthy

Amiya Chakravarty (1901–86)

Calcutta

A warm noontime contentment spreads over the towering
 trees
on the other side of the fence—
honeysuckle blossoms clamber up
the lattice gate and sway in the wind—
> as I step away and go down the path
> I take that simple scene with me—
> the idle plinking of a piano
> its drowsy tremolo
>> makes the spring sky ache:
> a south Calcutta alley.

> If I come back to earth
> again, I'll take this path.
> Beside the gate in the soft light I'll see
> red canna lilies—
> my eyes will sink into flowerbeds
> yellow and fresh blue, a thick coverlet of green grass—
> I won't know who owns that house or who lives there—
> the impatient spring ache
the idle plinking of a piano
> will be nectar, soothing my wayfaring heart—

towering trees serene,
> sweet season:

across the fence the world I love
is contented—knowing that, I can go.

Translated from the Bangla by Carolyn B. Brown and Sarat Kumar Mukhopadhyay

R.V. Pandit (1917–90)

My Goa

As a bride bedecked art thou, my Goa.
On thy vermilion lips I see the red, red earth;
The dazzling white Dudhsagar Fall is the *moghra* chaplet
in the knot of thy hair;
The domes of the temples are thy diadem,
And all the churches are the cunning pattern of thy bodice.
Those dimples in thy cheek are the Tiswadi islets;
Thou hast bound the Zuari river as a bright silver girdle about
    thy waist,
And the Mandovi is a river of gold around thy neck.
As a bride bedecked art thou, my Goa.

Thou wearest a garment of bright green fields,
And golden rice-ears are the gay filigree border thereof;
Thou hast put on a necklace of mango and cashew fruit,
And jackfruits are the golden keystones thereof;
Thy betel palms are as clasps upon thy ear-tips,
And the betel bunches as earrings in thy lobes;
The waving flowers in thy hair are coco palms that form a crest
    for thee,

O my Goa thou art like a bride bedecked.
The lakes and ponds cause thy fingers to glow as with jewels,
And the flowering trees that bloom on every side, are the sweet garlands about thy neck.
And the Agoada Fortress, the grim Fortress—what is that to thee?
The red *kumkum* on thy brow, that spells thy fate—
'Tis the blood of heroes who died for Freedom on the shores of Agoada.
Truly thou art a bride bedecked,
A bride bedecked, my Goa.

Translated from the Konkani by Thomas Gay

Anon, Gujarati Folk Song

Rain of the World

Pour down, O rain of the world,
Thou art the rain of four continents.
The earth, thy beloved is waiting for thee,
The joyous peasants are waiting for thee;
The nostril-bored bullocks are waiting for thee,
Thy beloved people are waiting for thee,
Pour down O rain of the world.
The birds and beasts are waiting for thee;
Rivers and trees are all waiting for thee;
Pour down O dark clouds pour down;
And fill the ponds and lakes with water,
And bring happiness and joy to the world.

Translated from the Gujarati by Madhubhai Patel

Jyotirmoy Datta (b. 1936)

Crabs on the Beach

I pass the afternoons watching
the activity of firebrigade-red
digger crabs on the beach at Digha
millions of tireless crabs
are engaged on some gigantic
excavation project stretching as far as eyes can see

but they are very unsocial
each digs his own tunnel
will a crab ever invite another
to his private and exclusive cave
they seem very curt and dry
wholly lacking in affection
they advance from their holes
with the jerky motion of spring-activated toys
and then eject a pinch of sand
with a swish of their rustless plastic claws
they are all the time either digging
or widening or cleaning their holes
they seem to lavish their entire affection
on their homecaves.

all of the crab
and not just his claws
is sheathed in nail
I am sure the crab would be cold and unmoved
even if his sweetheart embraced him

we the other children of the sea
have left her and wandered off
but Oedipus crab
sticks to the margin of sea and continent
each crab leads the life of a perpetual embryo
in the womb it has dug for itself in the sand
and the tidal circulation of the sea
fills up every hole with nourishment
every twelve hours.

Translated from the Bangla by the poet

Vikram Seth (b. 1952)

Flash

Bright bird, whose swift blue wings gleam out
As on the stream you dip and rise,
You, as you scan for parr and trout,
      Flash past my eyes.

Bright trout, who glints in fin and scale,
Whose whim is grubs, whose dream is flies,
You, with one whisk of your quick tail,
      Flick past my eyes.

Bright stream, home to bright fish and birds,
A gold glow as the gold sun dies,
You too, too fast for these poor words,
      Flow past my eyes.

But such drab words, ah, sad to say,
When all that's bright has fled and gone,

Praised by dull folk, dressed all in grey,
>> Live on and on.

English

Gajanan Madhav Muktibodh (1917–69)

A Single Shooting Star

A single shooting star
A distant star
shoots through the blue of space
Here, someone measures its speed,
records the rise and set.
But nothingness of space,
assumed to blue, must spell
an answer inaccessible.
To stretching scope
eye muscle's strain.

Astronomers describe
its pace and spatial shift;
account for its time concealed
in tunnels of shade.
Yet it tracks only itself,
oblivious to sketch
and sketcher, eye and scope.

With equal speed
another lone star seems
to move across the space
So in moving out of shades
of evil, reining self,
riding the void,

each star
becomes the image
seeing
its own fearless offspring—

because of this
I shall put faith in every man,
in every man's son.

Translated from the Hindi by James Mauch

Greece Chunder Dutt (1833–92)

Water Fowl

From the low hills that skirt these mighty meres,
And more than rival in their loveliness
The dreaming Indian's Happy hunting grounds,
In boyhood's careless prime, I once beheld
The wild fowl migrates. 'Twas a cloudless morn
In early spring; the sun had bathed in gold
The dew-sprent turf, and trees of giant girth,
Whose gnarled trunks, deep scarred and scathed with fire,
Raised by the neighbouring herdsmen to destroy
The rotting leaves, and withered and undergrowth,
And clear the pastures for the early grass,
Stood like grim warders of the lone hill side
On which I lay—a faint breeze stirred the leaves,
When from the fens a mighty rushing sound
Rose—the precursor of a wedge-shaped host
Of swans, and pelican, and clamorous geese,
White-collared teals, widgeons, and stately cranes
With flecks of vivid green upon their wings.
Northwards the phalanx streamed, and soon the sky

Was hid as with a veil of glancing wings!
And from the grassy slope my wondering eyes
Could at one single glance, with ease, survey
Myriads of birds! for hours and hours they flew,
With harsh shrill screams that echoed from the woods.
It was a sight to fire with wild delight
A youthful heart. I felt a keener joy
Than feels in far Caffrarian wilds the Boer,
(Lone tenant with his partner of a hut
And cherished garden 'mid the arid waste)
At a 'trek bokken', when the nimble deer
Sweep past his tiny farm, in such vast herds,
That to the welkin's verge the brown karoo
Seems a bright carpet to the gazer's eye.

Long years have past of joys and griefs and cares
Since that spring morn of which I speak, yet oft,
When I sit silent in long winter eves,
And gaze upon the fire in listless mood,
To my mind's eye return in vision clear,
Those gnarled trunks upon the lone hill side,
That cloud of out-stretched necks and restless wings!

English

Kalidasa (c. 5 CE–6 CE)

From The Loom of Time

Canto III

13
The dance-display ended, Love deserts the peacocks
to attend the honey-sweet concert of wild geese;

Beauty, Genius of Blossom-Time, forsaking
the Kadambā, Kutaja, and Kakubha,
the Sarja and Aśoka, now dwells, in the Sapta-parna.

14
Redolent of the fragrance of Śephālika blossoms,
resonant with bird-song in undisturbed quietness,
groves with lotus-eyed gazelles wandering in the glades
kindle restless longing in everyone's heart.

15
Playfully tossing lotuses, pink, white and red,
deliciously cooled moving fondly among them,
wiping away the dewdrops edging their petals
the breeze at daybreak rocks the heart with wild longing.

16
People rejoice to see the village-bounds
Crowded with large herds of cows lying undisturbed,
where ripe grain lies spread in heaps on threshing floors
and the air rings with cries of wild geese and sarus cranes.

17
The gait of wild geese surpass the rare charm of women's steps,
full-blown lotuses the radiance of their moon-bright faces;
blue water lilies rival the lustre of passion-glowing eyes,
delicate wavelets the play of their eyebrows graceful.

18
Śyāma creepers curving with tender flower-filled twigs
usurp the brilliance of women's jewel-loaded arms;

fresh jasmines peeping through vibrant Aśoka flowers
rival the sparkle of smiles brilliant as moonlight

19
Young women fill with a wealth of jasmine buds
their thick midnight-blue hair curling at the ends;
they place varied blue-lotuses
behind ears decked with fine gold earrings.

20
Globed breasts adorned with pearls sandal-misted,
wide curving hips with girdles strung with bells,
precious anklets making music on their lotus feet,
lit with happiness deep within
women now enhance their beauty.

21
A cloudless sky inlaid with the moon and countless stars
wears the exquisite beauty of lakes glowing
with the sheen of emeralds, and strewn with moon-lotuses,
wide open; and a regal swan floats serene.

22
Autumn skies are enchanting, star-sprinkled,
lit by a clear-rayed moon; serenely beautiful
are the directions of space, free of thronging rain clouds:
the earth is dry; waters sparkling clear;
breezes consorting with lotuses blow cool.

23
Wakened by the morning beams, the day-lotus
now expands to look like a lovely maiden's face;

but the moon-lotus droops with the setting moon
like the smiles of women whose husbands are far from home.

24
Seeing the glow of the beloved's dark eyes
in the blue-lotus,
hearing the tones of her gold girdle bells
in the love-mad murmur of wild geese,
recalling the rich red of her lower lip
in the Bandhuka's flame-clusters,
travellers, their thoughts whirling, lament.

Translated from the Sanskrit by Chandra Rajan

Sri Aurobindo (1872–1950)

The Tiger and the Deer

Brilliant, crouching, slouching, what crept through the green
    heart of the forest,
Gleaming eyes and mighty chest and soft soundless paws of
    grandeur and murder?
The wind slipped through the leaves as if afraid lest its voice
    and the noise of its steps perturb the pitiless Splendour,
Hardly daring to breathe. But the great beast crouched and
    crept, and crept and crouched a last time, noiseless, fatal,
Till suddenly death leapt on the beautiful wild deer as it drank
Unsuspecting from the great pool in the forest's coolness and shadow,
And it fell and, torn, died remembering its mate left sole in
    the deep woodland—
Destroyed, the mild harmless beauty by the strong cruel beauty
    in Nature.

But a day may yet come when the tiger crouches and leaps no
   more in the dangerous heart of the forest,
As the mammoth shakes no more the plains of Asia;
Still then shall the beautiful wild deer drink from the coolness
   of great pools in the leaves' shadow.
The mighty perish in their might;
The slain survive the slayer.

English

Bana (7 CE)

From The Deeds of Harsha

A Stallion Wakes from His Sleep

He stretches his hind-leg, and, bending his spine, extends his body
   upwards.
Curving his neck, he rests his muzzle on his chest, and tosses his
   dust-grey mane.
The steed, his nostrils ceaselessly quivering, with desire of fodder
rises from his bed, gently whinnies, and paws the earth with his
   hoof.

He bends his back and turns his neck sideways, till his face
   touches his buttock,
and then the horse, the curls matted about his ears,
rubs with his hoof the red corner of his eye, itching from sleep,
his eye, struck by his dew-drop scattering mane, waving and tossing,
his eye, to the point of whose quivering eyelash there clings a tiny
   fragment of chaff.

Translated from the Sanskrit by A.L. Basham

Anon, Punjabi Folk Song
Lullaby

Where does the Cuckoo sleep, Baby? Down by the great stone bank,
Where the lizards bask in the sunshine, and the monkeys play on the bank?
Where does the peacock sleep, Baby? Out in the jungle grass,
Where the jackals howl in the evening, and parrots scream as they pass.

What does the peacock drink, Baby? Cream from somebody's cup;
And if someone isn't careful, the peacock will drink it all up.
What does the Cuckoo drink, Baby? Milk from somebody's pan,
So run and stop the rascal as quick as ever you can.

What does the Cuckoo eat, Baby? Candy and all that's nice,
And great round balls of brown sugar speckled with silver and spice.
What does the peacock eat, Baby? Lollipops all day long;
But Baby must go to sleep now, for this is the end of the song.

Translated from the Punjabi by C.F. Usborne

Anon, Santhal Ritual Song
Erok Sim Bonga

Our obeisance to you, Mother Jaher Era.
On the occasion of the *Erok* festival we offer to you
young fowls, and freshly husked rice.
Accept it in pleasure
We pray to you:
For every seed we sow let there be twelve.

And let not disease attack them.
If they attack, please subdue them.
Do not allow weeds and grass to grow among our crops.
Do not allow disease and misfortune to befall our village.
Bring us the rain-bearing clouds in plenty.
Bring them in time.
Let the earth be green with our crops.
Let there be no hindrance to our movements.
Let there prevail among us
the spirit of mutual love and goodwill.

Translated from the Santhali by Sitakant Mahapatra

Sarojini Naidu (1879–1948)

The Bird Sanctuary

In your quiet garden wakes a magic tumult
Of winged choristers that keep the Festival of Dawn,
Blithely rise the carols in richly cadenced rapture,
From lyric throats of amber, of ebony and fawn.

The bulbul and the oriole, the honey-bird and shama
Flit among high boughs that drip with nectar and with dew,
Upon the grass the wandering gull parades its sea-washed silver,
The hoopoe and the kingfisher their bronze and sapphire blue.

Wild gray pigeons dreaming of a home amid the tree-tops,
Fill their beaks with silken down and slender banyan twigs,
But the jade-green gipsy parrots are only gay marauders,
And pause upon their sun-ward flight to plunder red ripe figs.

In your gracious garden there is joy and fostering freedom,
Nesting place and singing space for every feathered thing,
O Master of the Birds, grant sanctuary and shelter
Also to a homing bird that bears a broken wing.

English

From Jayavallabha's Vajjalagam (c. 8 CE)

Summer

Having burnt it all to ash
along with every animal,
the wild fire
shins up a dried-out tree
and surveys the forest again,
wondering what is left.

Translated from the Prakrit by Martha Ann Selby

Sri Jnanadeva (1275–96)

From Anubhavamrita, Canto IX

Life of the Opened Self

Now fragrance
        Develops a fine nose.
The ears of listening
        Grow.
Mirrors rise
        From the eyes.

The wind
>   Is fanning itself,
The head turning
>   Into a champak.
The tongue
>   Is an intense juice.
The lotus
>   Forges out a full sun.
The moonbird
>   Has become the moon.
Bees are flowers.
>   The bodies of men
Become woman.
>   The sleeper
Has become a bed.
The blossoms of the mango
>   Turn
Into singing koels.
>   The body itself
Becomes the rippling
>   Wind of the woods
On the shoulder
>   Of the Malaya mountain.
Flavours
>   Burst out their individual tongues.
Gold carves out
>   Its own ornaments.
The subject and the object,
>   The seer and the seen,
Are moved
>   Into a oneness beyond seeing.

Centuries of opening
    And falling petals
Do not disturb
    The stillness of being
Unalterable Chrysanthemum.
In that city
    Beyond all action
Experience arrives
    Like a throng
Of migrants
    Stunned.

Translated from the Marathi by Dilip Chitre

Rabindranath Tagore (1861–1941)

From Gitanjali, 100

Monsoon weather now I see
   all around humanity.
In an angry muttering
   it has come here, cloaked and shrouded.
Rising in a sky dense-clouded,
   furious at heart it dances—
and a mass of cloud advances
   over-running its own bounds.
Clasped in a close union
   clouds fly on unfaltering.
Who can tell what drives them on?
   From that drift the thunder sounds.
Monsoon weather now I see
   all around humanity.

Into the far-distant regions
    cloud-accumulations go
in their companies and legions.
    What propels them they don't know,
nor when they dissolve and fall,
    as the *Sraban*-torrents come,
from a great hillside to the sea.
    Do they comprehend at all
what land that was? Where it might be?
    How grand and splendid they become!
Yet it takes them unawares,
    the terrible life and death that is theirs.
Monsoon weather now I see
    all around humanity.

In that rumbling over there
    in the havoc of the north-east,
where a storm takes on its nature,
    what is whispered on the air?
What irrevocable future,
    in the deepening shadows pieced
on the horizon, in night-stillness
    carries its own speechless pain?
As it reaches to its fullness
    in the dark skies of the brain,
black imagination leads
    into what forthcoming deeds?
Monsoon weather now I see
    all around humanity.

Translated from the Bangla by Joe Winter

Subramania Bharati (1882–1921)

Wind, 9

Wind, come softly.
Don't break the shutters of the windows.
Don't scatter the papers.
Don't throw down the books on the shelf.
There, look what you did—you threw them all down.
You tore the pages of the books.
You brought rain again.
You're very clever at poking fun at weaklings.
Frail, crumbling houses, crumbling doors, crumbling rafters,
crumbling wood, crumbling bodies, crumbling lives,
crumbling hearts—
the wind god winnows and crushes them all.
He won't do what you tell him.
So, come, let's build strong homes,
let's join the doors firmly.
Practise to firm the body.
Make the heart steadfast.
Do this, and the winds will be friends with us.
The wind blows out weak fires.
He makes strong fires roar and flourish.
His friendship is good.
We praise him every day.

Translated from the Tamil by A.K. Ramanujan

From the Atharva Veda (c. 2 BCE)

Book XIX, Hymn 50
A Hymn to Night for Protection and Prosperity

Blind him and make him headless, Night! The serpent with the pungent breath.
Strike from his head the wolf's two eyes, and dash the thief against a post.
Those oxen that are thine, O Night, with sharpened horns and rapid pace,
With those transport us safe today o'er difficulties everywhere.
Uninjured in our bodies may we pass through each succeeding night,
And let malignities fail to pass, as men without a boat the depth.
As millet hurried through the air before us is beheld no more,
So cause the man to vanish, Night, who plans to do us injury.
The thief hast thou kept far away, the robber driver of our kine,
Even him who having covered up the horse's head would lead him off.
If dealing treasure thou hast come today, O highly favoured Night,
Cause thou us to enjoy it all so this may not pass away.
Do thou entrust us to the Dawn, all of us free from sin, O Night.
May Dawn deliver us to Day, and Day to thee, O glorious one.

Translated from the Sanskrit by Ralph T.H. Griffith

From the Isa Upanishads (c. 12 BCE–6 BCE)

6
Whoever sees
>All beings in the self (*ātman*)

And the self in all beings
>Does not shrink away from it.

7
For the one who knows,
>In whom all beings have become self,

How can there be delusion or grief
>When he sees oneness?

8
He has encompassed the bright, the bodiless, the unwounded,
>The sinewless, the pure, the unpierced by evil:

The wise seer, conqueror, self-born,
>He has arranged objects according to their nature
>Through eternal years.

9
They who worship ignorance
>Enter blind darkness:

They who delight in knowledge
>Enter darkness, as it were, yet deeper.

10
It is different, they say, from knowledge;
>It is different, they say, from ignorance:

So we have heard from those wise ones
> Who have revealed it to us.

11
Whoever knows knowledge and ignorance—
> Both of them, together—
By ignorance crosses over death
> And by knowledge reaches immortality.

Translated from the Sanskrit by Valerie J. Roebuck

Umashankar Joshi (1911–88)

Miles upon Miles

Miles and miles and miles pass through me
unmoving and still as the train rushes on.
Those distant hills cut their way in, sinking
in joy. Rivers flow in my veins, and behind
my wide eyes entire lakes dip and drown.
Fields flutter; their tremor brushes my limbs.
Houses spread out through my hands, and huts,
their yards rippling with the imprint of palms.
A creeper strays roofward . . . and
on that girl's blouse, design-like sits a butterfly.
Thus much only strung out on memory's line
As miles upon miles pass me through.

Worlds upon worlds pass right through me
bound to turning earth in chains of clay.
The Milky Way, herds of stars and planets,

jostling and wheeling, keep coming. In
leaps the antelope, the hunter behind, the scorpion.
Thirsty, I drink all of space. Storm's dance,
lightning's jabs, and the roar of the clouds,
summer's scorching winds and flowers of spring:
someone in there gulps it all down.
A tear from boundless compassion?—some shooting star.
Earth aspires to light?—a flashing firefly.
Thus much hope only in memory's store as
worlds upon worlds pierce me through.

Translated from the Gujarati by Suguna Ramanathan and Rita Kothari

Vyasa (c. 11 BCE–4 BCE)

From the Bhagvad Gita

The Way to Eternal Brahman, Section VIII

There is day, also, and night in the universe:
The wise know this, declaring the day of Brahma
A thousand ages in span
And the night a thousand ages.

Day dawns, and all those lives that lay hidden asleep
Come forth and show themselves, mortally manifest:
Night falls, and all are dissolved
Into the sleeping germ of life.

Thus they are seen, O Prince, and appear unceasingly,
Dissolving with the dark, and with day returning
Back to the new birth, new death:
All helpless. They do what they must.

The Yoga of Devotion, Section XII

Quickly I come
To those who offer me
Every action,
Worship me only,
Their dearest delight,
With devotion undaunted.

Because they love me
These are my bondsmen
And I shall save them
From mortal sorrow
And all the waves
Of Life's deathly ocean.

Be absorbed in me,
Lodge your mind in me:
Thus you shall dwell in me,
Do not doubt it,
Here and hereafter.

Devotion to the Supreme Spirit, Section XV

The light that lives in the sun,
Lighting all the world,
The light of the moon,
The light that is in fire:
Know that light to be mine.

My energy enters the earth,
Sustaining all that lives:
I become the moon,

Giver of water and sap,
To feed the plants and the trees.

Flame of life in all,
I consume the many foods,
Turning them into strength
That upholds the body.

I am in all hearts,
I give and take away
Knowledge and memory:
I am all that the Vedas tell,
I am the teacher,
The knower of Vedanta.

Translated from the Sanskrit by Swami Prabhavananda and Christopher Isherwood

Eunice de Souza (b. 1940)

Learn from the Almond Leaf

Learn from the almond leaf
which flames as it falls.
The ground is burning.
The earth is burning.
Flamboyance
is all.

English

Melanie Silgardo (b. 1956)

The Earthworm's Story

I lost this last bit of shine
scraping along the way.
The crow pecked,
the ant bit,
and the gravel sneered underbelly.
The damp gone, the leaves fall
heavy as plates, and clatter.
Above the fly stalks the air.
It does not matter
if that's your foot over me.

English

Siddhartha Menon (b. 1967)

Beetles

I have an affection
for the larger black beetles,
bulbous, gauche: I think I sympathize.

They are out of sorts
on surfaces, contrive to be lost in empty dustbins,
are seldom on an even keel.

They flounder anywhere—on clods,
on cement, and topple
quicker than a house of cards.

They are so much upon their backs, so
helpless as they claw
air, such easy meat.

You flip them right: they grope,
poise themselves and whirr like helicopters.
They do not cling to redemption.

Are they meant to be like this? There must
be a realm where every act
isn't the tragic-comic one—

where touchstones are less clear, the walls
less near. Not for surfaces,
yet there they are, rising and blundering,

there they are being flipped.
At times I see them pause, then burrow
impatiently, boring in.

English

Santan Rodrigues (1948–2008)

The Hang

It was no Christ on Calvary
When you came sweating up the runway
carrying your own self
to the end. Your arms lifted you up
as you propelled
your frail structure to a cross in the sky

to be nailed there.
And the wind moved piercing your side.
Till your weight
Laid you to rest in a sepulchre
of sand.

English

Anand Thakore (b. 1971)

Tusker Kills Mahout at Religious Ceremony

Nine weeks now, and the tamarind tree has put out a new branch.
A fresh wind from the west, the first rains.

The men barely notice me now on their way to the fields.

The womenfolk walk past me nonchalantly,
On their way to the river.

The village pundit is punctual about his weekly exorcisms:
Rosewater. Turmeric. Sandalwood. Ash.

Only the children still fear me.

***

A local poet has composed a paean
In praise of what he sees as my rebellion,

My willingness to be ruled by nothing
But an ancient impulse to break free.

The nation, he sings, has much to learn from this.

The villagers who hear him are amazed
That a demon so vile

Should have dared to lodge itself in *me*,
A beast half-divine, the mortal god of their tribe.
They tell him the same demon now lives in his songs.

***

Sure, they have their reasons, all of them,
Poet and pundit, men and women of the village,

For believing what they believe;
But all it was, really, was lust,

A minute's raw lust for a dead mate,
That tore me from my senses:

A huge haze came over me. A chaos
Of people and rocks, clouds, fields, hills and trees,

A compelling smell that meant: her skin.
Gravity deserted me, my light legs floated,

My body convulsed,
Then threw itself back before I knew it.

I trampled fences, crushed a thatched hut.
I uprooted a mango sapling not yet three summers tall.

When I lifted his broken body into my trunk,
I was not sure he had hit the ground,

I was that uncertain about where the earth really was.

Nobody understands I was trying to save him.

***

My new mahout is a good man.

He brings me fruit and wreaths of flowers at dawn
And says his prayers before he mounts me:

But I have only to think of her again, in that way,
And I am sure I will kill him.

English

'Are you looking for a god?'

Sankaracarya (c. 8 CE)

From Sivahandakahari

Let, Lord, your life-stream trickle down
Washing sin's dust away
And make a channel in my mind—
Cool thereby the fever of life
And calm its troubled waters;
Then find its riverbed in my heart—
So shall good prevail,
An unbreaking billow of bliss!

How often, Lord of beings, do we take
Nacre for silver, glass for diamond, flour
Mixed in water for milk, mirage for water!
So fools deluded after strange gods run,
Their minds unmindful of you, God of gods!

A man, a god, or a wild wandering beast
A cow, a bird, a worm or mosquito.
What matters whatever my birth be if but my heart
Longs for the bliss your lotus feet will rain?

Translated from the Sanskrit by P.S. Sundaram

Rasananda (c. 17 CE)

Many Many Aeons

After worshipping for many aeons
at long last, I've found you,
O dear Krishna!

I am not a milkmaid of yours,
yet you entice me with your flute,
Bolting the door of my heart
I shall make love, clasping
you in my womb.
You flirt, bumble-bee!
You went and hid in the field of the lotus!
I shall pluck the flowers
and put them into a basket.
If you are a fish, then I shall be
a crow on the river!
If you are soaring high, then
I shall draw you
with the string of love.
Says Rasananda Nabaghanachanda
Have you lost your sense?
If you are a dove, then I, as a vulture,
shall always be after you.

Translated from the Oriya by Sachidananda Mohanty and Smita Mohanty

Nammalvar (9 CE)

From **Love's Messengers**

2
The cold wind threads through my bones.

Remembering only my faults,
my lord doesn't show me any grace.
Go ask him,
    'What wrong did she do?'

Dear parrot, gnawing at a bone,
  please, go ask him.

I brought you up, didn't I?

Translated from the Tamil by A.K. Ramanujan

Vidyapati (15 CE)

Imaginary Re-union 2

Krishna is like my hand-mirror and the flower on my head,
He is like the black paste in my eyes and the betel in my mouth.
He is like the musk in my heart and the necklace round my neck,
He is everything to my body and the most valuable possession in
  my home.
He is like a wing for a bird and water for the fish,
I know him as the spirit of life to me.
Madhava tell me how it is with you?

Vidyapati says, both of you resemble each other.

Translated from the Maithili by Ajit Kumar Ghosh

Periyazhwar (Vishnuchittan) (9 CE)

From **Hush-a-bye Baby**

Brahma sent you in his love
This little cradle of pure gold
With rubies set on either side
And diamonds in between—

Hush-a-bye, my little dwarf
Who spanned the world.

Siva on his bull sent you
To wear round your waist, this beautiful belt
Made of gold and set with gems
Sparkling like pomegranate seeds.
Don't cry, don't cry, the owner of all—
Hush-a-bye, world-spanner.

Indra sent for my dear Lord
Who wears Lakshmi on his chest
And whose feet are like lotuses
With lovely anklets—and stood by.
Hush-a-bye, dear lotus-eyed.

Translated from the Tamil by P.S. Sundaram

Akkamahadevi (12 CE)

Like an Elephant, Caught

Like an elephant, caught
when he strayed from the herd,
remembering his mountain range,
I remember.

Like a caged parrot
sighing over his mate,
I remember.

Come this way, my child,
call me thus,

O Chennamallikarjuna, my Lord,
and show me the grace of your ways!

Translated from the Kannada by B.C. Ramchandra Sharma

Arun Kolatkar (1932–2004)

Yeshwant Rao

Are you looking for a god?
I know a good one.
His name is Yeshwant Rao
and he's one of the best,
look him up
when you are in Jejuri next.

Of course he's only a second class god
and his place is just outside the main temple.
Outside even of the outer wall.
As if he belonged
among the tradesmen and the lepers.

I've known gods
prettier faced
or straighter laced.
Gods who soak you for your gold.
Gods who soak you for your soul.

Gods who make you walk
on a bed of burning coal.
Gods who put a child inside your wife.
Or a knife inside your enemy.
Gods who tell you how to live your life,
double your money
or triple your land holdings.
Gods who can barely suppress a smile
as you crawl a mile for them.
Gods who will see you drown
if you won't buy them a new crown.
And although I'm sure they're all to be praised,
they're either too symmetrical
or too theatrical for my taste.

Yeshwant Rao.
mass of basalt,
bright as any post box,
the shape of protoplasm
or king size lava pie
thrown against the wall,
without an arm, a leg
or even a single head.

Yeshwant Rao.
He's the god you've got to meet.
If you're short of a limb,
Yeshwant Rao will lend you a hand
and get you back on your feet.

Yeshwant Rao
does nothing spectacular.
He doesn't promise you the earth
or book your seat on the next rocket to heaven.
But if any bones are broken,
you know he'll mend them.
He'll make you whole in your body
and hope your spirit will look after itself.
He is merely a kind of a bone setter.
The only thing is,
as he himself has no heads, hands and feet,
he happens to understand you a little better.

English

Arul Cellatturai (c. mid-20 CE)

Little House (6)

Our Mother is your mother.
Our father is your father.
You are our precious soul, right?
In our world, who else is kind?

You said you are the salt
in the surging ocean waters.
You declared you are the shining light.

We simple ones want to place
soft white rice in your mouth.

Come, we'll play in the little houses,
fixing them with fine sand from the Kavery river.

Our Lord and our King
with a straight sceptre,
don't destroy our little houses.

Holy one who flows with clear honeyed Tamil,
don't destroy our little houses.

Translated from the Tamil by Paula Richman

Muktabai (13 CE)

Open the Wattle-door, O Jnaneshwar!

Show mercy to me:
Open the wattle-door, O Jnaneshwar!

A Yogi of pure mind is one
who suffers the offence of the people.

When the world turns to conflagration out of anger
the speech of the saints should flow like water.

When the weapons of words cause torment
suffer it by accepting the advice of saints.

If the universe is cloth, then through the entirety runs
the single thread of the Brahma! Open the wattle-door,
   Jnaneshwar!

One becomes a saint only by suffering the abuses of the world:
he who is devoid of conceit attains greatness.
Where greatness dwells,
there dwells compassion.

Who can you be angry with,
when we are the all-pervading Brahma?

See all with equal regard,
open the wattle-door, O Jnaneshwar!

Translated from the Marathi by Pradeep Gopal Deshpande

Eesar Das Barhat (1538–1618)

Let the Pot with Just Water in It

Let the pot with just water in it
boil on the fire;
and, O you servant of God,
have faith in Him;
the Lord will provide the meal for you.
Where the wind and the rays do not reach,
farther than the sun and the moon,
and the firmament that holds them—
beyond them all is He;
and no one knows the way
that leads to Him.

Translated from the Rajasthani by Kesri Singh

Kanakadasa (16 CE)

Saku Saku

Enough, enough of this serving fellow humans, O Ranga
   enough, enough, I'm weary of serving other people

Lord of the universe, Rangaraya, I want the worship
   of your holy feet

Rising early in the morning, hurrying somewhere
   scurrying, anticipating the whims of somebody,
   like a slave I run so many errands each day,
   but always I return home empty-handed
      Enough, enough of this serving fellow humans ...

I left off ablutions, religious rites, the observance
   of silence, and daily sandhya prayers, became pitiable
   and low, I went to bad people, spent days like a dog.
   In my mind I boiled, harbouring all those evil greeds;
   happiness? I never found enough to fill up a sesame seed!
      Enough! Enough already! All this work for people.

Stuck like a fly fluttering hopelessly in a honeypot
   because of my hungers—O Vishnu—I too
   have my mouth wide open with greed—I'm stuck!
   Free me from the fetters of this bondage
   kindly give me the company of your devotees
   O Adikeshava of Kaginele, Lord of Venkatadri
   Madhava, Rangaraya!
      Enough! Too much! I've had about all I can handle

Free me, O Ranga, I'm sick of serving other people
I want to serve the Lord of the universe's holy feet.

Translated from the Kannada by William J. Jackson

Allama Prabhu (12 CE)

It's Dark Above the Clutching Hand

It's dark above the clutching hand.
It's dark over the seeing eye.
It's dark over the remembering heart.
It's dark here
    with the Lord of Caves
    out there.

Translated from the Kannada by A.K. Ramanujan

Bahinabhai Chaudhuri (1880–1951)

From **Bahinabai's Life and Thinking**

(As a woman) I have no right to listen to a reading of the Vedas.
The Brahmans have made a secret of the Gayatri mantra.

I am told I must not pronounce the sacred word 'Om'. I must not listen to philosophical ideas.

I must not speak to anyone about them. My husband was Jamadagni himself (if I did those things).

Says Bahini, 'My soul is very downcast. God has no compassion on me.'

Translated from the Marathi by Chandrashekhar Jahagirdar

From the Rig Veda (c. 17 BCE–11 BCE)
The Dove of Death
1. Gods, a dove has come here seeking someone, sent as a messenger by Destruction. We will sing against him; we will perform an expiation. Let all be well with our two-footed creatures, all be well with our four-footed creatures.
2. Let the dove that has been sent to us be kind; gods, let the bird be harmless in our houses. Let the inspired Agni relish our oblation. Let the winged spear spare us.
3. Do not let the winged spear attack us; it settles by the fireplace in the kitchen. Let all be well with our cows and with our men; gods, do not let the dove harm us here.
4. What the owl screeches is in vain; vain, too, the settling of the dove by the fire. I bow low before Yama, before death, who sent this dove as a messenger.
5. Drive the dove out, pushing him with a verse. Rejoicing in food, lead the cow around and wipe out all the evil traces. Let it fly forth, flying its best, and leave us strength to live.

Translated from the Sanskrit by Wendy Doniger

Guru Nanak (1469–1539)

Chet (March–April)

It is the month of Chet,
It is spring. All is seemly—
The humming bumble-bee
And the woodland in flower—
But there is a sorrow in my soul.

The Lord, my Master is away.
If the Husband comes not home, how can a wife
Find peace of mind?

Sorrows of separation waste away the body.
The *Koel* calls in the mango grove,
Its notes are full of joy.
Why then the sorrow in my soul?

The bumble-bee hovers about the blossoming bough,
O mother of mine, it is like death to me,
For there is a sorrow in my soul.

Nanak says: When the Lord her Master comes home to her,
Blessed is then the month of Chet.

Translated from the Punjabi by Khushwant Singh

Basavanna (1106–67/68)

Like a Monkey on a Tree

Like a monkey on a tree
it leaps from branch to branch:
how can I believe or trust
this burning thing, this heart?
It will not let me go
to my Father,
my lord of the meeting rivers.

Translated from the Kannada by A.K. Ramanujan

Devadurllabha Das (16 CE)

From Rahasya Manjari

The inner room too hot to sleep,
I came to the inner room on the south
To be with my Lord.
We smeared one another with water
Cooled with camphor and sandal paste
He ate cucumber, soft kernel of the tender palmfruit,
Green coconuts, candy laced with black pepper,
The morn-apple growing in water, and betel;
He made me eat all these after he finished his meal,
Contented I slept in his arms.

Translated from the Oriya by Rajendra Prasad Das

Janabai (c. 1298–1350)

God My Darling

God my darling
do me a favour and kill my mother-in-law

I will feel lonely when she is gone
but you will be a good god won't you
and kill my father-in-law

I will be glad when he is gone
but you will be a good god won't you
and kill my sister-in-law

I will be free when she is gone
I will pick up my begging bowl
and be on my way

let them drop dead says jani
then we will be left alone
just you and me

Translated from the Marathi by Arun Kolatkar

Bullah Shah (1680–1759)

Strange Are the Times

Strange are the times!
Crows swoop on hawks.

Sparrows hunt eagles.
Strange are the times!

The horses from Iraq are lashed
While the donkeys are caparisoned.
Strange are the times!

Those who wear long hair are kings
And the erstwhile kings are beggars.
Strange are the times!

Says Bullah, it's all ordained from above.
Strange indeed are the times!

Translated from the Punjabi by K.S. Duggal

Amir Khusrau (1253–1325)

Ghazal 257: Poverty Is More Pleasant than Majesty

Poverty is more pleasant than majesty;
depravity, more pleasant than piety.
Majesty has its headaches, and when
last I looked, beggary was more pleasant.
Since kings let no one approach them,
being indigent among the poor
is more pleasant.

When pride gets into someone's head,
being pals with a dog from the streets
is more pleasant.

When the heart breaks with melancholy
over some beauty, that breaking is more pleasant
than any salve. Public love play with idols
is more pleasant than all this devout hypocrisy.
Once won, there's no pleasure in love.
Separation, for those who play this game,
is more pleasant.

Put your base love out of your mind,
Khusrau. Love for the sacred secret
is more pleasant.

Translated from the Persian by Paul E. Losensky

Sheikh Mohamad (16 CE)

So It Is Done by God Gopal

So it has been done by God Gopal,
that nothing is sacred or profane any more.

Though the bush of *ketaki* is thorny,
inside grows the *kewada*.

The jack-fruit bears thorns on the body,
but conceals within life-giving water.

Though Sheikh Mohamad is a non-Hindu,
God Govind pervades his heart.

Translated from the Marathi by Pradeep Gopal Deshpande

Namdev (1270–1350)

From Returning from the Pilgrimage

I had heard that you are the Restorer of the fallen, so I came to
 your door;
Realising that you are not the Restorer of the fallen, I go back now ...

You give only when you receive, such is your generosity;
Why should I then hang around your door, the miser that you are?

You are not what you are renowned to be, so give up your claim;
Who has named you 'The Restorer of the fallen'?

Beating the gong, I shall proclaim to all three worlds;
that though known as the 'Restorer of the fallen,'
you are very treacherous.

Nama says, God, I expect nothing from you;
I touch your feet so that there should be love for me in your heart.

Translated from the Marathi by Pradeep Gopal Deshpande

Harinath Majumdar (1833–96)

Jaya—

Jaya
don't wake up Hara's wife,
I beg you.

Because she has to leave
she stayed up the whole night crying.

All night she was in pain;
only now she sleeps.
Alas, that moon-face is grey with grief.

When she wakes
Uma will abandon us for Kailasa city,
leaving Himalaya dark.
Kara has come to take her away;
that's why I ask you to delay.

For, as long as she sleeps
I can still gaze on her moon-face.

Translated from the Bangla by Rachel Fell McDermott

Sheikh Farid (1173–1265)

From Eight Poems

11
Do not belittle the Dust, O Farid!
No one equals its worth, indeed.
While we live, it's under our feet;
And over our head, when we are dead.

24
Engage yourself in the service of the Lord,
From every doubt be free.
Dervishes should, indeed, cultivate
The endurance of a tree.

27
Eager was she as a virgin;
When wed, concerns began.
Now her grief is only this:
She can't be a virgin again.

28
O dog of a Farid, why neglect your prayer?
This scarcely is the right way.
You must, indeed, visit the mosque
Full five times a day.

Translated from the Punjabi by J.S. Neki

Vipin Parikh (b. 1930)

I Want a God ...

I don't need a God
who can provide a release
from the cycle of births!
I want a God
who can
free me from railway timetables
restrain the blood racing
at traffic signals,
stop time from being
dragged away in a jumbo jet,
chastise the emptiness
seeking relief in
radio and television,

keep me away in the morning
from truth-cloaked news,
and stop me from being
sold off cheap in ads.
I want
a God who ...

Translated from the Gujarati by Pradip N. Khandwalla

Periyalvar (9 CE)

From Hymns of the Alvars

Who Shall Deliver Me from the Body of This Death?

Like tree that dwells on river bank
    I timid am
Lest in the pit of birth again
    I plunged am.
Lord, who art smell and taste and touch
And hearing ... I have dared thus much!

Like sailors caught in midst of storm
    I timid am
Lest in the pit of birth again
    I plunged am.
Lord of the Discus, though my word
Be cause for wrath, let it be heard!

Like sharing hut with serpent-mate
    I timid am
Lest into doleful births again

I plunged am.
Lord of the lotus eyes, my mind
Confus'd, no way to bear can find.

Like ant on firebrand blazing at both ends
   I timid am,
Lest into pit of destined woe
   I plunged am,
Eternal Sovereign, by thy hand
Thrust in, with all abatement bann'd.

The worm within the *neem* eats nought
   Save *neem* alone.
Thy rosy feet thy servant I
   Will love alone,
Thou Light Supreme, on serpent bed,
Who waning moon delivered!

Translated from the Tamil by J.S.M. Hooper

Mohammad Iqbal (1873–1938)

Man and God

You made the night, I lit the lamp in it.
You made the clay, I moulded it into a goblet.
In the wild wastes, mountains and forests that you made
Orchards, flower beds and gardens have I laid
It is I who ground stones and turned them into mirrors,
It is I who out of poison extracted its antidote.

Translated from the Urdu by Khushwant Singh

Eknath (1533–99)

Wonder of Wonders

Wonder of wonders
a thief stole a town
but when the trackers tracked him down
no thief no town

The town was entirely unfounded
the temple windblown
god confounded
the steeple shot across heaven

The foundations fled
to the recesses of hell
and the wall wandered
from door to door

The foundation the wall the temple
underneath all paradox
the meaning is simple

Translated from the Marathi by Arun Kolatkar

Puspadanta (8 CE)

From Sivamahimnahstava

Oh Lord! If the Giver of Happiness
Were to write for all time
With a pen made from a branch of the best of all celestial trees
Using the whole earth as Her leaf

If the mass of ink equaled the blue mountains and the ocean
Were the inkpot

Still it would be impossible to express
The fullness of your attributes.

Translated from the Sanskrit by Arthur Avalon

Akha (17 CE)

Vaishnav Struts About Town

Vaishnav struts about town
    sectarian in an ochre gown.
    At parsad he loads victuals
    on his plantain-leaf plate.

He showers praise
    on the steaming rice: Oh, it's great!
    Course follows course, fetching his applause.
    The more he is served, the more he wolfs down.

Replete now, paunch delirious,
    worship turns ever more serious.
    He sings devotionals and drums up a stew.
    Akha says: Put it down
    to the zap of youth.

Translated from the Gujarati by Gieve Patel

Ma Basanti Cakrabartti (20 CE)

Ma, If You Wore a Benarasi Sari

Ma, if You wore a Benarasi sari
and tied up Your hair,
You'd look so good—
and there'd be no harm in it, Ma,
no harm at all.

If instead of standing on daddy
You sat next to Him,
exchanging Your fearful form
for a sweet smile,
if there were no blood smeared on Your body,
You'd look so good—
and there'd be no harm in it, Ma.

What if Forgetful daddy didn't lie
like a corpse at Your feet
but spoke to You honeyed words?
Think how nice that would be!
The whole world I am sure
would be astonished: Siva and Kali
are playing new games
such an improvement!
You'd look so good—
and there' be no harm in it, Ma.

Translated from the Bangla by Rachel Fell McDermott

Joaquim Miranda (c. mid-18 CE)

From Jesus Entered the Garden

Verse 6
Said the Mother: My child, the time
You thirst for death, I know,
Angels of heaven, come to this hill,
Carrying with you pitchers of water,
The Creator thirsts for a drink of it;
He is gasping for life without it.

Verse 7
I abide by the foot of the Cross,
You have moved up to the skies.
If I were to give you water to quench
Your thirst, how would you drink it?
My hand does not reach there,
Find out a way to do it, my Lord.

Translated from the Konkani by Olivnho Gomes and Jose Pereira

Annamayya (1408–1503)

Imagine That I Wasn't Here

Imagine that I wasn't here.
What would you do with your kindness?
You get a good name because of me.
I'm number one among idiots. A huge mountain of ego.
Rich in weakness, in giving in to my senses.
You're lucky you found me. Try not to lose me.

Imagine that I wasn't here.

I'm the Emperor of Confusion, of life and death.
Listed in the book of bad karma.
I wallow in births, womb after womb.
Even if you try, could you find one like me?

Imagine that I wasn't here.

Think it over. By saving someone so low,
you win praise all over the world.
You get merit from me, and I get life
out of you. We're made for each other,
Lord of the Hill.

Imagine that I wasn't here.

Translated from the Tamil by David Shulman

Narsinh (Narsi) Mehta (1408–80)

If You Abuse Me with Your Language

If you abuse me with your language
All will know we are in love;
Therefore darling, I beseech you
Do not abuse me with your tongue.

You burst into my house cursing
Disguised as a godly beggar,
Be careful, do not press me roughly,

My husband is uneasy, anxious,
He will surely seek the truth.
He will discover we are familiar.
Do not abuse me with your tongue.

My envious sister-in-law will find out.
She will scold me very hard.
Narsi's Lord, I tell you truly,
I shall be banished from the house.
Do not abuse me with your tongue.

Translated from the Gujarati by Swami Mahadevananda

Anapiyya (19 CE)

From Napikal Nayakam Pillaittamil

Come So I Can Bedeck, with Anklets and Bells

Come so I can bedeck, with anklets and bells,
your feet like day-blooming lotuses.
Come so I can put on, with delight, your warrior's anklets
that confound the enemies who battle you,
like the ocean that wars with the land.

Come so I can adorn you with tinkling jewels.

Come so I can anoint with attar, rosewater,
the four perfumes, and most fragrant sandalpaste
your shoulders and chest towering like mountains
and clothe you lovingly.

So I can place you in the cradle
and rock you happily,
come joyously.

Muhammad, who has the truth,
come joyously, come.

Translated from the Tamil by Paula Richman

Mahadeviyakka (12 CE)

He Bartered My Heart

He bartered my heart,
looted my flesh,
claimed as tribute
my pleasure,
took over
all of me.

I'm the woman of love
for my lord, white as jasmine.

Translated from the Kannada by A.K. Ramanujan

Ksetrayya (mid-17 CE)

A Courtesan to Her Lover

Pour gold as high as I stand, I still won't sleep with you.
Why be stubborn, Muwa Gopala? Why all these tricks?

You set women afloat on your words,
break into their secret places,
deceive them with affectionate lies,
excite them in love play,
get together the whole crowd one day,
and then you steal away like a spinach thief.

Pour gold as high as I stand

You coax women's affections,
make them amorous and faint,
do things you shouldn't be doing,
confuse them, lie in bed with them,
and then you leave without a sound,
shaking your dust all over them.

Pour gold as high as I stand

You opportunist,
you excite them from moment to moment,
make mouths water,
show them love to make them surrender,
drown them in a sea of passion,
and by the time the morning star appears—
you get up and vanish.

Pour gold as high as I stand

Translated from the Telugu by A.K. Ramanajan, Velcheru Narayan Rao and David Shulman

Mirabai (1498–1546)

This Pain Has Driven Me Mad

This pain has driven me mad,
this pain no one can understand.
Only she knows what it means to be wounded
who's wounded, the fire trapped in her heart.
The jewel gleams only for the jeweller,

not for the fool who threw it away.
Lord of Meera, this hurt will only fade
when the Dark One comes to heal me.

Translated from the Hindi by Ranjit Hoskote

Palalikkuttar (c. mid-14 CE)

***From* Tiruccentur Pillaittamil**

You are truly great,
performing all three functions.

You created the entire wide world
around which Aruna drives his seven horses
in a chariot with fluttering banners.

You preserve the world you created.
You destroy it.

Your intention is to seize
entire cities of your enemies, isn't it?

Is it really prowess
to destroy the homes
we made as playhouses?

We are just little girls
with anxious eyes,
waists burdened
with the support of our heavy breasts,
and flower-like hands reddened
from sifting sand.

With your holy lotus feet,
sought by Indra and the other gods,
don't destroy the little houses of us little ones.

Rich one of Tiruccentur,
where the waves cast up pearls,
don't destroy our little houses.

Translated from the Tamil by Paula Richman

Kazi Nazrul Islam (1899–1976)

Let's Be Girls, Ma

Let's be girls, Ma,
and play with dolls;
    come into my playroom.
I will take the Mother's role, so I can
teach You how.

If You make one dull or wretched,
hold him to Your bosom;
who else will ease his pain?
One who gets no jewels and gems, Ma,
at least should get his mother.

Some will be quite naughty,
others lie about inside their homes,
but all play games of hide-and-seek
    (our world here has no death, Ma),
crying as they leave at night, returning with the morning.

This little boy,

You made him cry
>   You made him fear.
>   Now love away his fear,
cease to make him cry—

or casting You aside
he'll run away.

When this play is finished
lull him into sleep;
>   hold him in Your arms.

Translated from the Bangla by Rachel Fell McDermott

Sakalesha Madarasa (12 CE)
Both of Us Are Tired

Both of us are tired
justifiably so.
I am tired of this world you made
and of you, haunting me so.

In what way are you eminent
and I low
when you are a God
in this devotee's frame?

O Sakaleshwara, my Lord,
you know
and I too know!

Translated from the Kannada by B.C. Ramchandra Sharma

Tukaram (c. 1608)

God's Own Dog: VI

Pamper a dog
And it's spoilt for good
It'll loiter at your feet
And get in your way

That's how I've become
With You
Staying too damn close
All the time

I come wagging my tail
When You eat your dinner

Says Tuka,
O Lord
I don't even notice
If you are annoyed!

Translated from the Marathi by Dilip Chitre

Salabega (c. 17 CE)

O Sakhi, the Flute Plays in the Grove

O friend, tell me
who plays the flute
in the grove?
The bare trees bloom
at the sound of his flute.

The air stands still.
Stones turn into water.
The Yamuna flows upstream
and the fish seek the shore.
As the bell tinkles slowly,
freeing us from shame,
there's no time left to wear clothes.
Strange! the Rishi loses his poise
and succumbs to love.
The deer chases the tiger.
Says Salabega: I am Muslim by birth
But my heart is
at the feet of Radhakrishna.

Translated from the Oriya by Sachidananda Mohanty and Smita Mohanty

Ramprasad Sen (1718–75)

What a Joke!

What a joke!
She's a young woman
from a good family
    yes, but
She's naked—and flirts, hips cocked
when She stands.

With messy hair
roars awful and grim
this gentlewoman tramples demons
in a corpse-strewn battle.
    But the God of Love
    looks and swoons.

While ghosts, ghouls, and goblins
from Siva's retinue, and Her own companions
    nude just like Her
dance and frolic on the field,
She swallows elephants
    chariots, and charioteers
        striking terror into the hearts
        of gods, demons, and men.

She walks fast,
enjoying Herself tremendously.
Human arms hang from Her waist.

Ramprasad says: Mother Kalika,
preserver of the world,
have mercy!
Take the burden:
ferry me across this ocean of becoming.
Hara's woman,
    destroy my sorrows.

Translated from the Bangla by Rachel Fell McDermott

Tyagaraja (1767–1847)
Tell Me Why This Bad Mood Now

Tell me why this bad mood now,
dear Rama, please speak!

I held your feet with devotion
and called you my friend
and my shelter, so speak

Tell me why this bad mood now,
dear Rama, please speak to me!

Even to the wise son of the wind,
Hanuman, that fraction of Siva
when he knelt to you
You asked your brother to tell
the story of your trials—so
What can a nobody like Tyagaraja
expect? Tell me
Why this bad mood now
dear Rama, say something
to me

Translated from the Tamil by William J. Jackson

Purandara Dasa (1485–1565)

I Swear

You swear, so do I.
Both are named by your devotees.

Curse on me were I, Ranga, to worship others but you;
Curse on you were you to abandon me.

Curse on me were I to be deceitful in
Mind, body and wealth;
Curse on you were you not to fix Your mind on me.

Curse on me if I have the company of the wicked;
On you if you don't relieve me of worldly snares.

Curse on me if I don't cultivate friendship with the pious;
Curse on you were you not to cut my contact with the wicked.

Curse on me were I not to resort to you;
Curse on you were you, Purandar Vitthal, not to bless me.

Translated from the Kannada by Keshav M. Mutalik

Andal (c. 9 CE)

From Tiruppavai

Son of the Lord of countless cattle,
Huge, unfailing in filling to the brim
And flowing over the jugs held under them!
Lord, you have wisdom and energy,
A pillar of fire manifest,
Rise now! Like your routed foes
Seeking your door to fall at your feet
We too have come to honour and praise you.

Translated from the Tamil by P.S. Sundaram

Subramania Bharati (1882–1921)

Krishna the Omnipresent

I see your complexion, Krishna,
in the crow's dark feathers.

I see the divine green, O Krishna,
in the leaves of all the trees.

'tis your music, Krishna, that I hear
in all the sounds of the world.

And I thrill with your touch, Krishna,
when my finger feels the flame.

Translated from the Tamil by Prema Nandkumar

S. Joseph (b. 1965)

My Sister's Bible

This is what my sister's Bible has:
a ration-book come loose,
a loan application form,
a card from the cut-throat money-lender,
the notices of feasts
in the church and the temple,
a photograph of my brother's child,
a paper that says how to knit a baby cap,
a hundred-rupee note,
an SSLC book.

This is what my sister's Bible doesn't have:
the preface,
the Old Testament and the New,
maps,
the red cover.

Translated from the Malayalam by K. Satchidanandan

Kailash Vajpeyi

Momin

There were houses of worship
Earlier too,
There were killing fields as well.
This is the progress we have made:
Now the two are one.

Translated from the Hindi by Ananya Vajpeyi

Minal Sarosh (b. 1960)

On the Loft

When the mind
meditates, turns off all the taps,
and sits on the loft—
cross-legged, like a tank
full of water, it hears only
the single leaking drop,
trickling into the ears and
filling up the whole
ocean.

English

'I'm ever vigilant'

Ravji Patel (1939–68)

Whirlwind

When I'd finished my bath
I wiped my body
with the smell of the green fields.
The moment I whistled
cows jumped in
through the window,
carrying the morning's sunshine
on their horns;

buffaloes jumped in,
their bodies slick
with the waters of the lake
foul with fish-smells;

goats jumped in,
with lonely roads,
the muddy edges of roads,
deserted fields,
and peacock feathers
in their eyes;

I jumped in,
a whirlwind in the house.

Translated from the Gujarati by Hansa Jhaveri

Dhoomil (1935–75)

A City, an Evening, and an Old Man: Me

After taking the last drag,
I crush the cigarette in an ashtray
and now I'm a kindly man,
civil, suave.

On holidays I hate no one.
I do not have to fight
on any front.
I have finished the bottle of liquor
which says FOR DEFENCE SERVICES ONLY
and put it away
in the lavatory.
(Like all good citizens,
I draw the curtains
the moment I hear the siren.)

I've done nothing to make me
deserve a statue
on whose inauguration
responsible townsfolk
lose a busy day.
I've sat in a corner of my dinner plate
and lived an ordinary life.

The civility of prisons,
the courteousness of slaughter-houses,
are what I've inherited;
these qualities I've improved upon

and taken them two steps ahead.
(To be successful in life
it isn't necessary to read Dale Carnegie
but understand road signs.)

My lies are small ones,
but that is until you ask me the weight of a gun.
On the expression of a traffic cop
standing at a crossing
I've sighted the map of democracy.

And now I'm all smugness and satisfaction.
There's nothing I have to finish.
I've reached that turn in one's age
when the files begin to close.
Sitting on the verandah in my armchair,
I have few worries.
The sun sets on the toe of my shoe.
Far away, a bugle sounds.
This is the time when the soldiers return,
and the city, quietly, slowly,
changes its madness
to windowpanes and light bulbs.

Translated from the Hindi by Arvind Krishna Mehrotra

Nilakantha Dikshita (1580–1644)

From Peace

What a family to be born into! Can you believe
who turned out to be my parents?

And all the lectures I've heard—the finest professors,
the range of topics, class after class . . .
I've seen how bad the world can be. Tasted
every pleasure. What I've never managed
is a quiet heart. As you can see,
I've got it made.

My feet always know the way straight
to the crooked alleys,
My tongue follows its secret agenda:
to tell lies and lies alone.
My clever mind searches out the finest faults
in everyone. But when it comes to doing
what's good for me, I'm a lame,
dumb beast.

To make her happy, I didn't think twice
about throwing away my wealth or my life.
Her love was dearer to my heart
than the rapture of release.
And now that my life is spent,
and my money too, my dear wife
thinks less of me, Shiva,
Burner of Cities,
than a ball of fluff.

When they were little,
I would have killed
to provide for them.
I didn't sleep, I didn't eat,
but I put them through school.
Now these children of mine
think they were born out of thin air,

bringing with them great wisdom
from a previous life.
They don't remember
who they are.

My wife, my sons, closest friends,
my relatives, servants, whoever—
can't bear to part from me
even in their dreams.
But when the horde of Death's messengers
come knocking on my door,
not even one of them, Shiva,
Killer of Passion,
will volunteer to join me.

If you have the great good fortune,
of making friends with the king's close aides,
you've found your guru.
If they let you past the gate,
you're in heaven.
Then, if you get to meet the king in person,
it'll be like shaking God's hand.
And if you drop dead at your post in the palace,
as far as I'm concerned,
that's instant
redemption.

Pilgrimage to holy places,
worshiping the gods,
an obsession with rituals and charity,
mastery of the arts—
for people like me,
all these are only

ways of getting rich.
And then what happens?
We either bury the money in the ground
or surrender it to the king.

All the trouble I took,
ever since I was a kid
serving at the feet of my teachers,
to fathom the secrets of God—
look what came out of it:
the stuff of bedtime stories
that I tell yawning kings,
night after night,
to kill time.

Shade, water, clothing, food,
transportation, light—
where we mortals have to go,
not one of them is for sale.
It's a long road, and the journey
must begin with a certain something
that we, in our body's hunger,
can't seem to remember.

Translated from the Sanskrit by David Shulman and Yigal Bronner

Jayanta Mahapatra (b. 1928)

The Abandoned British Cemetery at Balasore, India

This is history.
I would not disturb it: the ruins of stone and marble,

the crumbling walls of brick, the coma of alienated decay.
How exactly should the archaic dead make me behave?

A hundred and fifty years ago
I might have lived. Now nothing offends my ways.
A quietness of bramble and grass holds me to a weed.
Will it matter if I know who the victims were, who survived?

And yet, awed by the forgotten dead,
I walk around them: thirty-nine graves, their legends
floating in a twilight of baleful littoral,
the flaking history my intrusion does not animate.

Awkward in the silence, a scrawny lizard
watches the drama with its shrewd, hooded gaze.
And a scorpion, its sting drooping,
two eerie arms spread upon the marble, over an alien name.

In the circle the epitaphs run: Florence R . . . darling wife
of Captain R—R—aged nineteen, of cholera . . .
Helen, beloved daughter of Mr. and Mrs.—of cholera,
aged seventeen, in the year of our Lord, eighteen hundred . . .

Of what concern to me is a vanished Empire?
Or the conquest of my ancestors' timeless ennui?
It is the dying young who have the power to show
what the heart will hide, the grass shows no more.

Who watches now near the dead wall?
The tribe of grass in the cracks of my eyes?
It is the cholera still, death's sickly trickle,
that plagues the sleepy shacks beyond this hump of earth,

moving easily, swiftly, with quick power
through both past and present, the increasing young,
into the final bone, wearying all truth with ruin.
This is the iron

rusting in the vanquished country, the blood's unease,
the useless rain upon my familiar window;
the tired triumphant smile left behind by the dead
on a discarded anchor half-sunk in mud beside the graves;

out there on the earth's unwavering gravity
where it waits like a deity perhaps
for the elaborate ceremonial of a coming generation
to keep history awake, stifle the survivor's issuing cry.

English

Mahadevi Verma (1907–87)

No Matter the Way Be Unknown

no matter the way be unknown, the spirit solitary

>	no matter darkness, like the new moon's enshroud
> in kohl-touched tears today wash this gathered cloud.
>		other eyes do not cry—
>		pupils lightless, lashes dry—
>		amidst a hundred lightnings here
> lamplight danced, although this gaze was watery.

>	others' may be the feet that retreat;
> others' that leave resolve to thorns and own defeat —

>   these feet that measure immortality,
>   pledged to pain, insensed with creativity,
>   by their propagation will secure
> in darkness dawn's golden tapestry.

>   others' will be the biography whose elements
> will merge with nothingness, in dust its monument.

>   that on which destruction falls today
>   I walk on everyday,
>   a continuum on pearls,
>   a fete of sparks, jubilant, fiery.

>   even if you send an embassy of laughter,
>   or spring, that makes the leaf-fall-dark of angry
>   forehead softer—
> you will find this breast unflustered,
> anguish-water, dreams' lotuses clustered;
> know, this unity in solitude
> in separation is binary:

no matter the way be unknown, the spirit solitary.

Translated from the Hindi by Vinay Dharwadker

Nissim Ezekiel (1924–2004)

Background, Casually

1
A poet-rascal-clown was born,
The frightened child who would not eat

Or sleep, a boy of meagre bone.
He never learned to fly a kite,
His borrowed top refused to spin.

I went to Roman Catholic school,
A mugging Jew among the wolves.
They told me I had killed the Christ,
That year I won the scripture prize.
A Muslim sportsman boxed my ears.

I grew in terror of the strong
But undernourished Hindu lads,
Their prepositions always wrong,
Repelled me by passivity.
One noisy day I used a knife.

At home on Friday nights the prayers
Were said. My morals had declined.
I heard of Yoga and of Zen.
Could I, perhaps, be rabbi-saint?
The more I searched, the less I found.

Twenty-two: time to go abroad.
First, the decision, then a friend
To pay the fare. Philosophy,
Poverty and Poetry, three
Companions shared my basement room.

2

The London seasons passed me by.
I lay in bed two years alone,
And then a Woman came to tell

My willing ears I was the Son
Of Man. I knew that I had failed

In everything, a bitter thought.
So, in an English cargo-ship
Taking French guns and mortar shells
To Indo-China, scrubbed the decks,
And learned to laugh again at home.

How to feel it home, was the point.
Some reading had been done, but what
Had I observed, except my own
Exasperation? All Hindus are
Like that, my father used to say,

When someone talked too loudly, or
Knocked at the door like the Devil.
They hawked and spat. They sprawled around.
I prepared for the worst. Married,
Changed jobs, and saw myself a fool.

The song of my experience sung,
I knew that all was yet to sing.
My ancestors, among the castes,
Were aliens crushing seed for bread
(The hooded bullock made his rounds).

3
One among them fought and taught,
A Major bearing British arms.
He told my father sad stories
Of the Boer War. I dreamed that
Fierce men had bound my feet and hands.

The later dreams were all of words.
I did not know that words betray
But let the poems come, and lost
That grip on things the worldly prize.
I would not suffer that again.

I look about me now, and try
To formulate a plainer view:
The wise survive and serve—to play
The fool, to cash in on
The inner and the outer storms.

The Indian landscape sears my eyes.
I have become a part of it
To be observed by foreigners.
They say that I am singular,
Their letters overstate the case.

I have made my commitments now.
This is one: to stay where I am,
As others choose to give themselves
In some remote and backward place.
My backward place is where I am.

English

Jaya Mehta (b. 1932)

When a Stone Is in One's Hands

Stone is history
an edifice
a sculpture

of Gandhi, Jesus, Buddha.
Stone is memory of
the Taj's opulence
a memorial stone
a foundation
a support
a weapon.

When did we learn all this?

When a stone is in hand
one experiences power
and forgets that what gets wounded
is hide
whether white or black
hurt by a sharp pebble.

When a stone is in hand
one forgets that
a fallen person
can be given water, even an enemy.

Such amnesia
when the hand grips a stone ...

Translated from the Gujarati by Pradip N. Khandwalla

Nirendranath Chakravarti (b. 1924)

Old Age

Don't wait for me any longer, folks.
The day's drawing on,
You'd better set out now.

I'll take a little time.
I'm not quite unencumbered like you people:
If I sit down somewhere,
Huge branches start to sprout within my breast,
And from my feet
Great roots begin to grow.
I can't rush out as soon as you snap your fingers.

So just you move on, folks,
Don't sit waiting for me any longer:
I'm going to be late.

Translated from the Bangla by Sukanta Chaudhuri

Firaq Gorakhpuri (1896–1982)

Annihilate the Stillness of the Evening

Annihilate the stillness of the evening, it's unfathomably dark
    Light the lamp of poetry, it's unfathomably dark

The benighted colonies of the world will begin to glow
    Sing elegiac songs, it's unspeakably dark

    I have lost my restive heart in the lands of grief
        Go, look for it carefully, it's dark, dark, dark

In this savage night you can see nothing at all
Let imagination not run wild it's impenetrably dark

        If she cannot attend the carnival of grief
        Invite her smiles today, it's incredibly dark

The tears that quivered in Adam's eyes after the Fall,
    Shed those tears, it's impossibly dark

    I see no end to this sad night
    Invent another night, it's intensely dark

Revive the memory of past resolutions
Kindle new lamps, it's real pitch dark

    His life was but a delirious sleep
Do not awake Firaq, it is frightfully dark

Translated from the Urdu by Noorul Hasan

Narayana (c. 12 CE)

From Hitopadesa

On Hunger

A woman will her child forsake
When hunger's pangs she can't evade,
As will the famished mother snake
Eat eggs that she herself has laid:
What sins will not the starving do?
Men grown gaunt turn pitiless too.

Translated from the Sanskrit by A.N.D. Haksar

Vinod Kumar Shukla (b. 1937)

Those That Will Never Come to My Home

Those that will never come to my home
I shall go to meet.

A river in flood will never come to my home.
To meet a river, like people,
I shall go to the river, swim a little and drown.
Dunes, rocks, a mountain, a pond, endless trees, fields
will never come to my home
I shall search high and low
for dunes, mountains, rocks—like people

People who work at the time,
I shall meet, not during my leisure hours,
but as if it was an important job.
This first wish of mine I'll hold on to, like the very last one.

Translated from the Hindi by Dilip Chitre

Mangesh Padgaonkar (b. 1929)

Lamp

Memory has smells, of grass damp
and crushed, has sounds of bird song
swarming in full-throated throng.
Commemorate these with the lighting of a lamp.

Memory has a tree, has wet black bark
And beneath, soft soil on which to lie.
Eye moved, there in the speechless orbit of eye,
Meteors split and shredded the dark.

Memory has a path, overtaken by flowers
An unrestricted growth where the feet pause, stop.
The earth quivered, there, like a dewdrop.
With splendid red dawn rewarded the stars.

When the smell of memory quickens again, on the damp
soil and the pressed grass quickens with bird song
swarming in full throated throng,
commemorate me with the lighting of a lamp.

Translated from the Marathi by Vinay Dharwadker

Melanie Silgardo (b. 1956)

Between

My London is where I am.
Comfortable city where we feed birds
and worry about the diminishing bees.
At my desk struggling for words
I would rather be watching the
tree fern unfurl its newest frond or
the woodpecker puncture the birch
with his rataratarata, while the
parakeet, foreign and raucous,
swoops and shrieks. Green wing
and scarlet beak how you bring
my Bombay back. In a flash I hear
crows and the hootootoot of cars in
gridlock, cricket commentary blaring,
and the clatter of stainless steel from
the neighbour's kitchen. I can smell the
familiar monsoon fug and feel the discomfort
of air conditioners. The heat rots everything
and the fridge is never big enough.
Uncomfortable city, bigger than life itself.
I dream between continents.

Work can wait, lunch can wait.
For now I simply want to knit moment to
moment, city to city, the two halves of my life.

English

Basudev Sunani (b. 1962)

Satyabhama

Satyabhama
Chuckled on the window seat
Of the bus, and then
Hid her face
In her hands

Was she shy?

Satyabhama
Faint, dark, like a slate,
Forgotten.

How could she
Have been otherwise?

It's two decades since
She was in class five
And I in two
In our village school.

On her cheek
The flush of self-confidence

To have learnt by rote
The alphabet.

Married to a dhoti-clad gentleman,
She is now in search
Of a suitable girl
For her son;

Persuaded by the villagers
She is now a candidate
In the local body election;

She said all this
Pressing her face
To the window-sill.

Satyabhama
Gives the feeling
Of someone intimate
Like the torn pages
Of an old book

From childhood
When eating porridge together
She taught me the art
Of sewing sal-leaf bowls.

There was nothing more
To share with Satyabhama.

By the time I was in class five
And she in class two
The bus had left.

I do not know
If I will meet her again.

If only I had had
A fleeting glimpse
Of her face.

Translated from the Oriya by Rabindra K. Swain

R. Parthasarathy (b. 1934)

Taj Mahal

Children on their way to school
barely notice it as it squats
on the river like a humped bull

swishing its tail occasionally
at the swarms of barefoot
tourists. They have been gone now,

the emperor and his favourite queen,
for some three-hundred-odd
years. But this marble flame,

Earth's other moon, how
it rubs expensive delicate salt
in the wound of unrequited love!

English

Shanmuga Subbiah (b. 1924)

Salutations

Yes! Oh yes!
Indeed I'm blessed!
By God's grace
I have two children.
It's rather strange,
But both
Are boys.
So?
I'm rheumatic,
My wife's consumptive.
The first boy,
Poor chap,
Is quite sickly.
The younger one,
So far,
Is okay.
But later on—
Who knows?
I'm a clerk.
Will this do?
Or would you like to have
More details?

Translated from the Tamil by T.K. Doraiswamy

Dhan Gopal Mukerji (1890–1937)

In Bedlam

They call me crazed, for I console the moon,
I know the hour when she began to weep—
It was when the poets were slain that night.
Lo, how they lie:
Those who were more restless than the sea
And more serene
Than the height-humbling eagle in his flight—
They are gone, gods and singers;
Only the moon remains,
Vainly carrying her silver lyre;
They call me crazed, for I console the moon.

English

Manohar Shetty (b. 1953)

Rumour

Hissed out by a salivating tongue,
I'm the nagging, unfinished whole.
A hint, a slack jaw, eyes rankling,
I'm the whisper growing harsher

With each passing ear; twisted
Around to suit my sly plotters,
I'm the invisible flame setting
Fire to dome, minaret, spire.

I'm fuel stored for the retreating
Mob, my bait greed, hatred and rage.

Only a few see through me
As rootless seed, poisonous weed.

But scotch me and another
Is born, a handmaiden made
Hungrier, more bitter, eyes
Streaked with smoke and fire.

English

Attoor Ravi Varma (b. 1931)

Sitting

At one sitting, I do all sorts of things
Like a multi-purpose machine
That grinds and churns and pounds.

With my one and only tongue
I speak many tongues
Like a hotel-plate that serves
Hot and sweet and sour things one by one.

Like a fan's reeling in steady speed,
Like a bulb's burning with the same glow
Above people who arrive, are ushered in and exit,
I'm ever vigilant.

My sitting, my looks, my gestures—
All, all are precise, measured
Like those of a Kathakali cast.

Colourless, tasteless, odourless,
Changing shape with the vessel—
That unique purity: That's me.

Translated from the Malayalam by R. Viswanathan

A.K. Ramanujan (1929–93)

Anxiety

Not branchless as the fear tree,
it has naked roots and secret twigs.
Not geometric as the parabolas
of hope, it has loose ends
with a knot at the top
that's me.

Not wakeful in its white-snake
glassy ways like the eloping gaiety of waters,
it drowses, viscous and fibered as pitch.

Flames have only lungs. Water is all eyes.
The earth has bone for muscle. And the air
is a flock of invisible pigeons.

But anxiety
can find no metaphor to end it.

English

Aziz Bano Darab (1934–2005)

Ghazals

So that I may meet myself
From a river I must turn into a waterfall

When I was growing up some well-meaning relatives
Gave me several masks and a tongue of stone.

Thoughtlessly, he turns the pages
When my face becomes a book.

Why would he take me out of myself,
Why should anyone put his hands in someone else's fire?

He keeps probing in the ashes of my past
He'll burn his fingers, if I'm not careful.

He's a weary traveler
I, a locked caravanserai
Even if he reaches me,
What will he find?

Translated from the Urdu by Qurratulain Hyder and Arlene Zide

Kunwar Narain (b. 1927)

Day by Day

I've a strange problem these days—
    my ability to hate with passion
    is failing me day by day.

I want to hate the English
   (who ruled us for two centuries)
   but Shakespeare gets in the way
He's done so much for me!

I try to hate the Muslims
   but Ghalib intervenes
   You tell me—can anyone
   disregard him?

I want to hate the Sikhs
   but Guru Nanak appears
   and my head bows of its own accord.

And these Kamban, Tyagaraja, Muttusvami . . .
   I keep telling myself—
   They are not mine,
   they are of the far South
   But my heart doesn't listen
   and makes them its own.

And that woman I once loved
   who deceived me . . .
   I could kill her if I met her!
   We do meet, but then
   the friend in her,
   or the mother, or the sister
   nourishes me with love.

All the time
   I wander like a madman
   looking for someone

I could hate to my heart's content
and feel light!

But the opposite happens
    sometime, somewhere
    I always meet someone
    Whom I cannot but love!

Day by day this love sickness is growing
    And suspicion has gripped me
    That one day this love
    Will send me to heaven ...

Translated from the Hindi by Lucy Rosenstein

Bal Sitaram Mardhekar (1909–56)

This Is the Order

This is the order
Of a dark world:
A wick of soot
In the heart of darkness.

A black plane
Zooms into darkness
Through black air.

There are no signals
Not red, nor green;
One cannot get lost
In the invisible.

Wherever I go
I am my own partner:
My eyes have turned
Into such walls.

Translated from the Marathi by Dilip Chitre

Tishani Doshi (b. 1975)

Homecoming

I forgot how Madras loves noise—
loves neighbours and pregnant women
and Gods and babies

and Brahmins who rise
like fire hymns to sear the air
with habitual earthquakes.

How funeral processions clatter
down streets with drums and rose-petals,
dancing death into deafness.

How vendors and cats make noises
of love on bedroom walls and alleyways
of night, operatic and dark.

How cars in reverse sing Jingle Bells
and scooters have larynxes of lorries.
How even colour can never be quiet.

How fisherwomen in screaming red—
with skirts and incandescent third eyes
and bangles like rasping planets

and Tamil women on their morning walks
in saris and jasmine and trainers
can shred the day and all its skinny silences.

I forgot how a man dying under the body
of a tattered boat can ask for promises;
how they can be as soundless as the sea

on a wounded day, altering the ground
of the earth as simply as the sun filtering through—
the monsoon rain dividing everything.

English

Padma Sachdev (b. 1940)

Sun

Sun, do not rise today.
Take away your light.
Light is sin's enemy
And sin
This moment
Is my desire.
To tread
With eyes closed
Those paths
Which vanished
Long ago.
To recall
Faces
Wiped away
By time.

To ask him,
To tell me again,
Who is stone
Who is old peepal
Who is cobra guarding a treasure
And to walk with me
as of old.

Translated from the Dogri by Shivanath

Jerry Pinto (b. 1966)

Window

What can you do with a window?
It will always remain four-cornered
Always be a savagery to the sky
Always offer enough room for only one head
Or one cloud
There's nothing open about a window

English

The Empress Nur Jahan (1577–1645)

On the Tomb of Us Poor People

On the tomb of us poor people
there will be neither a light
nor a flower, nor the wings of a moth, nor the voice
of a nightingale.

Translated from the Persian by Barakat Ullah

Kutti Revathi (b. 1974)

Breasts

Breasts are bubbles, rising
in wet marshlands.

I watched in awe—and guarded—
their gradual swell and blooming
at the edges of my season of youth.

Saying nothing to anyone else,
they sing along
with me alone, always—of
love,
rapture,
heartbreak

To the nurseries of my turning seasons,
they never once forgot or failed
to bring arousal.

In penance, they swell, as if straining
to break free; and in the fierce tug of lust,
they rise with the harmony of music.

From the crush of embrace, they distill
the essence of love; and in the tremor
of childbirth, milk from coursing blood.

Like two teardrops from an unfulfilled love
that cannot ever be wiped away,
they well up, as if in grief, and spill over.

Translated from the Tamil by N. Kalyan Raman

Jyotsna Karmakar (b. 1950)

To Grandmother, Long After

Long ago, grandmother gave me an amulet and said:
    Your heart will be drawn back to your home

I left the paper spread out on the three-legged table
and unable to find the stairs of the search for the secret of the
                                        people of the lost island
    lifting my hands in the darkness I said: Grandmother, you too!

Translated from the Bangla by Marian Maddern

Ranjit Hoskote (b. 1969)

Fern

This feathered leaf must have fallen from the hand
of the woman who turned around to see
if her child had strayed too close to the slope
of the fuming mountain or the hunting birds,
and left her footprint in ash that hardened
to rock. A spray of seeds released that noon
remains in the thick air, and this gift:

a leaf trapped between layers of mud
that volcanic fire baked into stone.
Drained of light and green, long spasm,
breath dusted with pollen:
a net of veins splayed on an altar
where the river turns in its sleep
and an old woman lights a lamp.

English

Adil Mansuri (1936–2008)

The City

The city at play on the river's sandbed
may vanish and never flash on memory's screen.

Let me breathe in deeply this sea of scents,
the smell of this fresh, wet mud.

Who knows if I will ever see again
these familiar faces, this glance, this glancing smile.

This window, this street, this wall, this house,
these lanes—eyes, have your fill of the city.

Embrace these loved ones. Who knows
what final partings lie in the years ahead.

O you who bid us goodbye, you live in our eyes;
what matter then if we find no fellow-travellers.

Touch this country's dust to your head, O Adil,
you may never ever tread this dust again.

Translated from the Gujarati by Suguna Ramanathan and Rita Kothari

Sitakant Mahapatra (b. 1937)

Time Does Not Fly

It is not time that flies.
It is men, all creatures
everywhere.

The cloud in brown coat flies away
waving goodbye to my father
as he sits like a portrait,
his head propped against the wall
of the front verandah of our house.

Next day, his back towards us,
father flies away and sinks
below the horizon
along with the setting sun.

Leaves fall
waving goodbye to the weeping tree.
And then the woodcutters come and fell the tree
and it waves goodbye
to the ancient soil on which it stood.

Suddenly one sees
houses, rivers, forests, paddy fields
swamps, wife and children, friends, relatives
the endless images, crafted by time:
everything rushing forward
into the darkness.

That darkness
is your only shadow.
Surely you should know
why we fly away, helpless,
and where.

Translated from the Oriya by the poet

Balachandran Chullikkad (b. 1957)

A Labourer's Laughter II

I searched in many books
for the truth concerning you
and I learnt that
cities and sagas
were made by you.

And I learnt that
all banners were starched
in your life-blood.

And I learnt that you
are the lord and master
of the spring to come.

I waited, at dusk, many a time
to chat with you,
feigning acquaintance.

Translated from the Malayalam by A.J. Thomas

Jeet Thayil (b. 1959)

Spiritus Mundi

I was born in the Christian South
of a subcontinent mad for religion.
Warriors and zealots tried to rule it.
A minor disciple carried his doubt
like a torch to temple and shrine.
I longed for vision and couldn't tell it.

The cities I grew up in were landlocked.
One, a capital, buff with architecture,
the other lost for months in monsoon.
One was old, one poor; both were hot.
The heat vaporised thought and order,
drained the will, obliterated reason.

I settled, 20 and morose, in a town
built by a patricidal emperor
whose fratricidal son imprisoned him,
for eight years, with a view of the tomb
he built for his wife, to remember her.
I was over conscious of my rhyme,

and of the houses, three, inside my head.
In the streets, death, in saffron or green,
rode a cycle rickshaw slung
with megaphones. On the kitchen step
a chili plant grew dusty in the wind.
In that climate nothing survived the sun

or a pickaxe, not even a stone dome
that withstood 400 years of voices
raised in prayer and argument. The train
pulled in each day at an empty platform
where a tea stall that served passers-
by became a famous fire shrine.

I made a change: I travelled west
in time to see a century end
and begin. I don't recall the summer
of 2001. Did it exist?

There would have been sun and rain.
I was there, I don't remember

a time before autumn of that year.
Now 45, my hair gone sparse,
I'm a poet of small buildings:
the brownstone, the townhouse, the cold water
walkup, the tenement of two or three floors.
I cherish the short ones still standing.

I recognise each cornice and sill,
the sky's familiar cast, the window
I spend my day walking to and from,
as if I were a baffled Moghul in his cell.
I call the days by their Hindu
names and myself by my Christian one.

The Atlantic's stately breakers mine
the shore for kelp, mussels, bits of glass.
They move in measured iambs, tidy
as the towns that rise from sign to neon sign.
Night rubs its feet. A mouse deer starts across
the grass. The sky drains to a distant eddy.

Badshah, I say to no one there.
I hear a koel in the call of a barn owl.
All things combine and recombine,
the sky streams in ribbons of color.
I'm my father and my son grown old.
Everything that lives, lives on.

English

Sitanshu Yashashchandra (b. 1941)

Solar

Sweet smelling rays shoot out from
that new-risen orange, the sun;
>   the neem, buried in the night,
>   a burst of flashing green;
>   and roots live coals that spark
>   off blazing birds.
>   So long now
>   Since
>   I looked
>   at you with
>   desire.

From here that dangling branch
is a bird winging through the wide sky.
It's *chaitra,* and rising gum drips from tree-trunks.
I seal my letter with this fresh and dripping gum.
I wrap up *vaishakh* in yellow cloth
and send the packet, look!—to you.
I am no scribbler of verses but a walker,
do you see, of these straight paths.

Translated from the Gujarati by Suguna Ramanathan and Rita Kothari

Susmita Bhattacharya (b. 1947)

Five Acts

School. See her run,
plaits swinging, Act I.

Home. Frock's gone
for Act II. Sari's on.

Marriage, Act III,
viz.: gold dowry.

Act IV's begun
(with luck) with a son.

Guru enters, Act V:
soul to stay alive.

With a futile sigh
the Curtain, from on high.

Translated from the Bangla by Joe Winter

Keki Daruwalla (b. 1937)

Map-maker

Perhaps I'll wake up on some alien shore
In the shimmer of an aluminium dawn,
to find the sea talking to itself
and rummaging among the lines I've drawn;
looking for something, a voyager perhaps,
gnarled as a thorn tree in whose loving hands,
these map lines of mine, somnambulant,
will wake and pulse and turn to shoreline, sand.

The spyglass will alight on features I've forecast—
cape, promontory—he'll feel he's been here,
that voyaging unlocks the doorways of the past.

And deep in the night, in the clarity of dream,
The seafarer will garner his rewards,
raking in his islands like pebbles from a stream.

2

Does the world need maps, where sign and symbol,
standing as proxies, get worked into scrolls?
You see them, mountain chains with raingods in their armpits
and glaciers locked like glass-slivers in their folds.
Desert, scrub, pasture—do they need shading?
They're all there for the eye to apprehend.
A family of cactus and camelthorn tells you
where one begins and the other ends.

These questions confound me, I'd rather paint
for a while—a ship on the skyline,
or cloud-shadow moving like a spreading stain.
Yet they live, pencil strokes that speak for rain
and thunder; and die—maplines ghosting round
a cycloned island that has gone under.

3

Forget markings, forget landfall and sea.
Go easy Man, I tell myself; breathe.
Gulls will mark the estuary for you,
bubbles will indicate where the swamps seethe.
Map the wrinkles on the ageing skin of love.
Forget Eastings, Northings—they stand for order.

Cry, if you must, over that locust line
flayed open into a barbarised border.

Mark a poem that hasn't broken forth, map the undefined,
the swamp within, the hedge between love and hate.
Forget the coastal casuarinas line.

Reefs one can handle. It's lust that seeks
out its quarry that one cannot map, nor that
heaving salt of desire that floods the creeks.

4

If you map the future, while a millennium
moves on its hinges, you may find
the present turned into an anachronism.
This too is important—what is yours and mine,
The silk of these shared moments. But having stuck
to love and poetry, heeding the voice of reason;
and experiencing the different textures of
a season of love and love's eternal season,

I put a clamp on yearning, shun latitudes, renounce form.
And turn my eye to the far kingdom
of bloodless Kalinga battling with a storm.
Dampen your fires, turn from lighthouse, spire, steeple.
Forget maps and voyaging, study instead
the parched earth horoscope of a brown people.

English

Lal Ded (1330–1384)

From I, Lalla: The Poems of Lal Ded

What the books taught me, I've practised.
What they didn't teach me, I've taught myself.
I've gone into the forest and wrestled with the lion.
I didn't get this far by teaching one thing and doing another.

Translated from the Kashmiri by Ranjit Hoskote

Pravin Gadhvi (b. 1951)

Shadow

'O Wood Cutter
Cut my Shadow'*

Whether I turn Hindu
Buddhist
or Muslim
I can't cleave this shadow.

Gone is the faeces pot
and the broom
but this shadow
does not depart.

Whether I change
name
work

---

* Lines from Lorca

Even the shadow of an untouchable was contaminating

address
or ilk
this shadow does not leave.

Whether I change
language
dress
or history
this shadow does not crumble.

Whether I compose a smruti
draft the Constitution
enact laws
or become a vote bank
this shadow can never be erased.
'O Wood Cutter
Cut my Shadow.'

Translated from the Gujarati by Pradip N. Khandwalla

Mrinal Pande (b. 1946)

Two Women Knitting

Rama said
Rama said to Uma
Oh my,
How time passes.
Ah me, says Uma
and both fall silent.

The two women cast on stitches
Skip stitches, slip the skipped stitches over,
Knit over purl,
Purl over knit.
After many intricate loops and cables
Their dark secrets still lie locked within
They have thrown the keys to their jewel casques in the lake.
Put the keys in, and the locks will bleed real blood.

Two women are knitting
Clicking steel against steel
Passers-by look up amazed at the sparks that fly.
Loneliness comes at every other row in their patterns
Though they have worn each others' saris
And bathed each others' slippery infants
Even though at this very moment their husbands
Lie asleep in the rooms upstairs
Shaking them in their dreams.

Translated from the Hindi by the poet and Arlene Zide

Anon, Rajputana Folk Song

A Child-Husband

I was so loved by my mother,
She married me to little Juvarmal.

While I grind, he is in my lap;
While I cook, he is in my lap;
When I go to fetch water, Juvarmal holds my finger, (as he walks beside me).

In my hand I have the sickle, on my shoulder the rake,
On my head I have Juvarmal's cradle.

The path is winding, and there is a green *peepul* tree;
I climb up it, and hang up the cradle of Juvarmal.

With the sickle in my hand I began to cut,
Juvarmal, who was sleeping in the cradle, cried.

O passer-by, on your way,
Please give a swing to Juvarmal, the child,

'Is he your brother or nephew? what is he?
Or is Juvarmal your child?'

'He is the son of my mother-in-law, and brother of my sister-in-law,
The child Juvarmal is my husband.'

Translated from the Rajasthani by Winifred Bryce

Gieve Patel (b. 1940)

The Ambiguous Fate of Gieve Patel, He Being Neither Muslim Nor Hindu in India

To be no part of this hate is deprivation.
Never could I claim a circumcised butcher
Mangled a child out of my arms, never rave
At the milk-bibing, grass-guzzling hypocrite
Who pulled off my mother's voluminous
Robes and sliced away at her dugs.
Planets focus their fires
Into a worm of destruction
Edging along the continent. Bodies

Turn ashen and shrivel. I
Only burn my tail.

English

Gagan Gill (b. 1959)

The Girl's Desire Moves among Her Bangles

The girl's desire moves among her bangles
They should break first on his bed
Then on the threshold of his house.

But why on the threshold?

Because a woman sits grieving inside the girl
A woman who's a widow
No, not really one
But a woman who'll surely become
A widow.

The girl's fear throbs in her veins
And moves across her bangles
The girl's desire throbs in her bangles
And they throb with her sorrow.

Sorrow?

Where's this girl's man?
The man who's in her mourning veins
Who fills her bangles with desire?

Her man lies caught
In someone else's body

Someone else's dream, someone else's sorrow
Someone else's tears
Each one of his sorrows, dreams, tears
Lies beyond the girl's mourning grasp.

But the girl's still a girl
The same primitive innocence in her
Fills her with madness, a deathwish
For which she will always punish the man
In the days to come.
When she will smash her bangles
On the threshold of his house ...

Translated from the Hindi by Mrinal Pande and Arlene Zide

Ali Sardar Jafri (1912–2000)

A Poem

Darkness,
Wearing the robe
Of man's blood,
Offers the mirage of hope
To those who cannot see.

Translated from the Urdu by Baidar Bakht and Kathleen Grant Jaeger

Valmiki (c. 600 BCE–250 CE)
From the Ramayana, Book VI, Canto CXVII
Sita's Disgrace

He saw her trembling by his side,
And looked upon her face and cried:

'Lady, at length my task is done,
And thou, the prize of war, art won.
This arm my glory has retrieved,
And all that man might do achieved;
The insulting foe in battle slain
And cleared mine honour from its stain.
This day has made my name renowned
And with success my labour crowned.
Lord of myself, the oath I swore
Is binding on my soul no more.
If from my home my queen was reft,
This arm has well avenged the theft,
And in the field has wiped away
The blot that on mine honour lay,
The bridge that spans the foaming flood,
The city red with giants' blood.
The hosts of King Sugriva led
Who wisely counselled, fought and bled;
Vibhishan's love, our guide and stay—
All these are crowned with fruit today.
But, lady, 'twas not love for thee
That led mine army o'er the sea.
'Twas not for thee our blood was shed,
Or Lanka filled with giant dead.
No fond affection for my wife
Inspired me in the hour of strife.
I battled to avenge the cause
Of honour and insulted laws.
My love is fled, for on thy fame
Lies the dark blot of sin and shame;
And thou art hateful as the light
That flashes on the injured sight.

The world is all before thee: flee:
Go where thou wilt, but not with me.
How should my home receive again
A mistress soiled with deathless stain?
How should I brook the foul disgrace,
Scorned by my friends and all my race?
For Ravan bore thee through the sky,
And fixed on thine his evil eye.
About thy waist his arms he threw,
Close to his breast his captive drew,
And kept thee, vassal of his power,
An inmate of his ladies' bower.'

Canto CXVIII
Sita's Reply

Struck down with overwhelming shame
She shrank within her trembling frame.
Each word of Rama's like a dart
Had pierced the lady to the heart;
And from her sweet eyes unrestrained
The torrent of her sorrows rained.
Her weeping eyes at length she dried,
And thus mid choking sobs replied:
'Canst thou, a high-born prince, dismiss
A high-born dame with speech like this?
Such words befit the meanest hind,
Not princely birth and generous mind.
By all my virtuous life I swear
I am not what thy words declare.
If some are faultless, wilt thou find
No love and truth in womankind?
Doubt others if thou wilt, but own

The truth which all my life has shown.
If, when the giant seized his prey,
Within his hated arms I lay,
And felt the grasp I dreaded, blame
Fate and the robber, not thy dame.
What could a helpless woman do?
My heart was mine and still was true.
Why when Hanuman sent by thee
Sought Lanka's town across the sea,
Couldst thou not give, O lord of men,
Thy sentence of rejection then?
Then in the presence of the chief
Death, ready death, had brought relief,
Nor had I nursed in woe and pain
This lingering life, alas in vain.
Then hadst thou shunned the fruitless strife
Nor jeopardied thy noble life,
But spared thy friends and bold allies
Their vain and weary enterprise.
Is all forgotten, all? my birth,
Named Janak's child, from fostering earth?
That day of triumph when a maid
My trembling hand in thine I laid?
My meek obedience to thy will,
My faithful love through joy and ill,
That never failed in duty's call—
O King, is all forgotten, all?'

To Lakshman then she turned and spoke,
While sobs and sighs her utterance broke:
'Sumitra's son, a pile prepare

My refuge in my dark despair.
I will not live to bear this weight
Of shame, forlorn and desolate.
The kindled fire my woes shall end
And be my best and truest friend.'
His mournful eyes the hero raised
And wistfully on Rama gazed,
In whose stern look no ruth was seen,
No mercy for the weeping queen.
No chieftan dared to meet those eyes,
To pray, or question, or advise.
The word was passed, the wood was piled,
And fain to die stood Janak's child.
She slowly paced around her lord,
The Gods with reverent act adored.
Then raising suppliant hands the dame
Prayed humbly to the Lord of Flame:
'As this fond heart by virtue swayed
From Raghu's son has never strayed,
So, universal witness, Fire
Protect my body on the pyre.
As Raghu's son has idly laid
This charge on Sita, hear and aid.'
She ceased: and fearless to the last
Within the flame's wild fury passed.
Then rose a piercing cry from all
Dames, children, men, who saw her fall
Adorned with gems and gay attire
Beneath the fury of the fire.

Translated from the Sanskrit by Ralph T.H. Griffith

Valmiki (c. 600 BCE–250 CE)

From the Ramayana, Book V, Canto 2

Lanka

The glorious sight a while he viewed,
Then to the town his way pursued.
Around the Vanar as he went
Breathed from the wood delicious scent,
And the soft grass beneath his feet
With gem-like flowers was bright and sweet.
Still as the Vanar nearer drew
More clearly rose the town to view.
The palm her fan-like leaves displayed,
Priyalas lent their pleasant shade,
And mid the lower greenery far
Conspicuous rose the Kovidar.
A thousand trees mid flowers that glowed,
Hung down their fruits' delicious load,
And in their crests that rocked and swayed
Sweet birds delightful music made.
And there were pleasant pools whereon
The glories of the lotus shone,
And gleams of sparkling fountains stirred
By many a joyous water-bird.
Around, in lovely gardens grew
Blooms sweet of scent and bright of hue,
And Lanka, seat of Ravan's sway,
Before the wondering Varna lay:
With stately domes and turrets tall,
Encircled by a golden wall,
And moats whose waters were aglow

With lily blossoms bright below:
For Sita's sake defended well
With bolt and bar and sentinel,
And Rakshases who roamed in bands
With ready bows in eager hands.
He saw the stately mansions rise
Like pale-hued clouds in autumn skies;
Where noble streets were broad and bright,
And banners waved on every height.
Her gates were glorious to behold
Rich with the shine of burnished gold:
A lovely city planned and decked
By heaven's creative architect,
Fairest of earthly cities meet
To be the Gods' celestial seat.

Translated from the Sanskrit by Ralph T.H. Griffith

Mirza Asadullah Khan Ghalib (1713–80)

On Drinking

Ghalib foreswore wine! But from time to time it's true
When dark clouds span the skies,
And nights are lit by the moon
He breaks his vow and takes a sip or two.

Translated from the Urdu by Khushwant Singh

'My heart's own love'

Punam Nambudiri (c. 16 CE)
From Ramayana Campu
The Moon-Rise
(Ravana tells the moon to shine when he visits Sita. The moon obeys.)

Like the face of Lady East,
like the mirror of Lady Night.
like the golden earring of Lady East,
like the wedding locket of the goddess of love,
like the ceremonial seat of the god of love,
like the white parasol held up
to welcome the advent of the god of love,
rose the moon in slow motion.

Like powdered camphor sprinkled on nectar
like the benign smile of the universe,
like the sea of milk that spreads far and wide,
like white ashes scattered around,
like lustrous white paint sprayed everywhere,
like pearls strewn all over
sweet moonlight swelled in the cool expanse;
seeing its radiance the entire brood of demons
played the game of love, each with his beloved,
revelled themselves in drinking fresh wine,
engaged in the mock fight of lovers,
made loud shrieks of ecstatic delight,
tried out new techniques of entertainment,
plunging themselves headlong into an ocean of bliss.

Translated from the Malayalam by V. R. Prabodhchandran Nayar

Habba Khatoon (c. 16 CE)

I Will Seek You Down the Wandering Brooks

I will seek you down the wandering brooks:
Don't tell me we shan't meet again:
The wild yellow rose has bloomed;
My iris buds ache to flower;
O let these eyes behold your form;
Don't tell me we shan't meet again.

Translated from the Kashmiri by Triloknath Raina

Mahe Jabeen (b. 1961)

A Love Poem

right then
as poetry happens
he comes and
kisses me

trying to find metre
in the sound of his feet
I casually close my eyes

youth
engulfs me
vague thoughts
that were taking shape
lose their consciousness

my poetic images
get mercilessly plundered

an unmasked love
kisses my naked forehead
a touch immersed in my eyes
shines provocatively
on my cheek
a look perches on the curve of my neck
and moves like a breeze

poetry freed from words
entwines us

lips publish love poems
with the author's consent

Translated from the Telugu by Velcheru Narayana Rao

Baladev Rath (1789–1845)

Oh, Pardon Me

Forgive me, O image of the goddess of love,
forgive me.
I didn't know
the princess was going to have a bath.

If a maid or companion
had come running and informed me

and I had not heeded her advice
and dared to go towards the pond,
then all this anger
would have been justified,
O narrow-waisted one!

O fair-haired one!
I didn't know
you were standing in the water
surrounded by maids,
and with all that beauty
of full, heavy thighs and breasts.

You held the corner of your saree
between your teeth
and faster than lightning
you ran, your anklets jingling noisy,
and stopped at the end of the platform
beautifying it with your presence.

Now that I have learnt a lesson
I would never repeat
this mistake, and if I did
you should destroy me with
your curses and punishment.
O lotus-eyed one, O full-bosomed one,
forgive me for this once.

Hearing Krishna's supplications
that precious gem of a woman
was elated and all on a sudden

made love to him.
So says the king of Astadurga.

Translated from the Oriya by Saubhagya Kumar Misra

Amaru (c. 800 CE)

She Neither Turned Away

She neither turned away, nor yet began
To speak harsh words, nor did she bar the door;
But looked at him who was her love before
As if he were an ordinary man.

Translated from the Sanskrit by John Brough

Palai Patiya Perunkatunko (c. 300 BCE–200 CE)

There Are Good Omens: The House-Lizard Chirps

There are good omens: the house-lizard chirps,
and my dark-rimmed left eyelid flickers.
My lover is gone,
but I know he will come (yes, I know—
money must be earned, ascetics must be fed,
but most of all, I know that
we will live our life in love).
Listen to what he said.

He said the heath was so hot,
you could not tread it
but he said the he-elephant

saves the last puddle of water,
though sullied by its young,
for its mate.
He said the sight would pain the eyes—
leafless trees, dry branches,
and no mark of pleasantness.
But there the he-dove would fan
with its soft wings, to console its
tired young loving mate.
He said the hot sun would scorch
all the bamboos on the hills,
affording no protection for those who would cross.
He also said the stag would give
its own shade, there being no other,
for his suffering mate.

Virtuous, from the trial of this forest,
he will not allow my beauty to fade;
I am certain he will come soon.

Translated from the Tamil by E. Annamalai and H. Schiffman

Vedanta Deshika (1268–1369)

From the Prologue of Mission of the Goose

Born in the flawless image of the Sun,
lending dignity to being human,
this god, never without Fortune,
was wide awake, eager to set off
to find Janaka's daughter.
He was ready to go,

now that Hanuman had returned.
Somehow or other, full of passion,
he got through the night
that seemed to stretch on forever
until dawn.

Early in the morning, sick at heart
since Janaka's daughter was far away,
and anxious to set in motion
the army of the monkey king,
he saw
the likeness of the full moon:
a regal goose
arrived right on time,
playing somewhere
in a lotus pond.

It walked Sita's walk.
Its shape was printed on her sari.
Its cry rang like her anklet.
It captured his eye.
Our hero's heart stopped for a moment
and he fused with her.
Fierce is the rule of Love
when he strikes at the right moment.

When he somehow breathed again,
Rama, Lakshmana's elder brother,
approached the goose with a gift
of lotus petals, hoping
to keep Sita alive with a message of love.

Even better than a real embrace
is getting news from your lover.

A goose knows nothing of messages, yet
Rama approached him with great respect.
(Not even Hanuman received such honour.)
In his utter madness he found a way
into the bird's heart. People shaken by separation
are reduced to begging help from clouds,
mountains, trees, and so on—to say nothing
of living creatures.

Translated from the Sanskrit by David Shulman and Yigal Bronner

Leela Gandhi (b. 1966)
Noun

Let me call you lover once
and I'll agree this love's a tenancy.
Just one tenacious arrangement
of our mouths, some tactile synergy
—you're good at that—to announce
the vowels, corporeally, with tongue's fluency,
then lips, catching the sharp descent
of teeth and sound. For this small bribery,
my lover-turned-landlord, overnight,
my occupancy will be light.
I'll pay what rent I owe in kind,
behave, keep passion confined
to small hours, the darkened stair,
and what gets damaged, lover, I'll repair.

English

Waris Shah (1722–98)

From **Heer-Ranjha**

1

Praise be to God the great,
Who on love this life has based;

Who was the first to love and dote
On Nabi, the prophet of our race.

Love exalts the saint and sage,
Love endows the man with grace.

Garden-like they smile and bloom,
Who the creed of love embrace.

24

Those whom the fire of love does burn,
Of the fire of hell are not afraid.

Those who pledge their hearts to love,
Are not concerned with earthly cares.

Flesh and blood are prey to death.
Faith alone can do and dare.

To hell will they be all consigned,
The false at heart, who stick nowhere.

Translated from the Punjabi by K.C. Kanda

Mustansir Dalvi (b. 1964)

Peabody

Babu Genu Dagadphode shells peas,
dropping the husk in a radius about his feet.
Unconcerned by stares in the 8.39 to Belapur,
he thinks of his wife and picks another pod.
Babu loves his Sumati, and she him,
or so he hopes, but has never verified.

De-leafing a cauliflower,
pulling strings off French beans,
his homecoming flurries drive the train on.
Which gives him greater pleasure?
The soft Pok! of a pod,
peas exploding on his palm in green orgasm,
or uncovering a misshapen pearl, tiny,
succulent, that he tucks away in his mouth,
with a scarce thought for his Missus.
By the time he is home, Babu Genu

will deplete a third of his load,
ring his doorbell with green fingers,
and greet his wife with emerald teeth.
Sumati sees, but just the same she loves her Mishter
for his trivial traveling kindnesses.
She thinks he loves her too, but has never verified.

English

Anon, Rajputana Folk Song

The Jewel Knight

My jewel knight, turn your horse, just once.
In Amrana, the parrots and peacocks are calling,
Yes, my jewel knight;
In Amrana the parrots and peacocks are calling,
Yes, my jewel knight;
And the black *koel* is calling in the garden,
O my clever Sodha, turn your horse back just once.

In Amrana there are *mahua* trees,
Yes, my jewel knight, there are *mahua* trees,
And from the *mahua* (flowers) drips the intoxicating juice,
O my jewel knight, turn your horse just once.

In the homes of Amrana the grinding stones are whirling,
Yes, my jewel knight, in each home the sound of grinding,
And the wheat is being ground into flour;
O my jewel knight, turn your horse just once.

In Amrana, the goldsmiths are at work,
Yes, my jewel knight, the goldsmiths are at work,
Do get an anklet made for me which will tinkle sweetly.

This Bhatiyal woman is standing under the shade of the balcony,
Yes, my jewel knight, the Bhatiyal woman is standing
under the shade of the balcony,
And shedding tears like a sad peahen;
O my jewel knight, turn your horse, just once.

There is thick darkness in Amrana,
Yes, my jewel knight, there is sick darkness in Amrana,
The palace and high buildings all look as if they were crying;
O my jewel knight, turn your horse just once.

Translated from the Rajasthani by Winifred Bryce

Bilhana (c. 10 ce–12 ce)
From Fifty Stanzas of a Thief

20

Still I recall my darling as she came,
Bent by her bosom's weight, to pleasure's bower,
House of the god who wounds with fiery darts,
Herself a beautiful and full-blown flower.
Her smile at me was radiance to bedeck
The clustered pearls which gleamed upon her neck.

21

Still I recall how my beloved spoke
When weary with our play; her tongue, confused,
Wished to assure me of her wild delight
But stumbled on the flatteries she used.
With timid murmurings and accents blurred
How charmingly she jumbled every word.

22

Still in another life I shall recall
What I recall at this my hour of dying:
The slender body of my royal swan

Amid love's lotus clusters languid lying;
Her eyes were closed in pleasure as we revelled,
Her garment loosened and her hair dishevelled.

23

Still could I see once more, as day declines
My loving mistress of the fawn-like eyes,
Carrying like two nectar-laden jars
Her swelling breasts, I would for such a prize
Renounce the joys of royalty on earth,
Heavenly bliss, and freedom from rebirth.

Translated from the Sanskrit by Richard Gombrich

Anon, Chhattisgarh Field Song

Complaints

How beautiful was the leaf—
When it was fresh;
It is yellow now.
How sincere were you to me—
When we were children
In youth, you have deceived me now.
In the leaves there is no flutter
Nor do the branches move.
O Sweetheart, you regard me as an enemy,
You don't speak a word to me.
It is a full moon night,
Yet the moon is nowhere to be seen.
My sweetheart has become mad,

He is not coming back.
Across the river
There is a mine of red clay
By your sweet words—
Why did you mislead me?
O, I was so innocent!
The evenings are disturbed,
Always by the crows
Here you made love to me
And went away to a distant village.
The moon rises,
And brightens the night!
O you are a woman!
You deceived me and went away.
The night is moonlit,
And the stars are twinkling
My *Raja* has become my enemy,
He does not speak to me.
In the mango leaves—
There is no flutter
My *Raja* has taken to silence,
He does not speak even a word to me.
I plucked the mango fruit,
Avowedly to eat it.
He deceived me,
By promising that he will come.
The rope you left tied to the cart.
O, I have newly come to you
For the first time;
And you have stopped talking to me.

Translated from the Chhattisgarhi by S.C. Dube

Anon, Punjabi Song

The Ballad of Laila

Last night distraught I wandered here and there,
All up and down Love's City sick at heart,
Till lo! I found myself all unaware
Caught in the tangles of my Laila's hair.

And all her raven tresses manifold
Entangled me around, and sudden bold
I grew, and being careless of my fate
My mouth I buried in her lips' pure gold.

And like a bee that pillages the tips
Of every crimson hyacinth and sips
Sweet honey from its petals—thus I lay
Drunk with the perfume of her honey-lips.

Said she: 'Thou art my heart's own love, I swear,
But those who trespass on this raven hair,
And rob the down from off these golden cheeks,
Must of the goodman of the house beware.

'He is a jealous watchman over me,
And Lord of all my dark locks' witchery.
he is my tyrant, and exceeding wrath,
And goeth about seeking to murder thee.'

'Let come what may,' said I, 'while thou art near
Thy locks protect me like a keen drawn sword.
Give me thy lips and this night without fear
I'll wander in that wilderness of hair.'

Said she: 'All else is folly; Love is best,
I will unlock the garden of my breast;
But thou, I know, will walk disdainfully,
And soon forget the lips that thou hast pressed.'

'Ah cruel one,' said I, 'unjust thou art;
The arrows of thine eyes have pierced my heart;
I am thy humble slave; thou knowest well
That never from thy side will I depart.'

'Hearken, ye hireling poets, do ye dare
Dispute my monarchy? Ye fools, beware;
For I am crowned with Laila's sovereign love,
And sceptred with a lock of Laila's hair.'

Translated from the Punjabi by C.F. Usborne

Chandidas (c. 15 CE)

The First Stage of Radha's Love

Radha goes out of her house too often;
Slowly she moves out, but back she comes;
Her mind is distracted, she breathes quickly.
She gazes at the *kadamba* trees:
Why is she in this plight?

She is not afraid of her elders or wicked people;
Maybe she is possessed by some evil spirit.
The end of her cloth is disorderly;
She does not arrange it properly.

She gets startled even when she remains seated;
Her ornaments fall on the ground.
She is only in her teens, the daughter of a king.
And moreover the damsel is a wife in a family.
For whom does she pine and why does the infatuation grow?
I do not understand the mystery of her behaviour.
From the state of her mind I presume that
She wants something beyond her reach.

Chandidasa says in all humility
She is trapped in her love of Krishna.

Translated from the Bangla by Ujjwal Majumdar

Shah 'Madho Lal' Husain (1539–93)

Open the Book, Brother Brahmin

Open the book, Brother Brahmin, demonstrate
when I'll meet my love face to face.

The woods are greening,
the marshes in bloom and
longing for my *mahi** swells my every limb—
the burden bows down Love's boughs.

Open the book, Brother Brahmin, show me
when I'll encounter my love.

* mahi: 'herder of buffalo' and 'beloved, sweetheart, swain' reference to the Hir-Ranjha story

See what manner of waters I cross,
rivers I ford, snakes I trample
over and over I face down lions—

Open the Book and say, Brother Brahmin,
When I shall face my love.

Other hazards loom above me,
they don't make me weak, nor give me pause;
desire draws me time and again to the reeds.

Open the Book, Brother Brahmin,
and show me
when I'll encounter my love.

Over and over cries out Shah Husain:
'Lord, I'm seeking the sight of you—
cast just one glance my way!'

Open your Book, Brother Brahmin, reveal
when I shall meet him face to face.

Translated from the Punjabi by Carla Petievich

Jayadeva (c. 12 CE)

From Gita Govinda

Song Seven

Seeing me surrounded by a gaggle of girls,
    my beloved has up and fled;

'My heart's own love' 195

I surely should have stopped her, but,
    feeling guilty, I let her go instead;
        Oh me, oh my, I am bereft!
        She's mad at me, she's up and left!

What will she do? What will she say
    after long separation rife with strife?
Nothing matters now—not family, fortune, home,
    nor, for that matter, even life;
        Oh me, oh my, I am bereft!
        She's mad at me, she's up and left!

I picture her: her brow is knit
    in jealous anger festered,
Her lotus flower face is flush
    as if by buzzing bees she's pestered
        Oh me, oh my, I am bereft!
        She's mad at me, she's up and left!

As I imagine making love with her,
    in my mind we are united;
So why search the forest for her?
    Why am I so benighted?
        Oh me, oh my, I am bereft!
        She's mad at me, she's up and left!

I realise, lithe lady, that jealousy
    rends and breaks your heart;
But how can I reassure you
    while we are so far apart?

>   Oh me, oh my, I am bereft!
>   She's mad at me, she's up and left!

You're driving me crazy:
   now I see you, now I don't;
Once you embraced me,
   and now you won't:
>   Oh me, oh my, I am bereft!
>   She's mad at me, she's up and left!

Please forgive me, my lovely—
   I swear I will behave;
Please let me see you once again!
   I'm burning up with passion grave;
>   Oh me, oh my, I am bereft!
>   She's mad at me, she's up and left!

Jayadeva comes from Kindubilva
   as the moon comes from the ocean;
And in this song I render Krishna's words
   with loving deep devotion.
>   Oh me, oh my, I am bereft!
>   She's mad at me, she's up and left!

Translated from the Sanskrit by Lee Siegel

Habba Khatoon (c. 16 CE)

Let's Go to the Upland Woods, My Friend

Let's go to the upland woods, my friend
Being gullible, he swallowed whole

Whatever was said to slander me,
Come back, my lover of flowers!

Let's go down the hill, my friend,
I'd give him the jewels I wear—
What if they cost two coins of gold?
Come back, my lover of flowers!

Let's go draw water, friend,
The world is lost in sleep and dreams,
While I stay awake to hear from you,
Come back, my lover of flowers!

Translated from the Kashmiri by Triloknath Raina

Kutti Revathi (b. 1974)

I've Brought This Summer Just for You

Your chest's meadow has dried up
You don't write to me these days.
There's a tumult of tears
in your seasoned letters.
Your body's so tender—like a blanket
with many arms I could cover myself with

There is no one else on this summer street, except
the postman carrying his load of gasping letters
and the girl who's forgotten her childhood secrets
When the strange bird of summer, which
drinks up all the water bodies in one gulp

arrives and perches quietly, the rocks too come awake,
Children refuse to play
beneath a sun that rises, blood-soaked, every day.
Inside a deserted house,
the telephone's been ringing for a long time.
Girls' eyes are afloat in the haze.

During a by gone summer, too hot
for trees to stand firm on their feet,
you had called my body a live expanse.
When I woke from sleep, I found
that the handbag where
I had hoarded your kisses
and our quarrels coated with the salt of tears,
had been flung open.
This summer that brings to mind
the acrid smell of a doused lamp,
I've brought along just for you.
Do write me letters. Do.

Translated from the Tamil by N. Kalyan Raman

Dom Moraes (1938–2004)

Asleep

The heat smells of lions and of yeast.
You talk unhappily to yourself in sleep.
I snore on the cool pillows of your breast
But fall awake as you slip down the slope
To your private valley of unhappiness
I cannot reach except with kiss and touch.

Your mouth I listen to is a small rose.
Awake, it does not tell me very much.

Time will not stop: and you are very tired.
Turn into my arms and truly sleep.
Turn into my arms and be desired.

The deep hurt in you like the sun disturbs
My dawns: but sometimes you are still in sleep,
Smelling of armpits and of wet herbs.

English

Harsha (c. 12 CE)

From Ratnavali

Miraculously found, and luminous
with feeling, my beloved
has slipped away, a brilliant necklace
lost before it could hang
upon my neck.

Translated from the Sanskrit by David Shulman

Anon, Goan Folk Song (17 CE)

On the Banks of a Lake

On the banks of a lake,
At the crow of a cock,
A landlord's son is busy angling,
With an umbrella over his shoulder.

That son of the landlord: Oh,
He is a wizard of a cunning fox;
He's merrily smooching away, there,
At the cheeks of Aunty Rosaline.

He is named Sebastian Henriques,
He spins away yarns to Mary,
With bait, hook, line and sinker,
He angles fine fish aplenty.

Translated from the Konkani by Olvinho Gomes

Ilanko Atikal (c. 5 CE)

From The Cilappatikaram, Canto 1

The Song of Praise

Let us praise the Moon. Like the cool, white parasol
Of the Cola king, his garland heavy
With pollen, he blesses this good earth.
Let us praise the Sun. Like the proclamations
Like the lord of the Kaviri, he travels
Ever around Meru crowned with gold.
Let us praise the Rain. Like the Cola king,
His kingdom shut in by the roaring sea,
He pours out abundantly his bounty from above.
Let us praise Pukar, this glorious city,
The fame of its royal seat of kings
Spread over the whole earth clasped
By the swelling waters.

Far famed and inimitable
Is the city of Pukar, known for its ancient families
Undisturbed since time immemorial.
Like the Potiyil or Himalaya, it too remains
As constant as the great men who adorn it.
Thus speak the wise ones who have heard
And known everything. In fame Pukar rivals
Heaven itself, blinds the Serpentworld in pleasures.
Here lived Manaykan, heir to a noble family,
Generous as the rainclouds. A perfect branch
Of his tree, a shining creeper of gold,
Was his daughter Kannaki, who was twelve years
Old, and loved by Kovalan. She was blessed
With virtues. So women adored and praised her:
'She is Laksmi herself, goddess
Of peerless beauty that rose from the lotus,
And chaste as the immaculate Arundhati.'

And here also lived Macattuvan, a man
Of immense wealth. Even the ruler
Of that great kingdom looked up to him as the chief
Among the noble families of his realm.
He was Kubera himself who gave away his wealth
To the needy. The fame of his son Kovalan,
Only sixteen years old, had already shrunk
The earth. Over and over again, in voices
Seasoned by music, with faces luminous
As the moon, women confided among themselves:
'He is the god of love himself,
The incomparable Murukan.' For it was love
That made them speak thus of the handsome Kovalan.

Their noble parents longed to see them
Take, on a favorable day, the marriage vows.
They rejoiced in the thought, and dispatched all over
The town girls resplendent in jewels
And mounted on elephants, to proclaim the news
Of their wedding. On the day the nomadic Moon
Drew near Rohini, drums resounded;
Conches, as usual, boomed. White parasols
Were held aloft, as in a royal procession.
The bridal pendant was taken around the town.

In the pavilion itself, the canopy of blue silk
Was inlaid with pearls. Burnished with gems
And diamonds were the pillars, their tops pendent
With festoons. Around the ceremonial fire, walked
Kovalan observing the holy rites
The venerable priest solemnized.
   Thus Kovalan
Married the fair Kannaki, spotless
As the bright star Arundhati. The eyes
That beheld this sight were indeed fortunate.
Young girls offered perfumes
And flowers. Others, a little older,
Looked sidelong as they chatted and sang
Among themselves. High-breasted women,
With serpentine hair, carried incense,
Sandalwood paste, and scented powders.
Matrons, with gentle smiles, went round
With lamps, vessels, and pots brimful
With shoots of sprouted palikai. All resembled
Golden vines, their disheveled hair

Plaited with flowers. With a rain of petals
They blessed the couple:
   'Your arms forever knotted
In embrace, inseparable in love may you
Remain, and unblemished be your life.'

Translated from the Tamil by R. Parthasarathy

Anon

The Dalliance of the Leopards

Very afraid
I saw the dalliance of leopards.
In the beauty of their coats
They sought each other and embraced.
Had I gone between them then
And pulled them asunder by their manes,
I would have run less risk
Than when I passed in my boat
And saw you standing on a dead tree
Ready to dive and kindle the river.

Translated from the Sanskrit by E. Powys Mathers

Anon

Love Song

I am playing on my flute of green bamboo,
My fingers are resting on the stops.

So how can I take you in my arms, O love,
When I'm playing on my flute of green bamboo?
Eat a little chilli and wait awhile.
My hands are full already, so how can we embrace?
I am playing on my flute of green bamboo,
And my fingers are resting on the stops.

Translated from the Gondi by Shamrao Hivale and Verrier Elwin

Anon

Distance Destroys Love

Distance destroys love,
So does the lack of it:

Gossip destroys love,
And sometimes

It takes nothing
To destroy love.

Translated from the Prakrit by Arvind Krishna Mehrotra

Anon

The Song of Phatmal (c. 1600 CE)

O Phatmal, you are the Rao of Hadoti,
and I a Brahmin damsel of Toda.
I had gone to fetch water from the village tank,
when the Hada Rao came with his soldiers.

No one will know
Ganga has been taken to wife.
So get me a set of red bangles.
I love a set of red bangles;
get me one of real ivory;
and get me a skirt from Agra,
and a shawl from Sanganer.

If you stay tonight I'll cook
an excellent jaggery porridge for you;
if you go, I'll pack some *choorma*
for the journey.
If you stay tonight
I'll don a robe of deccan silk;
if you go, a dark shawl will do.

But stay, my beloved,
do stay the night;
and let this be our night of pleasure;
at day-break tomorrow you may go.

Worth lakhs is your beautiful moustache, O Phatmal;
but worth crores,
a night spent with me!

Translated from the Rajasthani by Kesri Singh

Janna (12 CE–13 CE)

From The Tale of the Glory-Bearer

Young Yasodhara was happy in
the company of Queen Amrtamati,

whose looks were the very glass wherein
he dressed himself, and touched his features.
But things soon began to take
a new turn in the young prince's life.

Once, as it happened,
the king discharged his court duties
before time, and by the end
of day, went up the staircase
to the bed-chamber
to meet his beloved queen.
From the casements
rose a tiny column of
incense smoke like the grey-
winged dove that flew out, as if
at the behest of the love-god Mara,
to carry his message to
the minds of people.
Bees came hovering
round for the scent, and
the brush of their wings raised
the musk and camphor dust.
The blue sapphires
adorning the chamber
burned and glowed.
The bed breathed passion. It was
a swing-bed and at either
end were images of swans
inlaid with nine varieties of gems.

There they lay,
the young king and the lovely queen,
in bed in each other's arms.
Their eyes, cast, bit
into each other, their bodies
melted in the clasp, like those
fabled moon-stones
when the moon's rays fell on them.

....

In the small hours
of the morning, when the noise
of the last change of guards
at the palace gate died out,
the queen heard
a faint voice, and
was awakened. Enclosed
and lost
in the prison of her love's arms,
she heard:
the voice grew into song,
sweet and alluring in the dark silence.
It came to her
         like falling seeds
trouble the resting waters.
A tiny ripple
stirred
and grew. Soon it touched
her, tapped her gently, and

woke her out of her drowsy
slumber. Eyes wide open,
she stared in the dark,
and toward the direction of the song.
The voice came from the nearby
elephant stables. The song
went home to her, shook
her to the roots. Tired though
she was, her body rose again
tingling and all alive to the song.
She lost her heart to it,
to the possessor of that
divine voice. She paid him
    in her mind
the tribute
    of her entire body.

Translated from the Kannada by T.R.S. Sharma

Cempulappeyanirar (c. 1 CE–3 CE)

What He Said

What could my mother be
to yours? What kin is my father
to yours anyway? And how
did you and I meet ever?
    But in love our hearts are as red
earth and pouring rain:
    mingled
beyond parting.

Translated from the Tamil by A.K. Ramanujan

Allur Nanmullai (c. 1 CE–2 CE)

What She Said

Will he remember, friend?

Where the curve of the parrot's beak
holds a bright-lit neem
like the sharp glory
of a goldsmith's nail
threading a coin of gold
for a new jewel,

he went across the black soil
and the cactus desert.

Will he remember?

Translated from the Tamil by A.K. Ramanujan

Anon

Song

Dew on the bamboos,
Cooler than dew on the bamboos
Is putting my cheek against your breasts.

The pit of green and black snakes,
I would rather be in the pit of green and black snakes
Than be in love with you.

Translated from the Sanskrit by E. Powys Mathers

Annamayya (1408–1503)

A Woman Talking to Herself

Better keep one's distance

Than love and part—
especially if one can't manage
seizures of passion.

Make love, get close, ask for more—
but it's hard to separate and burn.
Gaze and open your eyes to desire,
then you can't bear to shut it out.

Better keep one's distance

The first tight embrace is easy,
but later you can never let go.
Begin your love talk—
once hooked, you can never forget.

Better keep one's distance

Twining and joining, you can laugh;
soon you can't hide the love in your heart.
Once the lord of the Lady on the Flower
has made love to you
you can no longer say
it was this much and that much.

Better keep one's distance

Translated from the Telugu by A.K. Ramanujan, Velcheru Narayana Rao and David Shulman

Shah Abdul Latif (1689–1752)

The Wayward Heart

O camel, cease thy lingering
And lengthen out thy pace.
This once my loved one bring me nigh.
Then in thine ears there cannot ring
The semblance of a yearning sigh.

O camel, cease to lag behind
And lengthen out thy pace.
This night I have it in my mind
To see my loved one's face.

For thee I bring the sandalwood.
Let others salt-bush eat.
This very night be thine the mood
To take me where my loved one stood
That there we twain may meet.

The camel, mother, for my needs
I brought and tied beside the tree.
Where he on wealth of buds might feast,
He, sneaking, on the salt-bush feeds,
The mean and miserable beast,
Undoing all my work for me.

The stupid brute I tell and tell
That in the milkbush there's no zest;
Yon poison bush is many's knell
But hath his silly head obsessed.

Around in plenty for his need
Is ripened scrub of sandalwood.
The sulky grumbler pays no heed
And makes me weep my tears in blood.

And wilt thou thus, O camel, pass
The sandalwood, nor drink thy fill?
Thou seekest not the fragrant grass
But spurnest it as something ill.
It must be thy distorted mood
That made thee find the salt-bush good.

Arise and bind him. Let him free
And he will lose himself and roam.
I feed him and he sulkier gets.
Put on the saddle when he frets.
With shackled feet still growl will he
But will not wander far from home.

To keep him fast I tied him up:
The shackles bound with tug and strain.
The beast has gone with hobbles on
To eat the salt-bush once again!
O Lord, into this camel's head
Put something that in sense doth share.
O save him, Lord of Mercy, save:
Such is Latif the poet's prayer.

Translated from the Sindhi by H.T. Sorley

Anon (c. 9 CE)

From The Muttollayiram

His Infatuates Complain

Look at the doors in this street!
All have worn-out hinges.
For mothers keep shutting them
and daughters keep throwing them open.
This happens
whenever the prince Kothai,
wearing fresh flower garlands
and riding a sturdy horse,
passes along the street
and love-mad girls
rush to have a glimpse of him.

Translated from the Tamil by M.L. Thangappa

Mir Taqi Mir

The Miracle of Wine

Last night she emerged, a little drunk
It was as if the sun was out.

My life I'd gladly give the wineglass
That drowned your modesty and brought you out.

Translated from the Urdu by Khushwant Singh and Kamna Prasad

'The broom's the limit'

Amrita Pritam (1919–2005)

Daily Wages

In a corner of blue sky
The mill of night whistles,
A white thick smoke
Pours from the moon-chimney?

In dream's many furnaces
Labourer love
Is stoking all the fires

I earn our meeting
Holding you for a while,
My day's wages.

I buy my soul's food
Cook and eat it
And set the empty pot in the corner.

I warm my hands at the dying fire
And lying down to rest
Give God thanks.

The mill of night whistles
And from the moon-chimney
Smoke rises, sign of hope.

I eat what I earn,
Not yesterday's leftovers,
And leave no grain for tomorrow.

Translated from Punjabi by Charles Brasch with Amrita Pritam

Balraj Komal (b. 1928)

Saba's Hands Wear a Bridal Henna Tint Now

Saba wears now
A bridal henna tint
On her delicate palms—
I offer her my blessings, good wishes—
Saba is grateful.
But does not say a word.

Saba's home
Is her apparel now.
She covers her head
With its roof
She bedecks her feet
With the soft touch
Of the marble floor;
She no longer sings
Of mountains, valleys,
Waterfalls, azure skies,
She is seldom drawn
To colourful verdant sights.

Saba, delicate as dew,
Her feet bound
Hangs, like a portrait
In the window frame;
Frail, she flows not
On sun-lit shores
She opens her lips, she smiles,
But says not a word

In whispers
To any one now.

Translated from the Urdu by the poet

Bhanudatta (c. 15 CE)
From Bouquet of Rasa

Mother-in-law can rant, and friends
condemn, and sisters-in-law reprove.
How am I possibly to sleep
another night in that house?
That cat of theirs is forever
springing out of the corner niche
to catch a mouse, and you see what all
she's done to me with her sharp claws!

Translated from the Sanskrit by Sheldon I. Pollock

Balaram Das (c. 15 CE)
From Lakshmi Purana

I am your first married wife, always remember this.
    Don't allege, Lakshmi lived in *my* house;
    She made away with ornaments
    worth thousands of golden rupees.
    Don't let loose on me, Lord, such infamy;
    take back the ornaments you once presented me.

Lakshmi untied the pearl tassel from her hair;
She took off the royal veil of fine silk

embroidered with gold and gemstones.
The Mother unfastened her netted waistband
of gemstones and jewels;
She took out the pearl nose rings.
From both her ears, she took off
    the large diamond danglers;
she took out her jade and gold necklace.
The goddess took out her anklets of fine silver;
she hastened to dislodge the rings off her toes.
Now how to describe her other jewellery sets?
When piled together
the gemstones and jewels and the ornaments radiated.
Lakshmi heaped the ornaments at one corner;
'Keep these,' she said, 'O Friend of the Poor.'

Lord Jagannath replies: 'What shall we do with these? We have no need for the ornaments. When a householder has to sadly separate from his wife, he has to provide for her food and clothing for six months. Carry along this jewellery; so that you can sell or exchange the ornaments to feed and clothe yourself.'

Goddess Lakshmi speaks:
    'Listen to me, carefully,
    O you God of the Universe!
    When you bring home another wife like me,
    present her these ornaments.
    I am leaving fallen and unsheltered;
    but bear my curse, Jagannath, the omniscient—
    if the sun and the moon really move in the universe,
    let you, Jagannath, the master of the universe,
    be denied a morsel of rice.
    For twelve years pitiable you shall remain,

dispossessed of food, clothing and water;
You, the vanquisher of Kaliya, the underwater serpent,
will get somthing to eat
only when it is served by me,
   a defiled chandaal woman.'

Translated from the Oriya by Lipipuspa Nayak

Sutapa Bhattacharya (b. 1942)

Draupadi

Love was the single fault
therefore I fell first of all!
I spend five nights in five rooms
all of them demand my labour, service, body
not my love.
Even he has his own Subhadra, Ulupi, Chitrangada—
each flower bloomed in a different Spring.

I am of no Spring, I am fire's daughter.
My unbound hair, become a thousand serpents, fills the air with poison;
In my eyes' desolate heat forest fires burn, a hundred saplings fall to ashes;
Yet there is no fault in that, such is the ruling!

Still, well and good, may your heaven remain yours;
with the one grave sin—which is my greatest virtue—
I will go with a smiling face towards hell.

Translated from the Bangla by Marian Maddern

Kamala Das (1934–2009)

The Stone Age

Fond husband, ancient settler in the mind,
Old fat spider, weaving webs of bewilderment,
Be kind. You turn me into a bird of stone, a granite
Dove, you build round me a shabby room,
And stroke my pitted face absent-mindedly while
You read. With loud talk you bruise my pre-morning sleep,
You stick a finger into my dreaming eye. And
Yet, on daydreams, strong men cast their shadows, they sink
Like white suns in the swell of my Dravidian blood,
Secretly flow the drains beneath sacred cities.
When you leave, I drive my blue battered car
Along the bluer sea. I run up the forty
Noisy steps to knock at another's door.
Through peep-holes, the neighbours watch,
they watch me come
And go like rain. Ask me, everybody, ask me
What he sees in me, ask me why he is called a lion,
A libertine, ask me why his hand sways like a hooded snake
Before it clasps my pubis. Ask me why like
A great tree, felled, he slumps against my breasts,
And sleeps. Ask me why life is short and love is
Shorter still, ask me what is bliss and what its price . . . .

English

Cantirakanti (b. 1961)

Wanted: A Broom

when he said Darling
he didn't ask for a paisa for anything
but when he said Marry Me
he asked for gold
money
stuff
plates and pots
everything
aiyo he even asked for a broom
to sweep the floor
I said
the broom's the limit
he got up and asked why

I said
so I can sweep you from my heart
and toss you in the trash

paying a life-subscription
just to get a male hooker
what am I
half-crazy
or a total fool

Translated from the Tamil by Martha Ann Selby and K. Paramasivan

Trilochan (1917–2007)

Champa Doesn't Know Her Alphabet

Champa doesn't know her alphabet
Whenever I sit down to study, she comes flying in
Quietly she listens to me
She's amazed
How do these black marks send out sounds?
Champa is Sunder's daughter
Sunder is a milkman:
He keeps cows and buffalo.
Champa takes the cattle out to graze in the pasture.
Champa is good
Fidgety and impish too
Sometimes she makes a mess
Sometimes she hides my pen
Somehow when I find it somewhere
And get it back—
All the paper's gone!
Given a hard time again!
Champa says: *all day you keep on poking at the paper
    is this work really good?*
This reduces me to lauaghter
and Champa falls silent again.
That day Champa came
I said to her: *Champa, you too come and read . . .*
This will come to your rescue in troubled times
Gandhi baba says that all must read and write.
Champa said straight out: *I won't! What is this?*
You always told me that Gandhi baba is nice,
how can he then, ask us to read and write?
No reading and writing for me, no way!

I said to Champa: *It's good to write*
Someday you'll get married.
For a while, your husband will stay with you
And then he'll set off for Calcutta.
Calcutta is very far away—
how will you read his letters?
Champa, it's good to read and write.
Champa said: *Look, what a liar you are!*
See for yourself, what studying has done to you!
So much learning and such lies!
Me, I'll never get married
and even if I do, I wouldn't ever let my husband go to Calcutta.
So, to hell with Calcutta!

Translated from the Hindi by Anamika and Arlene Zide

Arundhathi Subramaniam (b. 1967)

Tree

It takes a certain cussedness
to be a tree in this city,
a certain inflexible woodenness

to dig in your heels
and hold your own
amid lamp-posts sleek as mannequins
and buildings that hold sun and glass together
with more will-power than cement,

To continue that dated ritual,
re-issuing a tireless maze

of phalange and webbing,
perpetuating that third world profusion
of outstretched hand,
each with its blaze of finger
and more finger—
so many ways of tasting neon
so many ways of latticing a wind
so many ways of being ancillary to the self
without resenting it.

English

Sumangala's Mother (4 BCE)

'Tis Well with Me

O woman well set free! how free am I,
How thoroughly free from kitchen drudgery!
Me stained and squalid 'mong my cooking pots
My brutal husband ranked as even less
Than the sunshades he sits and weaves always.
Purged now of all my former lust and hate,
I dwell, musing at ease beneath the shade
of spreading boughs—O, but 'tis well with me!

Translated from the Pali by Margaret Macnicol

Anon, Gujarati Folk Song

My Husband's Home

In my husband's home my mother-in-law is a serpent;
Sneering she asks me to grind the mill all day long.

In my husband's home my sister-in-law is a dragon,
Snarling she asks me to spin the 'charkha' all night.

In my husband's home my elder sister-in-law is an angel of death,
Scolding me she eats away my soul all day and night.

Translated from the Gujarati by Madhubhai Patel

Soma (c. 4 BCE)

The Sceptic Says

The sceptic says—
That vantage ground the sages may attain
Is hard to reach with her two-finger wit
That is no woman competent to gain.

She replies—
What should the woman-nature do (to me)
With mind well set and knowledge faring on,
To me who rightly Dhamma can discern?
To him for whom the question may arise:
Am I a woman in these matters, or
Am I a man, or what not am I then—
To such a one is Mara fit to talk.

Translated from the Pali by C.A.F. Rhys-Davids

Rukmini Bhaya Nair (b. 1952)

Paranomasia

At Cambridge I learnt to lie with elegance
to turn to advantage a narrow bed,

a narrower scholarship, sail close
to the edge of the fens but be careful
not to sink, fence myself with books
but be careful not to think.

I thrust behind the lowered guards
of several visored dons, merry maid
though every night and blackmailed
in the mornings, a soupcon of malice
saw me to success, I learnt to trade
more and more for ever less and less.

and now I am a don myself, whose duty
is to see each shuffling undergraduate
develop deviously, sharp their skill
at feinting, secure a neat pass or two
but above all forget those clumsy truths
that send them far, far beyond the edge.

a queen anne bed, a unique dresser
I teach my acolytes finessed in pleasure
for the untutored minute comes
the cold fens circling wait, styxward slip
our familiar quarters, point encompasses point
and there's an end to all our hauteur.

English

Harindra Dave (1930–95)

The Speck

A speck, dreaming itself the sun,
rising, flying eastward, sinks in the west.
With heated gaze desiring
to dry the water into cloud,
and live, some day, a sun-disc in the sea,
it spins in a whirlpool's dark whorl.
Hearing the lamp,
scorched by the flame,
it asks the hurricane's speed, and beauty of the sky.
All watch, astonished,
the speck rise, struggling, to its feet.

Translated from the Gujarati by Suguna Ramanathan and Rita Kothari

Kadammanitta Ramakrishnan (b. 1935)

Tar and Broom

With a bucketful of tar and a broomstump
with a mouthful of filth and smut
with scabies on the head and ulcers on the feet
and sores all over the skin
I stand here at the porch of the world.
Villains, do you dare abuse me?
Why shut the door in my face

as though the holy place were your family plot?
Why such pretences, why such pretensions,
You, thorns of the vineyard!
Here I am with a bucketful of tar
to blacken the walls of the world.
Come on, then: I tell you if you dare obstruct me,
I will blacken your blanched faces too.
You are all carrion birds that scramble for funeral offerings
on the new moon day in the month of Cancer.
Didn't you crush with your fists
the jasmine buds that opened out amidst the pain of the night?
Didn't you in a herd slake your bestial lust
under the shade of the roadside tree?
I lay with my eyes open
pressing my finger to the ulcer on my foot,
The stone-pillow and the bed of sand and mud
were drenched in tears
when the pus oozed out from the gaping sore
and pain stuck to my very soul.
Didn't you then hold your noses and drive me out like a pest
with your palm-leaf broom, O my good people?
I then snatched away your broom
and its stump is my pen today.
With a bucketful of tar and a broom stump
and a song of hatred just aroused
I'll blacken your mansions
with the dirt from the gutter:
I'll paint you naked and black and provoke your gentility;
I'll smash your antiques in their coloured glass cases;
I'll plant thorns in the paths
of your beautiful gardens;

I'll draw graffiti that'll pain your eyes;
I'll throw filth upon you
and take off your dress of virtue.
My breath, reeking with camphor, will coat your perfume bottle with slime,
will dirty the water in your orchard lotus pond,
will draw a mandala with dark cloud ink on the white sky
and will dance on those squares a dance of fury.

Translated from the Malayalam by K. Ayyappa Paniker and Ray King

Mamta Kalia (b. 1940)

Compulsions

I want to pick my nose
in a public place
I want to sit in my office chair
with my feet up
I want to slap the boy
who makes love in a cafe
while I wait alone for the waiter
to bring me coffee and sandwiches
I want to pay Sunday visits
totally undressed
I want to throw away
all my cosmetics
I want to reveal
my real age

English

Tukaram (b. 1608–50)

Where Did It Go Wrong?

Where did it
Go wrong?
I was
Doing well.
What made me grab
This noose
That's around
My neck?

Now I'm tied
In too many
Knots.
I cannot
Move
Back
Or forth.

I have nothing
Left.
I am too deep
In debt.

My harvest
Has been
Looted.
My wife
And my children
Have to beg.

I borrow
Left and right.
Nothing
Seems enough.

Says Tuka,
It's best
I give up
All hope
And leave
All this
Where is
As is.

Translated from the Marathi by Dilip Chitre

Anon, Rajputana Folk Song

There Is No Limit to Desire

I would go to fetch water only when
I have a water-pot of gold,
    Then I would bring water.

The golden pot would be fit to carry
When I have a head-ring of pearls,
    Then I would bring water.

The head-ring would be fit to wear
When I have a priceless veil,
    Then I would bring water.

The veil would be fit to wear
When I have a necklace around my neck,
    Then I would bring water.

The necklace would be fit to wear
When my father is a king,
    Then I would bring water.

Translated from the Rajasthani by Winifred Bryce

Shakunt Mathur (b. 1920)

Waiting

Scolded
the old servant
for his usual slowness
Gave a good slap
to my darling son
for his mischief
To my daughter who'd been playing
gave a dozen hankies to hem
Ordered
the oldest one
to drink more milk
Washed
all the dirty clothes
Flipped through a few magazines
Darned some torn clothes
Put on some new buttons

Cleaned the machine and oiled it
Put the cover back on with care
Took out the half-finished sewing
and repacked it in a different way
Wiped the cupboards in the kitchen
Cleaned the spice jars.
And still
he
hasn't come home from the office.

Translated from the Hindi by Aruna Sitesh and Arlene Zide

Shobha Bhagwat (b. 1947)

Husbands

This woman has a job
so her husband is unhappy
this one sits at home
so her husband is upset
this one is very thin
so her husband is angry
this one is very plump
so her husband snaps at her
though this one has a lovely figure
her husband is grouchy
he is troubled by doubts
and simmers all the time
this one is very talkative
so her husband dislikes her

this one is very quiet
so her husband cannot stand her
this one has a messy home
so her husband complains
this one has a spic-and-span home
so her husband is morose
this one is always well-dressed
so her husband wonders, 'For whom?'
this one is always plainly dressed
so her husband says, 'She's dumb.'
Does this tight-rope balancing act
ever come to an end?
Where can one find a husband
who likes his wife?

Translated from the Marathi by Vinay Dharwadker

Bilqees Zafirul Hasan (b. 1938)

Dignity

'Bibi Sahib, my husband
would come home every night, dead drunk. Then he would batter me.
He wouldn't let me spend even a cent of his earnings.
How could I live with such a man? I left him,
left the village and came to the city.

Now I work in rich people's homes, such as yours,
I earn for myself and live by my labour.
What good is the vermilion in the hair part that adorns, but like
    a wound?

Now how could the Bibi Sahib explain to Dhaniya
that her story wasn't one of a kind
that she too endures something similar,
day after day, night after night.

But unluckily, she isn't Dhaniya. She is Bibi Sahib.
And this status has been given to her in reward (*bakhshish*) by her husband.
(One who has no status of one's own must live on charity alone.)
The dignity she attains by living with her husband:
Can a woman hope to find it elsewhere? Anywhere?

Feeling the gash on her forehead as she speaks,
'Dhaniya, you shouldn't have left your husband and walked away.'

Self-respect *is something*; but how should Dhaniya make Bibi Sahib understand this?

Translated from the Urdu by Mehr Afshan Farooqi

Anon

From The Gathasaptasati

Let Faithful Wives

Let faithful wives
Say what they like,
I don't sleep with my husband
Even when I do.

Translated from the Prakrit by Arvind Krishna Mehrotra

Anon, Gujarati Folk Song

Room Zoom

I went to the pasture to cut grass,
I got my wages,
I went to the bazaar,
A pan in my mouth,
A sheaf on my head;
I went to the goldsmith,
I saw the wristlet,
Bought the anklet;
Room zoom, room zoom
Ring the anklet bells.

Translated from the Gujarati by Madhubhai Patel

Bihari (c. 16 CE)

What One of Her Companions Said to Another

Friend, she's on top
I reckon,
resolute in love's combat,
for the bells of her girdle
jingle away,
while those of her anklets
are now mute.

Translated from the Hindi by Krishna P. Bahadur

'The sky between us'

Manohar Shetty (b. 1953)

Personal Effects

A few things he'll leave behind
To no one in particular:
A gold necklace from his mother
Melted into a wedding ring;

Two first editions with broken
Spines that may fetch
A small fortune, but too late
To pay the bills; a box

Of expired pills; a gold-nibbed
Fountain pen he refused
To write with; an Olivetti,
Its keys the seats
Of an empty stadium;

And clothes worn thin—he
Loved the comfort of old
Things: old letters, stopped clocks,
The patina in sideboards,
Fading photographs and paintings;

And, last, musty notebooks
And diaries empty of
Mythical poems and important
Jottings.

English

Anuradha Mahapatra (b. 1957)

Cow and Grandmother

Once she swam over the field like a heron, now the old woman
wearing plain white cloth thinks she is like a cow; a bee comes flying
to settle on the surface of the scalded pitcher; just at noon on the path
through the acacia grove darkness descends; sometimes she lifts on to her head
sheaves of rice; she looks for water at the neck of the dry pitcher, she gives
rice-water to the sick dog and the barren cow; she kneels and hides her face
in the straw; in the distance the cracks in the feet of the village wives
meet the field's cracks; at twilight jackals call; a girl reads the Gita
and, as drum and *ektara* tune up, goes swimming like the heron
over the white fields of Ranipur village; a patchwork of ripe berries
is spread over the empty courtyard; and in the turmeric grove
the young girl of long ago has become a blind grandmother; she knows
no science, but she can grow the *aparajita* vine over the sunny thatched house
and she knows the cow is old; still, when evening thickens
cow and grandmother are peaceful together in the grass, in the grasses' singing.

Translated from the Bangla by Marian Maddern

Markanda Das (15 CE)

From To the Cuckoo

(Yashoda, the mother of Krishna, expresses her sorrow on separation from her beloved son Krishna, before a cuckoo.)

Cuckoo! Keshaba has left for Mathura.
With whose permission did he leave?
He did not return, O cuckoo!

Cuckoo! To whom shall I give sugarcandy with milk?
The child who eats it has left.
He has left for Mathura. O cuckoo!

Cuckoo! The son left, did not return.
The deep woods of Vrindavan
Have lost their lustre. O cuckoo!

Cuckoo! This house is not home for Nanda.
This house is not beautiful
Without Govinda, O cuckoo!

Cuckoo! Nanda is made of stone.
He put collyrium in the eyes of his son,
Made him climb the chariot, O cuckoo!

Cuckoo! The sweet sound of the moving bells in the waist:
The women of Gopa were
Surprised to hear it, O cuckoo!

Cuckoo! Sometime in the past I hit him with a stick
Krishna has left me
For that one mistake, O cuckoo!

Translated from the Oriya by D.B. Pattanaik

Shakti Chattopadhyay (1934–95)

A Memory Comes Back

A memory comes back.
The whistle, the junction,
The level crossing, a slow train.
Will I see you in the window, reading Hart Crane?

The journey was long, a hundred and fifty miles,
At the end of which all I got is,
'You aren't so rich to be wasting money like this.'
How right you were. I was just a schoolteacher then, my dear.

We sat in the moonlight.
You took out a photograph
And said, 'Keep it.'
It's there in my wallet.

A memory comes back.
The whistle, the junction,
The level crossing, a slow train.
Honestly, do you still read Hart Crane?

Translated from the Bangla by Arvind Krishna Mehrotra

Srinivas Rayaprol (1925–98)

Married Love

Every evening
I am met at the gate by my wife
her hair in disorder and her dress in a mess

from the kitchen
and the girls hang on the leaves of the gate
while my ancient car rolls in.
One carries my bag, the other
my lunch basket.
The day's work is over and I am home.
I have forgotten them all day and now
suddenly remember that I must
disappoint them again
for my evening is planned
for a meaningless excursion to the bars.
And the coffee which my wife has served
is cold in my mouth
and the tales the children have brought from school
are dull on my ears.
In spite of my love for them
I must disappoint them again tonight

English

Dhurjati (16 CE)

My Chest Has Been Worn Away

My chest has been worn away
by the breasts of women rubbing against it.
My skin has been roughened
with love scars from their nails.
Lost in the straining of passion,
youth is gone.
My hair has started falling out,
I'm sick of it all.

I can't go on in this circling world.
O God of Kalahasti, make me desireless.

Translated from the Telugu by Hank Heifetz and Velcheru Narayana Rao

G.S. Shivarudrappa (b. 1926)

My Pocket

Do not put your hand in my pocket,
Brother. It is mine and no one else
Should meddle with it. It is not your concern.

My bank book, my debt account, my love letters,
It could be anything. But it is mine.
You cannot sort out my troubles. Let them
Be. Just give me your friendship.

No, do not worry about the contents
Of my pocket. I do not worry about yours.
Let the sky between us be clear
Of clouds. That is sufficient.

Translated from the Kannada by O.L. Nagabhushana Swamy

Natwarlal Pandya 'Ushnas' (1920–2011)

I, My Father

An amazing and strange new experience.
Entering for the first time a fatherless house,
An emptiness so musty and so vast.
Familiar objects spoke of earlier lives,
Yet curiously, seemed unfamiliar too.

Discarding travelling clothes, I wore an old
Loincloth of father's, left hanging out to dry.
And freshly bathed and dressed, sat down at prayer.

Reflected in the mirror was father's face,
Marked with sandalwood and ashes. I arose
From mid-day sleep—father's habit—athirst for mail.
Slept in father's cot that night, his very mattress.
And clearly saw my bier, my blazing pyre.
I saw my body burn; I my father!

Translated from the Gujarati by Suguna Ramanathan and Rita Kothari

Anon, Bodo Folk Song

Marriage Song

We have handed the bride over to you;
Take her home.
But be mindful of duties.
If you break limbs,
The loss will be your own:
For, she is your life's partner.
Others may not rate her high,
But she is a jewel to her mother.
Look to heaven and act accordingly.
She is now completely your charge.
She is not accomplished in ways of devotion and wisdom,
And spinning and weaving she knows not.
Yet you have selected her yourself.
Now stand by your selection,
In all virtue.

Translated from the Bodo by Mohini Mohan Brahma

Madeshwara (c. 14 CE)

From Male Madeshwara

Look here, Sankenne! I tell you:
If I leave you alone in this house,
Those nephews and brothers-in-law—
Pay heed to me, Sankenne:
Having traversed seven and seven fourteen regions,
I married you for the reason, my wife,
That you are beautiful, you are comely,
And that you befit my handsome features.
Hence, I won't go leaving you alone, my wife.
If I go, leaving you alone,

My aunt's sons will come here;
My uncle's sons will come here;
And my brothers-in-law will be here.
They will come here, feigning the need for fire;
They will come here feigning the need for hot water.
They will joke and chat with you;
They will use honeyed words.
They will see your figure and features;
They will see your beauty and charm;
They will make eyes at you.
Then, wife, they will caress you with love,
And they will cajole you to elope with them.
//Give alms to the sage on the mountain peak//

Alas! Master, my Master!
What sinful words you are uttering!
With such sinful words, don't make me a sinner, master.
Aren't my brothers-in-law the same as my father, master?
Aren't my cousins the same as my children, Guru?

Don't utter such sinful words, master;
I will bear your feet on my shoulders.
//Give alms to the sage on the mountain peak//

Hear me, O master!
Mother Earth and Sky above are my witnesses,
I will not swear an oath, master.
If I do, I will be unfit to be called a virtuous woman.

Sir, pay heed to my words;
Sir, go to the hills of wild honeycombs.
//Give alms to the sage on the mountain peak//

(Enraged by her refusal to swear an oath he says he will build a tiny hut for her in a desolate and tiny tribal village to stay in while he is away).

Shiva, Shiva! O Mother Earth! O Sky above!
Master, what are you saying?
To go to the desolate place where three mountain peaks meet,
To the silent valley near it,
To build a lonely hut in a tiny tribal hamlet there,
And to live there, far away from everyone—

Was I picked up from the streets by you?
Did I come to you of my own accord?
Was I bred and brought up all alone?
Mother and father I have;
Kith and kin have I;
Elder and younger sisters I have;
Friends and companions have I; and,
Relatives and acquaintances I have.

I cannot forget all these people;
Even if it means to lose my life.
//Give alms to the sage on the mountain peak//

(Sankenne still refuses to swear an oath of fidelity. In any case, she says, what would be the point in this desolate place.)

In this forest, on this path,
If a bangle-seller passes by,
Shouting 'bangles' 'Bombay bangles'—
A creature of a woman like you,
Just adores turmeric, kumkum, flowers and bangles.
Even when you are dying from hunger,
You will yearn for those things—
Then you will invite the bangle-seller with your gestures.
The bangle-seller approaches you . . . .

Translated from the Kannada by C.N. Ramachandran and Padma Sharma

Gnanakoothan (b. 1938)

Son to Mother

Get too chummy with girls
your ears will dry up, you said.
If you are naughty
God will strike you blind, you said.
When I worried you for things to eat,
It's bad for your tummy, you said
I got you in exchange for a
winnow of bran, you said.
What a lot of lies, Mother, you told me

when I was young!
What made you stop?
Or did you think
I could survive with truth?
Perhaps you thought
lies for grownups were beyond your ken
and left it to the government
to rule by the law.
I don't like it.
Wean me, mother, when you like,
But feed me your lies
for all time.
You love me, don't you?

Translated from the Tamil by Ashokamitran

Anjum Hasan (b. 1972)

In My Mother's Clothes

I feel the cool sweat from under my arms
soak her blouse timidly—shy, damp flowers
of my sweat on her blouse.

I wear her thirst blue and forest green
and burnt orange as if they belonged to me:
my mother's colours on my skin
in a dusty city.

I walk in her clothes
laughing inside, relieved
of the burden of being what one wears

since in my mother's clothes
I am neither myself nor my mother,

but more like that spindly
creature of six who slips onto
her fingers her mother's gold rings,
pulls on a huge cardigan that smells of sunlight and milk,
and conducts herself, drowsy with love, through rooms
with their curtains drawn against the honeyed light of June.

English

B.S. Mardhekar (1909–56)

Son-in-law

I've become a wedding-guest
in my own two-room home;
or a son-in-law, visiting
       his wife's family.

The friction gives me a fever;
quinine won't bring it down;
the salt wind from the invisible world
       stings my body.

The sound of distant temple bells
goes sour as it reaches me;
I catch it in the bowl of feelings
       and break down.

The machines that run all night
spoil the fruits of darkness;
I taste them and my feverish hate
    brings up my bile.

The fringe of lashes on my tired eyes
is the gauze of starlight in the sky;
and yet I don't dare
    go to sleep.

Translated from the Marathi by Vinay Dharwadker

Narasinh Mehta (1408–80)

Here Is a Palanquin

Here is a palanquin,
seated in it is a child groom,
the bride looks at it and laughs.

He is washed and placed inside,
his forehead marked with *tilak*;
The wedding guests grace the procession,
their heads sprinkled with coloured powder.

Made of green bamboos,
lifted by four men;
Wet white cloths on their heads,
the name of Rama on their lips.

They offer sweets to stray dogs,
and the dogs feel happy.
In front of the groom are faggots,
and flames follow him.
The groom is on his way to the bride's house,
the bride's mother is pleased to receive him.

Sparks of fire fly around the gate,
the flames dance around the hall;
Hurry up, you foolish mother of the bride,
the groom is at the gate.

Handsome is the dowry,
Crematorium is the name of the town;
The bride is Lady Red's daughter,
and is named Princess Pyre.
The groom stayed on at the bride's,
His people returned home;
They grabbed his money,
his marriage a good riddance for them.

They placed twelve pots and lighted twelve lamps,
and put a coin on the top;
'Go and tell his father,' they say,
he can now loudly mourn his son.'

Death took the groom away,
and freed him from flesh.
He merged into Narasinh's Lord,
and fulfilled himself.

Translated from the Gujarati by Niranjan Bhagat

O.N.V. Kurup (b. 1931)

Those Who Have Lost the Nectar

It has rained my son,
the courtyard has turned into a stream
and your joy, into paper boats.

You launch them one by one,
delighted
as you look at them intently.

As you sit like a legendary god
leading a fleet of ships to far off lands
in good weather
your father sits behind you
and enjoys the sight more.

Your ancestors
you haven't known, see it from afar.
Like their tears of joy, fall
the rain drops here and there.
The droplets of fresh rain
draw circles like flowers in the water . . .

In an instant, son,
your face is shadowed:
'Will it rain again, will the boats sink?'

We are those who have lost
the nectar of pure joy; we grieve over
things that might or might not come to pass.

Translated from the Malayalam by S. Velayudhan

Nirmal Prabha Bordoloi (b. 1933)

In the Smell of Rice Fields in Autumn

In the smell of rice fields in autumn
My father comes back to me;
In the fragrance of the new scarf
As I unfold it fresh from the shop
I find my mother again . . .

Where shall I leave myself
For my child
O, where indeed?

Translated from the Assamiya by Hiren Gohain

Daljit Nagra (b. 1966)

In a White Town

She never looked like other boys' mums.
No one ever looked without looking again
at the pink kameez and balloon'd bottoms,

mustard-oiled trail of hair, brocaded pink
sandals and the smell of curry. That's why
I'd bin the letters about Parents' Evenings,

why I'd police the noise of her holy songs,
check the net curtains were hugging the edges,
lavender-spray the hallway when someone knocked,

pluck all the gold-top milk from its crate
in case the mickey-takers would later disclose it,
never confessing my parents' weird names

or the code of our address when I was licked
by Skinheads (by a toilet seat)
desperate to flush out the enemy within.

I would have felt more at home had she hidden
that illiterate body, bumping noisily into women
at the market, bulging into its drama'd gossip,

for homework—in the public library with my mates,
she'd call, scratching on the windows. Scratching again
until later, her red face would be in my red face,

two of us along, she'd duck at my stuttered Punjabi,
laughing, she'd say I was a gora, I'd only be freed
by a bride from India who would double as her saathi.

Nowadays, when I visit, when she hovers upward,
hobbling towards me to kiss my forehead
as she once used to, I wish I could fall forward.

English

S.A. Usha (b. 1954)

To Mother

Mother, don't, please don't,
don't cut off the sunlight
with your sari spread across the sky
blanching life's green leaves.

Don't say: you're seventeen already,
    don't flash your sari in the street,

>   don't make eyes at passers-by,
>   don't be a tomboy riding the winds

Don't play that tune again
what your mother
her mother and her mother
had played on the snake charmer's flute
into the ears of nitwits like me.
I'm just spreading my hood.
I'll sink my fangs in someone
and lose my venom.
Let go, make way.

Circumambulating the holy plant
in the yard, making rangoli designs
to see heaven, turning up dead
without light and air,
for god's sake, I can't do it.
Breaking out of the dam
you've built, swelling
in a thunderstorm,
roaring through the land
let me live, very different
from you, Mother.
Let go, make way.

Translated from the Kannada by A.K. Ramanujan

Anon, Satpura Folk Song
On One Side of the Ganga

On one side the *Ganga*:
On another the *Jumna*.

In the space between the women are playing and singing.
Spread the blanket on the floor, oh brother.
Sit by the bride and comfort her,
Her heart is sad.
Call the carpenter from the town
Make a palanquin for the bride.
Call the merchant from the town, oh father,
Buy saris for the bride, oh father.
Her heart is sad.
Call the goldsmith from the town, oh father.
Call the goldsmith from the town.
Make a necklace for the bride, oh father,
Her heart is sad:
Call the Brahmin from the town, oh father,
Call the Brahmin from the town.
Let the wedding take place,
Her heart is sad.
The bride's heart is sad, oh father.
Her heart is sad.

Translated from the Gondi by Durga Bhagwat

Kampan (1180–1250)

From the Ramayana

Patalam 8; Jatayu Gives Up His Life

87.3503

Then, as she was speaking, Jatayus
appeared and said, like the thunder, 'You!
Where are you going? Where are you

going? Stop! Stop!' The flames
of his anger spreading through his eyes,
his heroic beak shining like lightning,
his body like huge, golden
Mount Meru coming through the sky.

88.3504

His two wings beat the air
as when a world ends, and the fierce wind
blows through the entire universe,
uprooting all the broad, strong mountains
till they rise in the sky and smash
one another to dust falling,
and the sea, swelling, surges up to be one
with the earth and both are destroyed.

89.3505

Trees with strong leafy tops curved down awhile
the clouds above soared high in the sky to avoid him.
'Up there! The great cruel Garuda is coming!' the cobras
thought, shrunk their hoods, skulked off and were deeply troubled.

90.3506

Elephants and yalis and every other sort of animal,
great trees from the forest and bushes and rocks
were torn away by the wind from his two wings
and sent soaring so that the sky seemed like the forest.

91.3507

'Where are you going? Where are you taking the wife
of the highest on your towering chariot along with
part of the earth? No I will cover the sky, all the directions!'
said he whose nature was to spread his protective wings.

Translated from the Tamil by George L. Hart and Hank Heifetz

Tulsidas (c. 1527–1623)

From the Ramayana

Childhood of Rama

One morning his mother first washed him and dressed him,
And then in his cradle she quietly placed him;

This done she prepared for her own household god
An off'ring of fit sacrificial food;

When the worship was done, with the god the meal shared,
She went to the place where the food was prepared;

Returning, her own son she saw with surprise
Was eating the food; she could scarce trust her eyes;

All worried she turned, at his bed took a peep,
And there saw the baby was still fast asleep;

Turning back to the altar, her son was still there;
Her heart jumped in great agitation and fear;

'One here, one there! Two babies! Marvellous spectacle!
Is it my mind at fault? Is it a miracle?'

Seeing his mother so deeply concerned,
The Lord to her worry a bright smile returned.

Then to her a sight of his wondrous true form,
His form universal, he showed;
In every hair of his body before her
A myriad bright worlds glowed.

Many Sivas, Brahmas, suns and moons with bright beams
Did she see; many worlds, oceans, woods, hills and streams;

She saw time and fate; virtue, wisdom and nature;
She saw things ne'er seen or heard by any creatures;

Illusion she saw also folding her hands,
With pow'r over all, tho' in trembling she stands;

All souls by Illusion she saw set in motion,
And that which her power breaks, faithful devotion;

O'ercome with the thrill, she could utter no sound,
But bowed with eyes closed and in rev'rence profound.

Translated from the Hindi (Avadhi) by the Rev. A.G. Atkins

Vinda Karandikar (b. 1918)

A Stalemate

She was not that simple:
there were twists and turns in her moods
like a creeper in a hedge

which avoids a neighbouring stone
and looks stealthily at a cactus far away.
Yet she reared a family
begot children
with eyes and noses like her husband's.
Suddenly she would pause and say
from behind the window bars
'Indeed, I am happy.'
He would say nothing, would only stare
at the clock on the wall,
afraid lest he miss the train.
Sometimes she would play at madness, deliberately;
it wasn't madness at all;
then, through the sieve,
go on looking at the moon;
laugh,
even when she couldn't.
Then he would feel, 'I must go to the dentist
to get her front teeth filled, if possible, with gold.'
Thus he lived, postponing one thing in the name of another.
And dared not speak, even to himself,
well aware of everything.

Translated from the Marathi by G. V. Karandikar

Adil Jussawalla (b. 1940)

Colour Problems in the Family

Mother forgot the features when the rest,
Pinker than Persia, found her future black.

So father turned up, obligingly darker,
His iron skin rich with inherited rust.

Yellow frogs, grandmother called us,
Sallow herself, brass with a touch of ash.

Then you, rose, known to be fair and just,
Said that colours that ran in my family
Had no place in your sun.

True.

They were colours I ashed on your shoulder,
Bled on your shirt as I spoke.
They were true, and continue to run.

English

G.J.V. Prasad

Desperately Seeking India

    In Delhi
  without a visa
    In Madras
  An Aryan spy

Kashmir's no vacation
They tell me it's a nation
And Punjab wants to die

In Bombay
I'm an invader
In Assam
An exploiting trader

They would throw me
From the hills
Kick me
From the plains

I promise
Never
To mention India again

English

Imtiaz Dharker

Bombay, Mumbai

You wear two names
like scaffolding, your smile held on
with bamboo sticks and sellotape
and string.

Salt swoops in on a sea-wind
and eats you bite by bite,,
making sounds like seagulls.
Paint, plaster, brick,
your lovely polished skin

gives in, peels and cracks,
but you fight back,
I am like that only,
you say, and toss your head.

White ants turn
your soul to diamond dust,
flood water slaps
at your glassy mouth, and you
smile back. You leave
doors open.
Absolution slides through the walls
of your heart.
You fall apart,
You make yourself again,
and shrug, I am like that only.

Which other city hands out
two different calling cards

one with the left hand,
the other with the right?

English

Vinod Kumar Shukla

Dhaulagiri

Seeing Mount Dhaulagiri,
I was reminded of its picture,
As I'd seen the picture first.

Among the pictures in my house
Are portraits of my ancestors.
I haven't seen my ancestors,
So whenever I think of them
I think of their portraits.

But not after seeing Dhaulagiri.
Now it's the ancestors who come to mind
And not their likenesses.

Translated from the Hindi by Arvind Krishna Mehrotra

'River of blood'

Keshav Malik (b. 1924)

In Praise of Guns

The clouds burst in praise of guns,
Especially when Cains rehearse
The ancient curse,

Then trumpeters trumpet the hearse
Of each brave son—
Circumcised and non.

God in heaven, who pours out in such fun,
When scorn answers in cold coin of scorn
Tooth for tooth, eye for eye.

From age to age so the show goes on—
The soul's gaze fixed
On mirroring pools of blood.

The clouds burst in praise of guns
In praise of sons—
A red thread running through a hole in the lungs.

Lightning and thunder commend violence,
The charioteer winks approval, let
Shot answer shot.

English

Sri Sri (1910–83)

Really?

Really?
Will all the world find happiness?
People see good times?
Really?

Really?
Does the world laugh
happily forever?
Does it overcome
its desire to kill?

Does the time when chains
tighten on slaves
end forever?
Do friendship and brotherhood,
their gentle ways,
win the day?

The dance of the oceans
with their hair dishevelled
and waves curled up—
will it end at last?
The boat's that caught
in the middle of the storm—
will it safely reach the shore?
Really?
Really?

Translated from the Telugu by Velcheru Narayana Rao

From an oral political narrative (c. late 19 CE)

The Bedas of Haligali

//Palla// (refrain)

Sad days came upon them—on those who wielded swords;
The angry fighters of Haligali—they were indeed doomed.

1. Nudi (unit of four or five lines)
//Chaala// (narration)

It was decreed from the foreign Company government:
The arms and weapons of all have to be seized by force;
Swords and scimitars, knives and sickles of all sorts.
Axes and lances, bows and arrows, muskets and shotguns,
Blades, bullets, powder—everything has to be seized;
Those who hide anything should be jailed for three years,
And those who resist should be put to sword.

//Yerra//(sing loudly)

Many will come forward of their own accord.
And surrender all the weapons they have;
If you offer them some job, in addition.
Gladly, they will give away all in their possession.

It was proclaimed through drumbeats
That such and such were the orders;
The brave fighters, coming to know of this,
Began to cry aloud, their eyes dim with tears.

//Chaala//

They collapsed on the ground, worried and sad.

2. Nudi

Obeying the orders, some gave up a few arms.
But expensive ones—they hid them inside.
'We have bought them, getting loans, and selling cattle;
How can we give them up?'—so, they buried them.
Then 'Joith Sahib,' a brave British officer arrived there,
And he searched every house; every nook and corner;
He was cunning, and he set one against the other;
And one let out the secret of another, almost gleefully.

Last section:

How can I list and describe
What was lost and looted?
They grabbed anything they could see.

Setting fire to the village, they left;
Haligali was reduced to ashes.
Such a rampage took place
No trace of Haligali was left.

I have described only what I could visualise.
May Kurtakoti Kamalesha bless both singers and hearers.

Translated from the Kannada by C.N. Ramachandran and Padma Sharma

Ajneya (1911–87)

Hiroshima

On this day, the sun
Appeared—no, not slowly over the horizon—
But right in the city square.

A blast of dazzle poured over,
Not from the middle sky,
But from the earth torn raggedly open

Human shadows, dazed and lost, pitched
In every direction: this blaze,
Not risen from the east
Smashed in the city's heart—
An immense wheel
Of Death's swart sun-car, spinning down and apart
In every direction.

Instant of a sun's rise and set:
Vision-annihilating flare one compressed noon.

And then?
It was not human shadows that lengthened, paled, and died;
It was men suddenly become a mist, then gone.
The shadows stay:
Burned on rock, stones of these vacant streets.
A sun conjured by men converted men to air, to nothing;
White shadows signed on the black rock give back
Man's witness to himself.

Translated from the Hindi by the poet

Amrita Pritam (1919–2005)

Ode to Waris Shah

I say to Waris Shah today, speak from your grave
And add a new page to your book of love

Once one daughter of Punjab wept, and you wrote your long saga;
Today thousands weep, calling to you Waris Shah:

Arise, O friend of the afflicted; arise and see the state of Punjab,
Corpses strewn on fields, and the Chenaab flowing with much blood.

Someone filled the five rivers with poison,
And this same water now irrigates our soil.

Where was lost the flute, where the songs of love sounded?
And all Ranjha's brothers forgotten to play the flute.

Blood has rained on the soil, graves are oozing with blood,
The princesses of love cry their hearts out in the graveyards.

Today all the Quaido'ns have become the thieves of love and beauty,
Where can we find another one like Waris Shah?

Waris Shah! I say to you, speak from your grave
And add a new page to your book of love.

Translated from the Punjabi by Darshan Singh Maini

Anon, Songs from the North (Kerala)

From Unniyarcha and Aromal Unni

Long past the midnight hour
statuesque Unniyarcha,
daughter-in-law
of the Attummanammel clan,

arose from her sleep,
astir with unease,
remembering an ominous dream.
She had seen Aromal Unni,
her brother, handsomest jewel
of the Puthooram clan
set out for his very first duel.
To the progenitors of her clan
she prayed and to the souls
of the dead that hover
around the battlefields, in fact,
to all the familial deities,
entreating, please save him,
save my brother Aromal Unni.
She straightened her clothes
and tidied her hair,
she lit a lamp to light up
the eastern gateway of the house.
She stooped to touch the earth
with her troubled brow.
She folded palms to salute the sun.
Then swept the courtyard clean
and cooked some rice with lentils
over the fluttering fragrant fire,
filled the pewters that held
five pints or more,
set out on banana leaves
the burnt husk of paddy
for brightening the teeth.
Then she called out,

as gently as she could,
Oh father, oh mother,
arise now from your sleep,
I have drawn the water
for your wash,
your breakfast of gruel
is cooked and ready.
The old ones asked.
Oh Unniyarcha,
why have you cooked our breakfast
so early, the cock has only begun
to crow.
I have my reasons.
said Unniyarcha
I dreamt of my brother
going out for a duel.
I saw him go out
to fight his very first duel.
I must therefore hasten home
to make sure that he doesn't.
The dream certainly had
a message meant for me.
The old man said,
dreams are untrustworthy.
Besides, pregnant that you are,
you cannot walk your way home.
Oh, but I must go, she cried.
I must stop him
before it is too late.

Translated from the Malayalam by Kamala Das

Imtiaz Dharker (b. 1954)

Gaddi Aa Gayi

It happened like this. Their country
slipped out of their hands and broke
like a cup or an earthen pot.
They never spoke as if they remembered
the shape it used to have.

They never cried over spilt blood,
at least not in front of us. It was as if
you reassure a guest. 'Oh don't mind that,
it was only a cheap old cup and anyway
broken china brings good luck'.
And a whole generation swallowed
the nightmares that sounded like trains.
Gaddi aa gayi tation the
Gaddi aa gayi tation the

When the train came in to its destination,
the station drank up the names
of their aunts and uncles,
their neighbourhoods and cities
and our mothers and fathers swallowed
the nightmares that sounded like trains
Gaddi aa gayi tation the
Gaddi aa gayi tation the

They swallowed the things they remembered
and the cousins who had gone away
with the ghost of the place
that broke with the cup. One day when

my mother was planting potatoes in another
country, she dug up a fragment of china
and looked at it as if she remembered
something that had never been spoken
Gaddi aa gayi tation the
Gaddi aa gayi tation the

something she dug out of the nightmares,
something unbroken.
She said the neighbours from the other side
were kind. They took her in and hid her.
They pretended she was one of their own
until they could send her home
Gaddi aa gayi tation the
Gaddi aa gayi tation the

to the country with a different name
to the station on the other side
on another train

English

Faiz Ahmad Faiz (1911–84)

The Morning of Freedom, 15th August 1947

This pock-marked daylight, this morning that reeks of night
Is not the morning we looked for
Is not the morning the good companions longed for
When they set forth across the wasteland by starlight,
Seeking the shore of night's dead ocean,
Some anchorage for the vessels of grief.

Starting out, those friends
Found traps on young blood's mysterious highways;
Allurements called from the land of pleasure.
Arms beckoned, lips blew a kiss.
But the face of the morning was their heart's desire,
The thighs of daylight gleamed near,
Tense with desire, they knew nothing of weariness.

People say that the light and the darkness are parted.
People say that feet and destination have met.
The afflicted are far better off, people say.
The pleasures of union are blessed,
The rigours of parting forbidden.

That fire in their hearts, that longing in their eyes
This 'blessed union' will never assuage.
When did the breeze of morning rise,
Where did it go?
On the roadside the lamp glows, just the same.
The night hangs heavy just the same
Our hearts and eyes still look for salvation,
Let us move on now,
We have yet to arrive.

Translated from the Urdu by Kathleen Grant Jaeger and Baidar Bakht

Robin Ngangom (b. 1959)

Flight

The warning disguised as a message
came before the village was up and about,

and when they left
they didn't carry pots or blankets
or even machetes.
As they went to the outpost of guardians
they left chickens running in the yard
and the dog lazing on the steps.

Flights like theirs
Do not have destinations,
And only once did they wish for wings.

The taste of the herd will return them
To dark and dingy towns where
They will sell used clothes, wild meat and herbs.
The most vulnerable will sell bodies.
Because in spite of the land mines
They still shared limbs.

Words like 'the end of history'
Will not resonate anywhere in their lives.
They do not have meat and drinks left
To offer to embedded scribes.
As newspapers have died on them. Like before
Their fates will go unreported, arousing
Only a shred of curiosity somewhere.

Translated from the Manipuri by the poet

Anon (c. 16 CE)

From Purattirattu

How Do I Know This Is My Son?

How can I be sure? How do I verify?

that this is my son;
> how do I verify?

Eyes are submerged in a sea of arrows,
the wreathed head severed by sword,
the bleeding mouth struck with sharp arrows
frothing for quite some time,
the chest pierced by poisoned shafts,
the thighs discoloured,
as the valiant hero lay on a bed of arrows
like a *kalarci* flower turned upside down!

Translated from the Tamil by P. Maruthanayagam

Tenneti Suri (1911–58)

Here Comes God

Hey, here comes god,
lifeless in bronze,
parading the streets,
riding his wooden horse.

Ask him about wages, fellows.
Tell him we don't have
enough to eat.

The wise men tell us
even stone hearts melt.
Let's see if that's true.

Bow down to him,
see if he listens,
and let go if he doesn't answer.

Hold up your hands
millions at once
raise your voice
so the sky itself shivers.

Ask him about the wages, fellows.
Tell him we don't have
enough to eat.

Translated from the Telugu by Velcheru Narayana Rao

K. Ayyappa Paniker (b. 1930)

Philistines

We have destroyed the enemies of culture,
We have,
now we do their work
better than they.

Translated from the Malayalam by the poet

Auvaiyar (c. 100 BCE–250 CE)

Elegy (for Anci)

This bright burning pyre
of black half-burned faggots,
pieces picked as if by a gypsy
in a field fire,

may it burn brighter
till it burns down to a handful.

Or rise in flames
and reach out to heaven.

> The fame of our sun-like king,
>> his white umbrellas cool
>> as the moon,

>> will not blacken,
>> will not die.

Translated from the Tamil by A.K. Ramanujan

Khadar Mohiuddin (b. 1955)

From Birthmark

A Certain Fiction Bit Me

A certain fiction bit me
   a distortion
      a slander

August 10, 1955
that's the day I was born

   in a small village
      in a remote corner of Krishna District

Long before I was born
   my name was listed among traitors

History depicted
   son as stepson,
      divided brother from brother
and left me alone

Textbooks laughed at me
   in my childhood

I was just becoming a person
when this history drove strange fears
      deep into me
          tortured me, threw me
             to the howling winds

The present makes me responsible
   for things I've nothing to do with

The present casts around me
   shadows of suspicion

Shadows watching me
     over my head
        always, all ways
They squeeze my existence into numbers

They see 1947
   in the umbilical cord, freshly cut
      its end still wet with the blood
         of the baby born in my house

      Hindi-Hindu-Hindustan
      Muslim go to Pakistan

      Another place to go as well
      You will know its name as hell

Helpless in the theatre of slogans
   I'm imprisoned in the present

No constitution pats my back
The throne of three lions
    smiling behind their whiskers
        takes no notice of me

I have no human form
  except as an alien
    as some kind of memorial to 1947
      in the mind
        of the first class citizen

Translated from the Telugu by Velcheru Narayana Rao

Akbar Ilahabadi (1846–1921)

Satirical Verses

Akbar, if I stick to the old ways
Saiyid tells me bluntly: Those values are shoddy
If I adopt the new style,
People from my community raise a public outcry
If one talks of moderation; it's neither here not there
All have stretched their legs too far
This side insists don't touch even 'lemonade'
The other feverishly summons, '*Saqi*, bring the cup.'
One side regards the whole book of planned management as unclean
To the other, the bag of English mail is God's word itself
Thus Majnun suffers hardship both ways:
In Laila's company and in Laila's separation.

Translated from the Urdu by Mehr Afshan Farooqi

Rangrelo Bithu (16 CE)

Praises Galore to the Land of Dhat

The low hills are stony, russet and bare,
with no trees on them save the stunted thorny cactus.
You wouldn't hear the call of a peacock
in all the land.
Hyenas, porcupines and monitor lizards
are the only creatures that you'd come across.
The people are starved;
hunger drives them afield
in search of the prickly grass
whose seeds I have seen them eat.
Such as the Jadavs of Jaisalmer.

The senior queen drives her donkeys
to a distant pond to fetch her water;
alone she must go,
and bestirring with her hands
the water
to clear its surface
of the floating dirt and debris,
fill her pots;
and load them on to the wooden frames
on the donkeys' backs
and drive them home,
trudging all the way,
tired and exhausted.

The king's chief bard is pot-bellied;
he wears his lower garment
in a loose unseemly manner;

he is lame in both his legs;
and groans at every step he walks.
The carpet on which the Rawal's court assembles
is worn, with large holes in it;
his poets are all stupid
and cannot distinguish between
a buffalo and an elephant;
to them coarse wool
and silk are just the same.
Such is the land of Dhat!
Praises be to the land of Dhat!

The comely women all go
to fetch water at dawn;
they return past midnight
dishevelled and distraught;
their dishevelled children
pine for them all day.
Such, indeed, is the land of Dhat!
Praises galore to the land of Dhat!

Translated from the Rajasthani by Kesri Singh

Vanparanar (c. 100 BCE–250 CE)

A Woman and Her Dying Warrior

I cannot cry out,
I'm afraid of tigers.
I cannot hold you,
your chest is too wide
for my lifting.

Death
has no codes
and has dealt you wrong,
may he
shiver as I do!

Hold my wrist
of bangles,
let's get to the shade
of that hill.
Just try and walk a little.

Translated from the Tamil by A.K. Ramanujan

Sarala Das (15 CE)

From the Mahabharata

O Chaitana,
As silence fell upon the field of Kurukshetra,
Emerged Manogobinda from under the mighty bell.
Stood he, Manogobinda, to the east of the river of blood.
Climbed he the auspicious column raised for the Bharata war.
Watching the river of blood, the king, Managobinda,
Beat his forehead, surveying all around.
'O Destiny,' he cried,
'I gained such a fortune, so vast,
On the strength of my merits of previous birth.
And sank it all in a trifle, such is my feeble fate.'

Sat there lamenting, the king of the Kurus, atop the auspicious pillar.
Saw he then floating down the carcass of Duhshasana.

Drew it he close into his lap, the proud monarch.
And fell to mourning.
'O brother mine, Duhshasana, the one great fighter on the earth,
O clear young lad, Duhshasana,
Virtuous, righteous, brave, and wise,
Foremost honoured in the world of warriors.
O dear boy, you hauled Draupadi by the hair,
And stripped her in the hall of the great court.

....

Where dear boy, did you put by all those virtues and pledges,
And now come floating, stretched upon this river of blood?
What use have I, dear, for this life of mine?
Shameless am I to be thus alive, allowing you to perish.

....

Little of the night is left to sing your virtues.
Would you, my brother bear me across this stream of blood?'

Translated from the Oriya by Madhusudan Pati

Mirza Mohammad Rafi Sauda (1713–80)

From The State of the Realm

Look, you fellows who are here,
Young or old, don't ever claim from now
That you have a tongue in your mouth—
I have heard great Sauda's discourse.
My God! What organisation, what flow!

I just asked him, 'Sir, be pleased to say
If there is any way to survive here
In minimal comfort?'

He said, 'Better be quiet, man; even
Angels can't answer this question.
What can I say? Today there are
Hundreds of ways to earn one's bread.
Here is a brief account.

'If you acquire a horse, and serve
in some grandee's cavalry, then
by God, your pay will be paid in
the Upper World. And in the Qazi's mosque,
dwell donkeys; young and old just wait
for the Mulla to give the call for prayer;
and when he calls, they gag him and say
'Shut up, you lout, there is no muslimness now.

．．．．

'For a hundred rupees or two a month, if one
were to serve as a rich man's physician:
Let the patron just sneeze and he glares
At his tame doctor. He calls for a bow
And arrow to ward off even the hint
Of a breeze. When the Navab eats,
His doctor's blood pressure goes up.
The patron hogs all sorts of things and if
His belly aches as a result, then God
Help the doctor; even if he were
Avicenna, he would be declared a fool

In short, they don't hire doctors.
They hire soldiers to fight with death.

Translated from the Urdu by Shamsur Rahman Faruqi

Ajneya (1911–87)

Kalemegdan*

On this side
in a long moat
between the rampart and the inner wall
carefully ordered
stacks of weapons from the last war:
tank trunks, mutilated cannons, flat-nosed mortars—
their unblinking blind eyes
staring at the sky.

On that side
on a mound
between the rampart and the wall,
half overgrown by disorderly thickets
ruins of a monastery and a church
darkness surging from frameless windows
as if seeking men on the earth . . .

God, my poor God,
who murdered you more?

Translated from the Hindi by Lucy Rosenstein

*Translator's note: Kalemegdan is the name of a fortress, situated at the confluence of the Danube and Sava, which has been turned into a museum.

Raghuvir Sahay (1929–90)

Cycle Rickshaw

It may sound like socialism to say
we should treat horses like human beings,
especially when one of them happens to be a human being.
When we jump guiltily off a rickshaw,
and then feel sorry we've deprived the poor man of his livelihood
and finally tip him out of pity—
in all three cases we're a trial to him, and he has to endure us.
It is only when we haggle over the fare
that we approach equality.
Come, you engineers of the twenty-first century,
let's invent a cycle-rickshaw in which
the passenger and horse can sit side by side
and just go for a spin.
And what good will this do, you may ask?
Well, if there's a disagreement between you and the horse,
at least he won't have to turn round and get a crick in his neck.

Translated from the Hindi by Harish Trivedi and Daniel Weissbort

Jaysinh Birjepatil (b. 1933)

The Secunderabad Club

The Empire rests there.
Dull cherry orchard thud
Of cues from the Billiard Room,
Heirloom of a half-finished game.

Bearers in white man this khaki outpost,
Playing host to snickery ghosts,
Mutton-chop good looks, peaches and cream,
Flash on their sepia consciousness.

Someone dissolves with a cool splash
In the desegregated pool.
An irate Koi-Hai glares,
Thumps the table with a pseudo-Sandhurst air.

On the wainscot of the Men's Bar,
Mid-century Club Presidents turn brown:
Their portraits shine in the mirror—
None breaks rank.

To whom do these memories belong?
They sprout in vases,
White ants building colonies,
Chota pegs served for auld lang syne.

Out in the dark a cart creaks by
In the land of the vanishing empires
Adipose waddlers chew betel-nut
In the corridors of power.

Bearers stoop under the white man's burden.
The Empire is frozen
In their look of reproof
As fish-knives are used for stirring the soup.

English

Shrikant Varma (1931–86)

Process

What was I doing
When
Everyone was saying 'Hail'?
I was also saying 'Hail,'
And was afraid,
as everyone was.

What was I doing
When
Everyone was saying.
'Aziz is my enemy'?
I too said
'Aziz is my enemy.'

What was I doing
When everybody was saying,
'Don't open your mouth'?
I also said,
'Don't open your mouth,
Say what everyone says.'

The shouts of 'Hail' have ceased,
Aziz has been killed;
Mouths have been silenced.

Bewildered, everyone asks
'How did it come to pass'?

As others ask
So I ask,
'How did it come to pass?'

Translated from the Hindi by Vishnu Khare

Tabish Khair (b. 1966)

Remembering Tiananmen

Sometimes, I sigh for life—
So many farewells, meetings how few.

I

Sitting silently in the willow-breaking pavilion
What can we do but remember; remember
The days that had been dragon-ridden,
The young men and women who had loved too much
And let their love bear leaves without the deeper root.

II

In China, once when the ky-lin had shrieked,
Someone had made poems of the injustice all felt,
Of every heart's desire not yet fulfilled.
Unheard, from the shadows he had leapt into the dark,
Leaving us only with memories of dragon-boats and
dumplings.

III

All good things soon come to an end, our elders had said
When we stood in Tiananmen Square making poems.
Today, when we hide in the willows, awaiting almond blossoms,
We told you so, they seem to say shaking the snow in their hair.
Having planted no cherry tree, the old can afford to be wise.

English

Lakhmi Khilani (b. 1935)

When That Day Comes

When that day comes
The soldier touches his mother's feet
Looks at his wife with affection
Kisses the forehead of his child ...

When that day comes
The soldier carries lethal weapons with him
Ties bombs and missiles around his neck
And tries to pretend that he is stone-hearted ...

When that day comes
The soldier reaches the battlefield
To save his nation
Fights with the soldier of the other nation.

When that day comes
The day passes by and the night too passes away
The earth looks red

The sky looks red
Nothing else but the red colour remains.

When that day comes
The soldier smiles with his eyes closed
He lives in order to spread peace in the world
He fights in order to bring peace in the world
He dies in order to bring peace in the world
And finally reaches that world of peace
When that day comes . . .

Translated from the Sindhi by Madhu Kewlani

Kunwar Narain (b. 1927)

Ayodhya, 1992

O Rama
Life is a bitter fact
and you are an epic.
> You cannot win over
> the unthinking
> that now has not ten or twenty
> but a million heads and hands;
> and who knows with whom your ally
> Vibhishana too now stands.

What more can our misfortune be
that your kingdom lies shrunk
to a stage of dispute so petty.

Ayodhya is not your war-free realm now
But a warrior's Lanka of old,

And 'Manas' not your virtues
but slogans that elections hold.

O Rama, where are these times
and where your golden days:
Where your noble glory
and where these wily ways!

We humbly pray, O Lord, that you return
securely, with wife and home,
to some scroll—some sacred tome;
these jungles are not the jungles of yore
that Valmiki used to roam.

Translated from the Hindi by Apurva Narain

Vyasa

From the Mahabharata

Bhishma and Parsurama Engage in Combat

Parasurama, excited,
deluged me with twelve
terrible weapons,
so radiant and swift,
that I cannot, O Bharata,
describe them in words.

For how is that possible?
When the arrows converge
from different directions
like the twelve suns that blaze
at the world's dissolution,
one feels only fear.

When the arrows like nets
came rushing, I blocked
them with arrows like nets.
With twelve of my arrows
I baffled the power
of the twelve fierce suns.

Parasurama-mahatma
replied with more arrows
with golden shafts
and golden wings.
They sped through the air
like radiant meteors.

These too I repulsed
with my shield and my sword,
and replied with a shower
of divine arrows
intended to kill
his charioteer and horses.

When he noticed the swarms
of gold snake-arrows
released at his chariot,
Parasurama-mahatma
the Haihaya lord,
shot divine missiles.

And suddenly a swarm
of arrows descended
like a swarm of locusts,
devouring my body,

devouring my horses,
devouring my chariot.

Those arrows devoured
my chariot, my horse,
my charioteer too.
They crumbled the wheels,
the axle, the spokes,
the yoke of my chariot.

To the best of my powers,
I hurled on my guru
a counter-discharge;
the violent impact
made that Brahmin hero
a blood-dripping mass.

I bled with his arrows,
he bled with mine.
And late in the evening,
when the sunrays vanished
in the hills of the west,
the combat ended.

Translated from the Sanskrit by P. Lal

Book XI

Gandhari's Lament for the Slain

Stainless Queen and stainless woman, ever righteous ever good,
Stately in her mighty sorrow on the field Gandhari stood!

'River of blood' 303

Strewn with skulls and clotted tresses, darkened by the stream of gore,
With the limbs of countless warriors is the red field covered o'er,

Elephants and steeds of battle, car-borne chiefs untimely slain,
Headless trunks and heads dissevered fill the red and ghastly plain,

And the long-drawn howl of jackals o'er the scene of carnage rings,
And the vulture and the raven flap their dark and loathsome wings.

Feasting on the blood of warriors foul *Pisachas*[1] fill the air,
Viewless forms of hungry Rakshas[2] limb from limb the corpses tear!

Through this scene of death and carnage was the ancient monarch led,
Kuru dames with faltering footsteps stepped amidst the countless dead,

And a piercing wail of anguish burst upon the echoing plain,
As they saw their sons or fathers, brothers, lords, amidst the slain,

As they saw the wolves of jungle feed upon the destined prey,
Darksome wanderers of the midnight prowling in the light of day!

Shriek of pain and wail of anguish o'er the ghastly field resound,
And their feeble footsteps falter and they sink upon the ground,

[1] pisachas: ghosts, goblins
[2] rakshas: demons

Sense and life desert the mourners as they faint in common grief,
Death-like swoon succeeding sorrow yields a moment's short relief!

Then a mighty sigh of anguish from Gandhari's bosom broke,
Gazing on her anguished daughters unto Krishna thus she spoke:

'Mark my unconsoled daughters, widowed queens of Kuru's house,
Wailing for their dear departed, like the osprey for her spouse!

How each cold and fading feature wakes in them a woman's love,
How amidst the lifeless warriors still with restless steps they rove.

Mothers hug their slaughtered children all unconscious in their sleep,
Widows bend upon their husbands and in ceaseless sorrow weep.

Mighty Bhishma, hath he fallen, quenched in archer Karna's pride,
Doth the monarch of Panchala sleep by foeman Drona's side?

Shining mail and costly jewels, royal bangles strew the plain,
Golden garlands rich and burnished deck the chiefs untimely slain,

Lances hurled by stalwart fighters, clubs of mighty wrestlers killed,
Swords and bows of ample measure, quivers still with arrows filled!

Mark the unforgotten heroes, jungle prowlers mid them stray,
On their brow and mailed bosoms heedless sit the birds of prey,

Mark the great unconquered heroes famed on earth from west to east,

Kankas[3] perch upon their foreheads, hungry wolves upon them feast!

Mark the kings, on softest cushion scarce the needed rest they found,
Now they lie in peaceful slumber on the hard and reddened ground,

Mark the youths who morn and evening listed to the minstrel's song,
In their ear the loathsome jackal doth his doleful wail prolong!

See the chieftans with their maces and their swords of trusty steel,
Still they grasp the tried weapons,—do they still the life-pulse feel?'

Translated from the Sanskrit by Romesh C. Dutt

Anon, Political Song

This Night Is Endless

This night is endless
The rice jars are empty
My eyes fill with tears
and my heart is anguished
How will I look after my mother?

I cannot stay much longer.

I hear the mountains tremble
as the people march upon them
and the mansions of the rich crumble

[3] kankas: birds of prey

Do not keep me, then, mother
as I too must go
to make the bright sun rise.

Translated from the Bangla; translator unknown

Pash (1950–88)

No, I Am Not Losing My Sleep

No
I am not losing my sleep over
how and when
you'll strike
to finish me off
frankly, I couldn't care less
about it
because
I don't have the patience
of a watchman
to be on an eternal guard
to sift and filter
countless moments
to await
the time slot
your henchmen have fixed for me.

No
I don't waste my time thinking about such trifles
nor am I sentimental about

my memories of my village
and the folks I left behind
No I don't think now about
such things as
the fine hues of red
when the sun sets over the village
nor do I care about
how she feels.

Translated from the Punjabi by Suresh Sethi

Narayan Surve (b. 1926)

Lifetime

A whole lifetime assigned to me:
even the light when I was born
was assigned to me;
I said the things I was assigned to say.
Cursing under my breath,
I walked the street assigned to me;
I came back to the room
assigned to me;
I lived the life I was assigned to live.
They say we go to heaven
if we follow the path assigned to us.
Between the four pillars assigned to us
I spit:
there.

Translated from the Marathi by Vinay Dharwadker

Sarveshwar Dayal Saxena (1927–83)

Red Bicycle

A red bicycle
Stood against the thorn-bush
All night.
I heard the policemen's whistles
And the sound of their heavy boots.

Next morning
A boy turned up from somewhere
And started ringing
Its moist cold bell.

A patrol car, its siren on,
Screeched to a halt.
The boy saw the starlike
Blue lights on its roof.
And forgot the bell.

Then the car left with the boy.

For the first time
I saw the window bars' shadow
Fall across the floor of my room
And was afraid.

Translated from the Hindi by Arvind Krishna Mehrotra

Nirala (1899–1961)

Breaking Stones

By a road in Allahabad
I saw a woman
breaking stones.

No tree to give her shade,
A dark skin,
Firm tightly cupped breasts,
Eyes fixed on the ground,
Thoughts of the night before
Going through her mind,
She brought down the heavy hammer
Again and again, as though it were
A weapon in her hand.
Across the road—
A row of trees, high walls,
The mansions of the rich.

The sun climbed the sky.
The height of summer.
Blinding heat, with the loo blowing hard,
Scorching everything in its path.
The earth under the feet
Like burning cotton wool,
The air full of dust and sparks.
It was getting to noon,
And she was still breaking stones.

As I watched,
She looked at me once,
Then at the houses opposite,
Then at her ragged clothes.
Seeing no one was around,
She met my eyes again
With eyes that spoke of pain
But not defeat.

Suddenly, there came the notes of a sitar,
Such as I had not heard before.
The next moment her young body
Quivered and as sweat
Trickled, down her face, she lifted
the hammer, resuming work,
As though to say
'I'm breaking stones.'

Translated from the Hindi by Arvind Krishna Mehrotra

Chandrashekara Patil (b. 1939)

Once Upon a Time

Once upon a time,
my friends,
this sky knew no limit
and this earth, no boundary.

Whatever you shouted then
became a song. But
none listened.
Wherever your feet took you

became a path. But
none to follow you.

But when lips are sealed
and feet chained,
just a struggle of the feet
(the chains may not be broken, but . . .)
you might light up
the milky way in the sky.

Just an attempt to break the silence—
(you may not produce a syllable, but . . .)
the earth might
break out into a chorus.

Translated from the Kannada by the poet

Purandara Dasa (1484–1564)

Where Are the Untouchables

There are no untouchables, they aren't even
In the neighbourhood of the untouchables.

He is an untouchable who under his wife's
Control insults his parents;

She, an untouchable who, having borne
Many children and now old, hates her husband.

He is an untouchable who, having studied
From a teacher, torments his elders;
She an untouchable who, attracted by other men,
Dislikes her own husband.

He was protected by a master but being
Ungrateful he quarrelled with him. He is an untouchable.
She in poverty scolds her husband every now and then;
She, indeed, is an untouchable.
He is an untouchable who, wallowing in
Sin, has free sex with other women.
She is an untouchable who quarrels,
Argues and is epileptic and evil-natured.

He is an untouchable who, not sympathising
With the distressed, lives without concern.
She who is involved in love-acts in her
Youth, is a real untouchable.

One who knows not the holy waters and
God's sacred flowers is an untouchable.
She, not engaged in
Other-worldly knowledge hates the sages, is an
untouchable.

He is the greatest untouchable who worships
Not Narayan, father of Brahma.
She is a low untouchable who has abandoned
The real master, Purandar Vitthal.

Translated from the Kannada by Keshav Mutalik

Gieve Patel (b. 1940)

Continuum

Do you ascribe to me coarse feelings
And obsessiveness

The way I grossly return
To nerve endings?

I am continuum with the century's skin.
I am horribly bruised each time it is struck.

But why isolate, you say, mere anatomy
In the poet's abundant chamber;
Why endlessly squint at ragged fibres?

A chorale daily rises
From the world's forsaken cellars
Where tormentor coaxes
A song from an object:
A song of ravaged pitch,
The century's folk song.
And would you have me ignore it?

English

Anon

From Bharath

An Epic of the Dungri Bhils

Pandu, the King
One day the Sun declined behind the western hills.
The Sun declined behind the western hills.
The parakeets returned to their nests.

Lamps were lit at every niche in the palace.
Lamps were lit at every niche in the palace.
Pandu, the king, had drifted into deep slumber.

Pandu, the king, dreamt a dream.
He dreamt a dream.
Iyaro, the God of Hunting, appeared in his dream.

'Go out hunting in the Meru-Sumeru mountains,
                    O king,' said the deity.
'Go out hunting in the Meru-Sumeru mountains.'
The king awoke with a start.

'What a strange dream I had,' pondered he.
'What a strange dream I had!'
He kept tossing and turning in bed.

The waking cock's crowing heralded the day.
The waking cock's crowing heralded the day.
The first streak of light brightened the sky.

Pandu, the king, pondered for a while.
He pondered for a while.
He cleaned his teeth and rinsed his mouth.

Pandu offered prayers to the rising Sun.
He offered prayers to the rising Sun.
He picked up his bows and arrows.

Pandu's bow was full six cubits long.
His bow was full six cubits long.
His quiver contained seven long arrows.

Pandu, the king, put up a hide on the mountain.
The king put up a hide on the mountain.
But not a single animal came that way.

The Sun rose high in the sky.
The Sun rose high in the sky.
The earth turned into a heated hearth.

The king was thirsty, his throat became parched.
The king was thirsty, his throat became parched.
In search of water he set out.

By following a trail of animals,
By following a trail of animals,
Pandu reached the Khanda lake.

Pandu quenched his thirst with the water of the lake.
He quenched his thirst with the water of the lake.
He erected a hide to conceal himself.

Pandu saw a pair of deer coming by.
He saw a pair of deer coming by.
Holding his breath, the king waited for them.

The stag and his doe approached the lake.
The stag and his doe approached the lake.
As they came near, the king took aim.

Tambur: O maharaj.

Translated from the Gujarati by Nila Shah

'Sleep on your left side'

Arvind Krishna Mehrotra (b. 1947)

Bhojpuri Descant

I
Piss after dinner,
Sleep on your left side:
You'll never fall sick.

II
If landlords are saints,
Pestles are bowstrings.

III
Witty landlords,
Wheezy thieves:
Lynch them.

IV
A servant who knows
The secrets of the house,
A pretty wife,
Spetched clothes,
A wicked king:
They need careful handling.

V
A shoe that pinches,
A sharp-tongued wife,
The first-born a daughter
An unproductive farm,
A duncish brother:
They cause endless grief.

VI

A brown she-elephant,
A bald wife,
Rain in winter:
Signs of luck.

VII

Three oxen, two wives:
Death's at your doorstep.

VIII

A spendthrift son,
A cross-eyed buffalo,
A moody ox:
Get rid of them at once.

IX

An ox with six teeth
Will quickly change hands,
An ox with seven
Will butt its owner,
An ox with nine
Will rush in nine directions
And won't spare even the family priest.

X

To inspect the teeth
Of a skewbald ox
Is a waste of time.

XI
The thin-tailed ox
With reindeer's piss
Brings prosperity.

XII
The blue-flanked ox
With purple horns
Can't be wrong.

XIII
One plough is death,
Two's survival,
Three's good business,
Four's a kingdom.

XIV
A wise farmer does his own tilling,
The one less wise walks beside his team,
But the farmer who goes looking for tillmen
Forfeits his seed.

XV
A small ploughshare
Tickles the field.

XVI
A kite's screech from atop a ruin:
Sign of rain.

XVII
A chameleon
Scrambles up the bole
Tail-first: Expect a flood.

XVIII
Clouds throughout the day,
A clear sky at night:
Famine.

XIX
The clouds from the west are misers.

(After Ghagha)

English

Bhavabhuti (c. 725 CE)

From Act 2

Rama's Last Act

This is the very same forest I am seeing again today
where once—it was many years ago—I long sojourned,
both hermit and householder devoted to my own *dharma*,
who came to know the sweet taste of worldly pleasures.

Those are the same mountains, where peacocks used to cry,
those, the same forest-reaches with their deer in heat,

those, the riverbanks with their lovely reeds and vines
and rushes blue-black and thickly clumped together.

And what looms in the distance there like a wreath of clouds
is Mount Prasravana. where the Godavari River runs.

On that mountain's high peak the king of vultures once lived
and on the lower slopes we enjoyed our leaf-thatched huts
by the Godavari. where the forest lay spread out
alive with cooing birds, splendid with dark trees.

Translated from the Sanskrit by Sheldon I. Pollock

Gopal Honnalgere (1942–2003)

How to Tame a Pair of New Chappals

don't keep them together
don't allow them to talk to each other
they may form a trade union

don't leave them anytime near
a wall-clock, law-books, calendar, national flag
gandhi's portrait or newspaper
they may come to know about
independence day, satyagraha,
holidays, working hours, minimum wages and corruption

don't take them to your temple
they may at once come to know you are weak
your god is false and start biting you

don't take them anytime close to your dining table
they may ask for food
or cast their evil eyes on your sumptuous dinner

first use them only for short walks
then gradually increase the distance
they should never know the amount of work they have to do

pull their tight straps loose
let them feel happy
they are growing bigger
smear some old oil on the rough straps
let them feel they are anointed

now they are good subdued labourers
ready to work overtime
for your fat feet

English

Dharmakirti (c. 7 CE)

The Tradition

No one behind, no one ahead.
The paths the ancients cleared have closed.
And the other path, everyone's path,
easy and wide, goes nowhere.
I am alone and find my way.

Translated from the Sanskrit by Octavio Paz

Siddalingaiah (b. 1954)

I Must Have a Word

I must have a word
with cactuses and thorny plants.
I must put a question
to the moon
whose light is stolen.
I must free
the blood-red roses
from their thorns.

Wells without water,
shameless politicians,
cops who move
with clubs
like thorny bushes,
Oh world,
I must have words with you.

We must speak
while there may be time
to grow the colour green again
in this, our world,
daily done to death,
our mountains trucked away,
our clinging grass
plucked up, the desert sands
allotted all the land
as if in triplicate,
passed on by bureaucrats,
who take the bribes of winds.

And each branch burns now
along with the voice of reason,
allowed to wither,
held in jails, barred
like woodsheds.

All the great
fruits wither, mango,
jack-fruit, wisdom of the ages,
the soft plum of gentleness.
Oh world, I must stop you,
We must have words, and now.

Translated from the Kannada by Sumatheendra Nadig and David Ray

Vallana (c. 900 CE–1100 CE)

The Oblique Invitation

Traveller, hurry your steps, be on your way:
the woods are full of wild animals,
snakes, elephants, tigers and boars,
the sun's going down and you're so young to be going alone.
I can't let you stay,
for I'm a young girl and no one's home.

Translated from the Sanskrit by Octavio Paz

Ravidas (1376–1448)

I've Never Known How to Tan or Sew

I've never known how to tan or sew,
    though people come to me for shoes.

I haven't the needle to make the holes
    or even the tool to cut the thread.
Others stitch and knot, and tie themselves in knots
    while I, who do not knot, break free.
I keep saying Ram and Ram says Ravidas,
    and Death keeps his business to himself.

Translated from the Hindi by J.S. Hawley and Mark Juergensmeyer

Jibanananda Das (1899–1954)

A Strange Darkness

A strange darkness found the world today.
The blind have clearest sight: that is the way.
To move, the world must take the fine advice
Of the heartless, ignorant of pity's sway.
While those for whom it is naturally understood
To do what's tested, or to say what's good—
To strive for spirit's aim that is past price—
Vulture and jackal have their hearts for food.

Translated from the Bangla by Joe Winter

Kabir (c. 14 CE)

Let's Go

Let's go
Everyone keeps saying, as if they know where Paradise is.
But ask them what lies beyond
The street they live on,
They'll give you a blank look.

If Paradise is where they're heading,
Paradise is not where they'll end up.
And what if the talk of Paradise is just hearsay?
You better check out the place yourself.
As for me, says Kabir, if you're listening,
Good company is all I seek.

Translated from the Hindi by Arvind Krishna Mehrotra

Vemana (c. 17 CE/18 CE)

Why Marry?

Why marry?
Why have children?
Why fall into grief?

It's madness—

Like lifting
a heavy stone
from the ground
>onto
>your
>head.

*

A blister on a rich man's back
becomes quite newsworthy.

Who has heard of a wedding
in a poor man's house?

*

Fast,
and you'll be born
as the village pig.

Practice rigors,
and you'll be born
poor.

Bow to stones
and you'll turn into
a lifeless statue.

Translated from the Telugu by J.S.R.L. Narayana Moorty and Elliot Roberts

Kanaka Ha Ma (b. 1964)

Series of Omens

Don't disbelieve omens
Omens are clues
Warnings from the soil

Shrivelling up again and again.
Dying even as they sprout—
A broken clay lamp,
A discarded puppet, suffocated in its own swaddling.
A neglected *devi* in the corner of a village, unworshipped, wrathful
A series of nightmares.

The residue of past karma
Or this life's folly—
Torment churning ceaselessly in a whirlpool—
Finally ends

Next morning.
Sunshine

The clues connect—
A line of a poem read somewhere
Two birds flying in the sky
Sparrows nesting in a loft
The odour of *neelanjana*, always burning
The creeper in the backyard, flowering ...

Translated from the Kannada by the poet and Priya D'Souza

Anon (c. 13 CE)

From The Art of the Courtesan

Grasp those who are sincere in love;
Ensnare the noble ones with a show of affection;
Win over the poets by a display of passion;
Give food and clothes to maids;
Respect greatly the man useful in future;
Take you my counsel, my daughter.

Charm the celibate ones with words, the friends with smiles,
The dependants with gifts,
The family men with affected indignation,
The lovers with bewitching glances,
The foolish ones with tears of joy,
The king with enticing charms;
The sensualists with tact;
The noble ones with magic potion,

The poets by lending your ears to their verses,
And your own relations in other ways.

Translated from the Malayalam (Manipravalan) by P. Narayana Kurup

Ravji Patel (1939–68)

That Afternoon

See, the sarus crane has flown
From the patch at the edge of my field.
Mother, let the buttermilk go back into the pot,
And wrap up the bread.
There's no life left in this tobacco and pipe.
Let the fire smouldering below these ashes
Die; and let me
Lie down in the shade of the mahua tree.
Never mind if the whole sky
Comes pouring down,
Or the grass grows as tall as myself.
Hey, you there,
Don't let the bullocks draw the plough
Over that patch at the edge of my field.

Translated from the Gujarati by Suguna Ramanathan and Rita Kothari

Rabindranath Tagore (1866–1941)

They Call You Mad

They call you mad. Wait for tomorrow
        and keep silent.

They throw dust upon your head. Wait
>   for tomorrow. They will bring
>   their wreath.

They sit apart in their high seat. Wait
>   for tomorrow. They will come
>   down and bend their head.

English

From Jayavallabha's Vajjalagam (c. 8 CE)

What She Told Her Daughter about Unchaste Women

Dear daughter, don't cry
That you have been married to an old man.
It is a nice village
Which has arbours nearby;
And a temple hidden by trees.
Frequented by numerous youths.

Dear daughter,
There are hemp fields to the east
And *asoka* groves to the west;
To the south there is a banyan tree.
Surely, one can't find such a village
Unless one had done meritorious deeds earlier.

Daughter clear,
The stigma of chastity

has never touched our family—
With blessings from gods
And Brahmins—
Until this day.

Translated from the Prakrit by H. V. Nagaraja Rao and T.R.S. Sharma

The Dhammapada (c. 4 CE/5 CE)

From The Fool

Chapter V

60. Long is the night to him who is awake; long is a mile to him who is tired; long is life to the foolish who do not know the true law.

61. If a traveller does not meet with one who is his better, or his equal, let him firmly keep to his solitary journey; there is no companionship with a fool.

62. 'These sons belong to me, and this wealth belongs to me,' with such thoughts a fool is tormented. He himself does not belong to himself; how much less sons and wealth?

63. The fool who knows his foolishness, is wise at least so far. But a fool who thinks himself wise, he is called a fool indeed.

64. If a fool be associated with a wise man even all his life, he will perceive the truth as little as a spoon perceives the taste of soup.

65. If an intelligent man be associated for one minute only with a wise man, he will soon perceive the truth, as the tongue perceives the taste of soup.

Translated from the Pali by F. Max Muller

Namdeo Dhasal (b. 1949)

Stone Masons, My Father, and Me

Stone masons give stones dreams to dream;
I set a match to fireworks.
    They say one mustn't step into
    one's father's life:
        I do; I scratch
    his elbows,
        his armpits.

Stone masons give stones flowers;
I play horns and trumpets.
    I overtake the Parsi who stands
    turned to stone
        by the bodies of four women
    bent like bows.
I see my father's bloodied rump.
    In the chaos of the dark
    I smoke a cheroot
        and smoulder with memories
    till my lips get burnt.

Stone masons inseminate stones;
I count exhausted horses.
    I harness myself to a cart; I handle
    my father's corpse; I burn.

Stone masons mix blood with stones;
I carry a load of stones.
    Stone masons build
    a stone house.
    I break heads with stones.

Translated from the Marathi by Vinay Dharwadker

Kabir (c. 14 CE)

Listen Carefully

Listen carefully,
Neither the Vedas
Nor the Qur'an
Will teach you this.
Put the bit in its mouth,
The saddle on its back,
Your foot in the stirrup,
And ride your wild runaway mind
All the way to heaven.

Translated from the Hindi by Arvind Krishna Mehrotra

M. Gopalakrishna Adiga (1918–92)
Do Something, Brother

Do something, brother:
something, anything:
You mustn't be idle.
Pull out this plant, nip this little leaf,
crunch that flower.

There's grass, run
your faggots through.
Butterflies, parrots, sparrows—chase
them, hold them, cage them, pluck
their wings and pull their fur and feather.
There in the garden grow, for the wild elephant's feet,
jasmine and the banana's gold.

All over your walls
virility's master switchboards
itch for your fingers. Close
your eyes and pull twenty down.
Earth, water, the skies, they are all
your geese with golden eggs.
Gouge them: slash them.

'Do, or die,' they say.
For your genius' galloping dance
disasters are the test
Brother, act, act at once, do something.
Thought's weights and measures
are all for the past,
for the dead's undying ghostly treasures

There's the forest, cut it
clean to the stump, slit it for your buntings.
You have the axe, the sickle, the saw
and the knife; go, harvest all the world
with a flourish of your hand—

But
winter mists:
light foggy walls that line
the space between your face and mine:
the road sighs and breaks in two
under the eyes,
a couple of mountain peaks rear their hoods
and lower upon your head;
or lightning winks from sirens
that sing on every tree:
do they plunge you
into anxieties and dilemmas of reason?
No, no, this won't do.
You are a simple man,
and that's your strength.
Horse-sense and the blinkers
are your forté.
Eat what comes to the hand; crush what you touch;
cut the hindering vines.
Mother Earth herself, though tired,
lies open to the skies: there's still flesh
upon her bone marrow for your hunger.
Come, come, brother, never forget
that you are a man.

Then there's the well. Rope
the wheel and axle, pull all
the water out. Reach the last dryness
of the rock: group, grope with the grappling iron.
'V for Victory', brother.
Gain the God's own arrow,
and aim it straight to the heart
of God's own embryo-world.
Do something, anything,
anything, brothers.
Idle men
are burdens on the land.
Do brother, do something.
Keep doing something all the time
to lighten Mother Earth's loads.
This is right. This is natural.
This is the one thing needful.

Translated from the Kannada by A.K. Ramanujan

Asvaghosa (18 CE)

From Buddhacarita

Canto 3

Then at one time he (Prince Sarvartha Siddha, the future Buddha)
    heard some songs
composed about the parks, with their soft meadows
and adorned with lotus pools,
their trees sounding with cuckoos.

Then after hearing of the lovely nature
of the parks of the city, which were loved by the women,
He set his mind on an excursion outside,
like an elephant shut inside a home.

Then the King having heard of the feelings
of that desired object his 'son'
gave orders for a pleasure trip,
suited to his affection, fortune and age.

He diverted from the Royal Way
the distressed press of common people,
Thinking: 'Let not the Prince, whose thoughts are delicate,
have his mind disturbed.'

Then after very gently driving away
those who were lacking limbs and those whose senses were defective,
Those who were disabled by age and so on, the pitiful, in all directions,
they made the Royal Way very beautiful.

Then, when the Royal Way was made beautiful.
the famous Prince, with disciplined followers,
Descended from the top of the palace at the proper time
and went to the King, being given leave.

Then indeed the King, his fear welling up,
kissed his son's head, gazed at him for a long time,
And ordered: 'Go!' with a word,
but through affection did not let him go with his mind.

Then he mounted a golden chariot,
yoked with four quiet horses
Bearing trappings of finest gold,
whose charioteer was brave, wise and true.

Then with a befitting retinue
he reached the road which was scattered with
brilliant bouquets of flowers,
Hung with garlands, with trembling bunting,
like the Moon with a constellation in the sky.

Very slowly he entered the Royal Way
which was as if strewn with halves of blue waterlilies,
As he was being looked at by the citizens all around,
their eyes expanded wide with curiosity.

Some praised him for his charming qualities
and others saluted him for his brilliance,
But some wished him fortune (sovereignty)
and length of life, because of his cheerfulness.

Hunchbacks and groups of mountain tribesmen and dwarfs
slipped out of the great houses,
And women from the little houses;
they bowed as to the banner in the procession of the god (Indra).

Then hearing the news from the servants:
'The Prince is going!'
Women went to the balconies of the palaces wishing to see him,
being given leave by their elders.

Obstructed by untied girdle strings,
their eyes confused as they awakened from sleep,

Putting on their ornaments at the news,
they gathered noisily through curiosity.

Frightening the multitudes of house-birds
with loud noise on the stairs and balconies of the palaces,
with clamour of girdles and sounds of anklets,
rebuking each other's haste.

Canto 8

Then the groom depressed,
when his selfless master had gone to the forest,
Made an effort to restrain his grief on the road,
yet his tears were not exhausted.

But the road which he had traversed in one night
on his master's order, with that horse,
That same way now took him eight days,
as he reflected on the absence of his master.

And the strong horse Kanthaka wandered
pained in feelings, dispirited,
Though adorned with jewellery
he was as if shorn of beauty, without him.

And returning towards the forest of asceticism
he neighed violently, pathetically, over and over again;
Though hungry on the road he did not approve, nor take
either young grass or water,

Then gradually those two approached the city called Kapila,
deserted by that illustrious one who was devoted to the welfare
   of the world;

It was as if empty,
like the sky deprived of the Sun.

Translated from the Sanskrit by A.K. Warder

Kynpham Sing Nongkynrih (b. 1964)
Lines Written to Mothers Who Disagree with Their Sons' Choices of Women

For managing to love
an object of scorn
they place around my neck
a garland of threats.

And the world is cold this winter,
cold as the matrimonial column
they lecture to my sewn-shut ears,
or the stares that stalk
the woman of my choice.

But the cherries are pink
and festive as her love.

Leave cherries to winter, mother,
love to seasoned lovers.

Translated from the Khasi by the poet

Siddaramayya (12 CE)
Know How to Tell

Know how to tell
a mahout from a goatherd
and learn to sit as the simian sits.

Know the ways
of the mad man's mind
Know how to shed the darkness within.

Kapilasiddhamallinathayya,

let me in on the views
of a child.

Translated from the Kannada by B.C. Ramchandra Sharma

Vijay Nambisan (b. 1963)

Madras Central

The black train pulls in at the platform,
Hissing into silence like hot steel in water.
Tell the porters not to be so precipitate—
It is good, after a desperate journey,
To rest a moment with your perils upon you.

The long rails recline into a distance
Where tomorrow will come before I know it.
I cannot be in two places at once:
That is axiomatic. Come, we will go and drink
A filthy cup of tea in a filthy restaurant.

It is difficult to relax. But my head spins
Slower and slower as the journey recedes.
I do not think I shall smoke a cigarette now.
Time enough for that. Let me make sure first
For the hundredth time, that everything's complete.

My wallet's in my pocket; the white nylon bag
With the papers safe in its lining-fine;
The book and my notes are in the outside pocket;
The brown case is here with all its straps secure.
I have everything I began the journey with,

And also a memory of my setting out
When I was confused, so confused. Terrifying
To think we have such power to alter our states,
Order comings and goings: know where we're not wanted
And carry our unwantedness somewhere else.

English

Sarangapani (18 CE)

A Wife's Complaint

How is this household
going to survive?
Tell me what to do
with all these lewd antics
of lord Venugopala,
scion of the Gokula clan.

Takes no care of his house.
Finds good advice bitter.
Wants special meals.
Hangs out with pimps.

Tell me what to do

Sleeps in whorehouses.
Throws away money on sluts.

Scratches his creditors
for luxuries,
with not a drop of ghee
in our house.

Tell me what to do

But there's no end of dancing songs,
not to speak of the lute.
He bet on cocks at the fights

Tell me what to do

I have a single sari to wear and to wash.
Can't even mention a second blouse
Tumeric has become my gold,
and my ears are bare.

Tell me what to do

And then I have to listen daily
to his affairs with those women.
Even my curses don't stir him.

It's been seven years
since we've been to bed.
Women of my age
are mothers of children.

Tell me what to do

Translated from the Telugu by A.K. Ramanujan, Velcheru Narayana Rao and David Shulman

Devara Dasimayya (c. 11 CE)

Fire Can Burn

Fire can burn
but cannot move.

Wind can move
but cannot burn.

Till fire joins wind
it cannot take a step.

Do men know
it's like that
with knowing and doing?

Translated from the Kannada by A.K. Ramanujan

Hemacandra Suri (12 CE)

O Learned Man

O learned man,
rare are those
who are wise
and perfect in every way,
those that are clever
are taken to be cheats;
and those that talk straight
are dull as bullocks.

Translated from the Prakrit by H.V. Nagaraja Rao and T.R.S. Sharma

Sami (1743–1850)

Six Shastras, Eight Puranas, and Four Vedas

Six Shastras, eight Puranas, and four Vedas the same truth proclaim:
Why wander like maniacs from place to place?
Seek divine communion, igniting eternal flame,
And behold Him even in the market place.

Translated from the Sindhi by Shanti Shahani

Vijayalakshmi (b. 1960)

What Shall We Sell Next?

Come, tradesmen,
With bulging bags of gold;
They are calling you
to sell the river, the wind,
the sunlight and the rain,
to sell the beauties of the fourteenth night,
to sell the pure notes of the dawn's music,
for you to buy.
Come, you can snuff out
the beauties of the tall, blue hills,
And root out the green trees of the forest.
You man come and pack
the cold and the mist; don't forget!
They are calling you
with an ironed out smile on the lips,
they who are determined
to make mincemeat of the land

and sell it out.
See, they are trumpeting,
you may cut the land
with your butchers' knife:
But there is something more to sell:
The men who adorn their neck
with the trump card of discretion
A hundred thousand men.
Even their flesh is worth nothing
who will now come to buy them?

Translated from the Malayalam by C.P. Sivadasan

Anon

From Sutrakritanga (c. 6 BCE–3 BCE)

A Celibate Monk Shouldn't Fall in Love

A celibate monk shouldn't fall in love,
and though he hankers after pleasure he should hold himself in check
for these are the pleasures which some monks enjoy.

If a monk breaks his vows.
and falls for a woman,
she upbraids him and raises her foot to him.
and kicks him on the head.

'Monk, if you won't live with me
as husband and wife,
I'll pull out my hair and become a nun,
for you shall not live without me!'

But when she has him in her clutches
it's all housework and errands!
'Fetch a knife to cut this gourd!
Get me some fresh fruit!'

'We want wood to boil the greens,
and for a fire in the evening!
Now paint my feet!
Come and massage my back!'

'Get me my lip salve!
Find my sunshade and slippers!
I want a knife to cut these leaves!
Take my robe and have it dyed blue!'

'Fetch me my tweezers and my comb!
Get me a ribbon to tie my hair!
Now pass me my looking-glass!
Go and fetch me my toothbrush!'

'Fetch the pot and the drum and the rag-ball,
for our little boy to play with!
Monk, the rains are on the way,
patch the roof of the house and look to the stores!'

'See to getting that chair upholstered!
Fetch my wooden-soled slippers to go out walking!'
So pregnant women boss their husbands,
just as though they were household slaves.

When a child is born, the reward of their labours,
she makes the father hold the baby.

And sometimes the fathers of sons
stagger under their burdens like camels.

They get up at night, as though they were nurses,
to lull the howling child to sleep,
and, though they are shame-faced about it,
scrub dirty garments, just like washermen . . .

So, monks, resist the wiles of women,
avoid their friendship and company.
The little pleasure you get from them
will only lead you into trouble!

Translated from the Prakrit by A.L. Basham

A.K. Ramanujan (1929–93)

The Guru

Forgive the weasel his tooth
forgive the tiger his claw

but do not forgive the woman
her malice or the man his envy

said the guru, as he moved on
to ask me to clean his shoe,

bake his bread and wash his clothes.

Give the dog his bone, the parrot
his seed, the pet snake his mouse

but do not give woman her freedom
nor man his midday meal till he begs

said the guru, as he went on
his breakfast of eggs and news

asking me to carry his chair to the dais.

I gave the dog his bone, the parrot
his seed, the pet snake his mouse,

forgave the weasel his tooth,
forgave the tiger his claw,

and left the guru to clean his own shoe
for I remembered I was a man born of woman.

English

'Light like ash'

Mamang Dai (b. 1959)

A Stone Breaks the Sleeping Water

I wish I had inherited fruit trees.
Tall, full grown trees
with flowering branches and ancient roots
nothing vanishes so surely as childhood
the life of clay, the chemistry of colour
this I realise in the season of dying
in the month of the red lotus
when a stone breaks the sleeping water

Where eyes meet the dawn
claiming the course of a river, a stream
I wish I could fulfill impersonation of a life
and inherit each simple hour
protected by innocence.

Now when it rains
I equate the white magnolia with perfect joy
Spring clouds, stroke of sunlight
The brushstrokes of my transformed heart.

English

Joy Goswami (b. 1954)

A Mound of Earth, a Heart

A mound of earth a heart
Crowned by a set of bones, playing
Bones. Dice. Bones.

A mound of earth, a heart
Could you claim the right to spade and shovel
Digging hands bare?

Clumps come away lumps of earth
Flesh earth flesh earth—
Dice. Bones. Dice.

Far off, the lacerated world
Is still afloat, could you offer it a fistful
Of earth a handful of heart—

Would you dare?

Translated from the Bangla by Sampurna Chattarji

Pranabendu Dasgupta (b. 1937)

Man: 1961

In a big wind, in a ruined house
trembling, he holds
with one hand the woman at his side,
while the other confuses him,
lacking a place to rest.
On a margosa tree the pigeons settle.

Facing a harrowing hill,
facing the darkness of
a heaving, wearisome sea,

he cannot find
a private view, a landscape of his own.

In a big wind, in a ruined
house he sways, he trembles.

Translated from the Bangla by Buddhadeva Bose

Anon, Kashmiri Song (c. 18 CE)

Nostalgia

I made nosegays of jasmine in the garden,
And went to the bazaar after six long months,
There I met my dear father;
He met me there and took me to his attic.
There he made a cushion for me to sit on;
He lit a lamp and placed it in the cranny,
He opened a book and read it to me;
Softly I began to reveal my heart,
Silently I began to shed big tears;
Fondly he placed his hand on my head.
'My daughter, you return to your in-laws,' he said;
'The house of your in-laws is now your abode.
Your father's house to you is of no avail.'

A mother's house is the royal house;
A brother's house is just a hope.

Translated from the Kashmiri by Shafi Shauq

B.B. Borkar (1910–84)

Cemetery

A cemetery within earshot, at least for the mind;
be accustomed to its proximity,
above all, at dusk
Read over its arched entrance
the terse message of the dead:
My turn today, yours tomorrow.

Sit on the cold cement seat
distilling that moral,
bathing in the equinoxial wind
to the soft sound of falling leaves.
On the wings of the soul
roam in the ash-blue sky.
Returning carefree to your former serenity,
make detachment burning-hot, intense,
like rising stars;
turn the leaves minute by minute
close to you, delectable.

Enlightened, see the pyres of your dear ones
come alive,
and your own pyre too;
in the dance of the fire, contemplate Eternity.
Become a flame of prayer
till the mark of grace is on your forehead
—the moon's curved form in sandalwood paste.
And the body limp like a plantain-leaf
to fertilise the living earth with inspiration.

Translated from the Marathi by Vrinda Nabar and Nissim Ezekiel

G.S. Sharat Chandra (1935–2000)

Facts of Life

My father, teetotaler, vegetarian,
took two baths a day,
one at dawn the other
before his evening obeisance
to Lord Shiva at the temple.

Cleanliness of forms,
the given and the gifted,
adherence to principles,
honesty, truth, purity,
were things he'd die for.

Yet he died of a malignancy
whose virtue was pillage,
whose form spread
from viscera to vision,
from body to soul.

Now he who loved roses
lies buried within the limits
of his caste's cemetery
by the river Kabini
where the banyans sway,

where transients and pilgrims
come to celebrate Shiva's victory
over one demon or another
see its tall crabgrass
their revelries to defecate.

English

Bhatti (c. 6 CE)

From The Death of Ravana, Canto 18

Vibhishana's Lament for Ravana

Grief envelops my heart, it is as if my being ceases, grief wipes out my sight, without you I lose my strength.

Who does not know that no one else but you was so fond of his relatives? I call into the void, how can I smother my rising anguish?

......

Even though bereft of you we continue with our duties and we decide on life: a curse on the greed that wrecks obligation

If you do not give me word I will crush my own body, for the recollection of your virtues is increasing my grief.

Who will laughingly take off his own garland and garland me? Who will bring me near to his seat? Who will speak sweetly to me?

I shall not go back to Lanka so long as I live. When will I have delight if I never see you?

For within an hour I will die afflicted, my kinsmen slain. I gave good advice in council, I never did anything displeasing to you.

Translated from the Sanskrit by Oliver Fallon

Dursa Adha (1533–1654)

On Hearing of Pratap's Passing Away

You are gone, O Pratap, and no more.
But whilst you lived,
Your steed remained unbranded,
And your turban unlowered in obeisance to mortal man;
Still you defied dread sovereign Akbar—
Steadfastly from the very beginning;
And minstrels sang of your exploits
Throughout the land.

Never once did you go to the *Navroz* fairs,
Nor ever to the royal camps, nor court,
To stand in submission before the Emperor
Beneath his balconies.
Greatest among all you were;
And unbeaten—indeed in triumph—
O Gehlot King, you departed this world.
At the news of your passing away, O Pratap,
In speechless wonder
Did the Emperor bite his lip;
And he heaved a sigh of dismay,
And tears welled up in his eyes.

Translated from the Rajasthani by Kesri Singh

Adil Jussawalla (b. 1940)

Nine Poems on Arrival

Spiders infest the sky.
They are palms, you say,
hung in a web of light.

Gingerly, thinking of concealed
springs and traps, I step off the plane,
expect take-off on landing.

Garlands beheading the body
and everybody dressed in white.
Who are we ghosts of?

You. You. You.
Shaking hands. And you.

Cold hands. Cold feet. I thought
the sun would be lower here
to wash my neck in.

Contact. We talk a language of beads
along well-established wires.
The beads slide, they open, they
devour each other.

Some were important.
Is that one,
as deep and dead as the horizon?

Upset like water
I dive for my favourite tree
which is no longer there
though they've let its roots remain.

Dry clods of earth
tighten their tiny faces
in an effort to cry. Back
where I was born,
I may yet observe my own birth.

English

Ramakanta Rath (b. 1934)

Reports of Your Passing

Reports of your passing away
have reached us here.

Don't count me
among your widows,
or among those who carry your body
in funeral procession.

Your body, mercifully,
is far, far away.

In the parting of my hair,
the vermillion mark
is brighter than ever.
Now stop joking,
become the bridegroom,
and come.

I wear
the bride's heavy silk
and gold.
My bangles
tinkle and snub
all scandals.
You no longer are
anyone's father, son, husband.
You are the pure naughtiness
of our last night together,
the voice,
that teases me,

and the touch that deflowers
the virginity of my loneliness.
Just when I'd start crying
you arrive and tickle
my lifeless longing
into unrestrained laughter.

When they deposit your body
on the pyre,
all that you ever meant to them
will be consumed by the flames.
They would return home
and, a few days later,
would fill your absence
with thoughts of you
and a thousand other things.

My joy today
is uncontrollable.
If you had not died for them,
you would not have become
entirely mine.

Since everyone believes you are dead,
my journeys to the river bank
will now be without fear.
They will forget me,
or sleep like the dead
when I hold you in my arms,
when your hands traverse

my body,
when I renounce all power
to resist, or to speak,
and when it is utterly impossible
for me to die,
or to live.

Translated from the Oriya by the poet

Indira Sant (1914–2000)

Absence

I learn a hundred things.
I made a thousand decisions.
But at the destined time,
I wasn't around.

I'm still not around,
wiped out that very second
as the wild lightning
Flashes out, disappears,

It was all over with me
Though I was there alright.
The quivering eyelids,
The parted lips,
The rapid breath,
The very same woman.

Translated from the Marathi by Vrinda Nabar and Nissim Ezekiel

C.P. Surendran (b. 1959)

The Colours of the Season's Best Dream

Senile dinosaurs wearing white
Block traffic tonight.
Here in the city we drink chilled smog
And eat pickled soot.
We wear snakeskin suits
And our beauties this winter
Look like bruised fruit.
Ambulant screams of red and blue,
And all windows weep
Without seeming to hurt
Sponsors of laundered teeth. Colgate it is.
Smile now, smile right, pursue
The winner through thickets of red light.
The only trouble is the hole
in your baby's heart
The baby, oh the baby
Flies birds out of his oriental eyes
And his fingers curl like burnt paper
And are light like ash in your skeletal hands.
A moon blooms in the mirror in the doctor's room,
Trick or treat, it's blue like the baby's face.

English

Kedarnath Singh (b. 1934)

Remembering the Year 1947

Kedarnath Singh, do you remember Noor Miyan?
The fair-looking Noor Miyan

The dwarfish Noor Miyan
After selling *surma* at Ramgadh Bazaar,
he would be the last to come home...
What, you remember such trivia too, Kedarnath Singh?

You remember the school...
The tamarind tree.
The Imam bada...
You remember from the beginning to the end
the multiplication table of nineteen
Can you, from addition and subtraction on your forgotten slate,
deduce why
leaving your colony one day
Noor Miyan had gone away?

Do you know where he is at present?
In Dhaka or Multan?
Do you know how many leaves fall every year in Pakistan?
Why are you silent, Kedarnath Singh?
Are you weak in mathematics?

Translated from the Hindi by Pradeep Gopal Deshpande

Nita Ramaiya (b. 1941)

The Year 1979

This is the year
Of my mother's glance up through the water
At all of us
Submitting the joys and sorrows of sixty-eight years to the Machhu River.

This is the year
Of of my brother's last scream
Hoarding his twenty-three years in the flood waters
Overflowing in his sparkling eyes and shining shoes.

This is the year
That made
Study Literature Politics Ideologies
Understanding Intelligence Wisdom stammer.
How can I explain to my son
Lighting the courtyard of my parents' house
That I am being pounded, pounded
At every step I take within this house?

This is the year
Of the invisible scene hanging
Between
The mood of my ten-year-old son
And
My devastation.

This is the year
Of the thirst of the shameless
Deranged river.

Translated from the Gujarati by the author

Gagan Gill (b. 1959)

I Won't Come and Tell You

I won't come and tell you

that these days I'm a star
lonely as stars

I won't come and tell you

that these days
there is broken glass
in my breath

that gods pass
one by one
inside me
to revive an ancient ache

that these days
my soul is sitting hidden
inside the flesh
like a dislocated bone

that the sparrows
that used to fly
within me
have begun to tire

that there was nothing there for them to sit on
no tree, no cage, no rooftop.

that the nail
that used to poke through
has grown larger
than the heel.

Translated from the Hindi by Arlene Zide and the poet

Eunice de Souza (b. 1940)

Songs of Innocence

I
Who made you?
God made me.
Why did he make you?
To know him, to love him
to be happy with him forever
in this world and the next.

II
orange berries in the backyard
goldfish in the pond
the sun high in the sky
uncles who make you feel tall

no myth in such memories
no chill in the dawn
marigold mood
before the fall

III
I crave your dream of innocence:
a profusion of flowers blooming
for themselves
birds big enough to swallow avocado stones

But green can be humid as the womb...
Avoid, friend, the man who has never known
a dry season.

IV
Searching for roots
I find the caretaker dead
the white ants burrowing
grand-aunt clothed in cobwebs.

Her clock
crumbles in my hands.

Pink cement houses
surge up among the fronds.

I hear the pigs forage
and know this is not home

This never was home:
grandfather left as a young man ...

He had a well of sand.
To him more sand was given

English

Anon, Punjabi Song

Life in the Desert

We came: the dust-storm brought us. Who knows where the dust was born?
Behind the curtains of Heaven and the skirts of the silver morn.
We go where the dust-storm whirls us; loose leaves blown one by one,

Through the light towards the shadows of evening down the tracks
of the sloping sun.
We are blown of the dust that is many and we rest in the dust
that is one.

We have pitched our tents; we feast and we play on the shifting
sands of life.
We are drunk all day with the things of the world, with laughter
and love and strife.
But the sentry of death stands waiting, and the long last march
must be done;
For the camel bells tinkle, the load must be strapped, and we fare
forth friendless alone
Into the Western darkness that shrouds the last ray of the sun.

Translated from the Punjabi by C.F. Usborne

Meena Alexander (b. 1951)
Looking through Well Water

I hear grandmother singing,
she is singing in well water
I see her face as the waves stir
over cloudy white pebbles.

At the well's mouth
fern fronds dark as hair
on an infant skull
nibble into stone.

She didn't give birth to me
but when I look into the well

it's her face I see, slight
freckled bones bent into water.

I'll tell you what divides us:
a ridge of cloud, two oceans,
a winter in my fireless room
high above Van Cortlandt Park
also death, the darkest water
crashing through pebbles, fern
fronds, bits of speckled shell.

I hear the koel crying in well water
its beak is glazed with blood
it's tilted on a nest of clouds
afloat and burning.

English

The Dhammapada (c. 4 CE/5 CE)

From Old Age

Chapter XI

146. How is there laughter, how is there joy, as this world is always burning? Why do you not seek a light, you who are surrounded by darkness.

147. Look at this dressed-up lump, covered with wounds, joined together, sickly, full of many thoughts, which has no strength, no hold!

148. This body is wasted, full of sickness, and frail; this heap of corruption breaks to pieces, life indeed ends in death.

149. Those white bones, like gourds thrown away in the autumn, what pleasure is there in looking at them?

150. After a stronghold has been made of the bones, it is covered with flesh and blood, and there dwell in it old age and death, pride and deceit.

151. The brilliant chariots of kings are destroyed, the body also approaches destruction, but the virtue of good people never approaches destruction—thus do the good say to the good.

152. A man who has learnt little, grows old like an ox; his flesh grows, but his knowledge does not grow.

Translated from the Pali by F. Max Muller

Henry Derozio (1809–32)

The Poet's Grave

Be it beside the ocean's foamy surge,
On an untrodden, solitary shore,
Where the wind sings an everlasting dirge,
And the wild wave in its tremendous roar,
Sweeps o'er the sod!—There let his ashes lie,
Cold and unmourned; save, when the seamew's cry,
Is wafted on the gale, as if 'twere given
For him whose hand is cold, whose lyre is riven!
There, all in silence, let him sleep his sleep!
No dream shall flit into that slumber deep—

No wandering mortal thither once shall wend,
There, nothing o'er him but the heaven shall weep,
There, never pilgrim at his shrine shall bend,
But holy stars alone their nightly vigils keep.

English

Dom Moraes (1938–2004)

Wrong Address

Objects of the wrong shape
share these rooms with me.
My body collides with them,
for I mismanage my body.

I feed plants on my balcony
to remind myself I am alive.
But this is the wrong climate
for the least gesture of love.

She, wannest, most delicate,
most tender half of me once,
becomes cold and separate,
mostly for the wrong reasons.

Growing old here is a waste.
A wrong key turns the lock.
The wards fall on my words
and truly I would like to go.

For here the months abrade
the gradual sounds of grief

to gutturals I don't know.
It's the wrong end of my life.

English

Balmukund Dave (1916–93)

Moving House

Rummaging through the house again we found
scraps of Lux soap, a toothbrush, an old broom,
a leaking bucket, tin box, and lidless bottles,
thread and needle, specs (broken), clips and pins!
Taking down the nameplate on the door,
we placed it face down in the departing lorry.
We looked around again one last time at where
those first ten years of married life went by:
our son, a boon so long desired, was born;
from where we took him to the fire's last embrace.
Suddenly from some corner camp, a voice:
'*Ba-Bapu*, you've left nothing here but me.'
Our eyes were full of pricking grains of grass;
our leaden feet tied down with iron weights.

Translated from the Gujarati by Suguna Ramanathan and Rita Kothari

B.C. Ramchandra Sharma (1925–2005)

On the Death of a Friend

We haven't learnt a thing from the king
who ordered the sea to stop.
We beat our chests and retreat but hope

for miracles forgetting
that earth is three-fourths water.

Only the very young
dare the heaving waves as they build
with sand. Lazily the sea flicks its tongue
and licks before it levels the pyramid
and the castle in a final surge.
Ripples of laughter
chase the sand to the water edge
and the children build again.

We are the Magi
wise before time and too old
for sand and castles in the air.
No star beckons us and we are weary
with running between sea and sea.
Propelled by fear
we rise on wings of prayer
to the top of a tree.
Blinded by sun and blinded by rain
we grope flap and fall to rise and hope again.

Loaded with gifts we come every year
to placate the element, pills
for sleep pills for high blood pressure
and pills to ensure
the smooth working of the glands.
Stretches of white sand
for the children. For you and me church bells
and the band on the stand
to smother the roar and the rising fear.

Words die with every breath
and meaning dies to lie like flotsam
littering the beach. Yes, I use them
to talk of him and his death,
the passage of a little wave
into a little cave
deep within the sea.

Saved from predatory birds at birth
he was a gift like the land
from a capricious sea.
He stayed and played for a while
while the sea smiled
and taught us how to play a losing hand
without breaking the rules.

Counting the granules
of sand still in the hollow of my palm
I know that he took away from me
the terror of the inevitable sea.

Translated from the Kannada by the poet

Anon, Marsiya (c. 14 CE)

Come, O Sisters, Let Us Wail for Our Brothers

Come, O sisters, let us wail for our brothers,
And go bare-foot in the last hour of the night to Karbala.
Let us implore them to wake and return home:
'Your only sister is dying for you on the roadside.

Who gave you the last bath and wrapped you in the shroud?
And who was there to close your eyes?'

Translated from the Urdu by Naji Munawar

Toru Dutt (1856–77)

Our Casuarina Tree

Like a huge Python, winding round and round
The rugged trunk, indented deep with scars,
Up to its very summit near the stars,
A creeper climbs, in whose embraces bound
No other tree could live, but gallantly
The giant wears the scarf, and flowers are hung
In crimson clusters all the boughs among,
Whereon all day are gathered bird and bee;
And oft at night the garden overflows
With one sweet song that seems to have no close
Sung darkling from our tree while men repose.

When first my casement is wide open thrown
At dawn, my eyes delighted on it rest;
Sometimes, and most in winter, on its crest
A grey baboon sits statue-like alone
Watching the sunrise; while on lower boughs
His puny offspring leap about, and play;
And far and near kokilas hail the day;
And to their pastures wend our sleepy cows;
And in the shadow, on the broad tank cast
By that hoar tree, so beautiful and vast,
The water-lilies spring, like snow enmassed.

But not because of its magnificence
Dear is the Casuarina to my soul:
Beneath it we have played; though years may roll
O sweet companions, loved with love intense,
For your sakes, shall the tree be ever dear.
Blent with your images, it shall arise
In memory, till the hot tears blind mine eyes!
What is that dirge-like murmur that I hear
Like the sea breaking on a shingle-beach?
It is the tree's lament, an eerie speech
That haply to the unknown land may reach.

Unknown, yet well-known to the eye of faith!
Ah, I have heard that wail far, far away
In distant lands, by many a sheltered bay,
When slumbered in his cave the water-wraith
And the waves gently kissed the classic shore
Of France or Italy, beneath the moon,
When earth lay tranced in a dreamless swoon:
And every time the music rose before
Mine inner vision rose a form sublime,
Thy form, O Tree, as in my happy prime
I saw thee, in my own loved native clime.

Therefore I fain would consecrate a lay
Unto thy honor, Tree, beloved of those
Who now in blessed sleep for aye repose,
Dearer than life to me, alas! were they!
Mayst thou be numbered when my days are done
With deathless trees, like those in Borrowdale,
Under whose awful branches lingered pale
'Fear, trembling Hope, and Death the skeleton,

And Time the shadow;' and though weak the verso
That would thy beauty fain, oh fain rehearse,
May Love defend thee from Oblivion's curse.

English

Nida Fazli (b. 1938)

Prayers for the Dead

If different graves
did not have
separate epitaphs
the same grief
would lie reposed
in all of them
a mother's son
a sister's brother
a lover's fiancé.
You may say your prayers
at any of the graves
and quietly
depart.

Translated from the Urdu by Balraj Komal

Waris Shah (c. 18 CE)

From Kissa Heer

Ranjha Writes to the Bhabis

Life moments gone do not return
Fortunes do not stage a comeback

The word once out will not be put back
into the mouth

The arrow released will never be
back in the bow

The soul once it's left will not re-enter
the dead body

Life has deserted me and I am a
living corpse.

Only if nature alters its course
will Ranjha return to you

Says Waris Shah: Who really wants me back? None.
Brothers and Bhabhis, you are
only playing tricks and pranks
I will not be fooled

Translated from the Punjabi by Gurcharan Singh

Kapilar (c. 3 BCE–2 CE)

A Time Was When the Wine Cask

A time was when the wine cask
Remained open; plentiful rice
Cooked with sumptuous meat
By cutting down sheep was offered.
Such was your rich friendship.
Today Pari is dead. I weep
And am taking leave of you

With glances, O famous mountain!
I go in search of grooms
To stroke the dark tresses
Of the girls who wear bangles
Made by expert craftsmen.

Translated from the Tamil by Prema Nandkumar

Manmohan Ghose (1869–1924)

Can It Be?

I mind me how her smile was sweet
    And how her look was gay.
O, she was laughter, joy complete!
    And can she now be clay?

I see the roses on her grave
    They make my sad heart bleed.
I see the daisies shine like stars.
    And is she earth indeed?

All lovely things with beauty are,
    And just deeds shine as just.
And faith and truth and duty are.
    And is she only dust?

The great sky keeps its solemn blue:
    Fresh earth is wildly fair.
Can all things be, and I and you—
    She nothing, she nowhere?

English

Mirza Asadullah Khan Ghalib (1713–80)

Lament of Old Age

Your gaze travelled from my heart to my core (in such a fashion)
That in one glance it was both my love and my passion.

Where has the headiness of youth's evening drink gone?
It's time to get up and go, gone are the sweet dreams of dawn.

This bewitching pattern of footprints—to whom do they belong?
Was it my beloved scattering rose petals as she went along?

My (very) vision blinded me like a veil
As every eye fell upon your face unveiled.

I cannot tell the difference between yesterday and today
Since you left, all are the same, everything falls away.

Asadullah Khan, time has taken its toll and left you for dead
What happened to all the carousels, where's youth fled?

Translated from the Urdu by Khushwant Singh

Notes on the Poets

This information is taken mainly from the books/sites in which the poets are represented.

Adha, Dursa (1533–1654) Rajasthani court poet contemporary of Akbar and of Rana Pratap.

Adiga, M. Gopalakrishna (1918–92) Poet, academic, editor, pioneer of Kannada Navya movement, also wrote fiction.

Adigal, Prince Ilango (c. 12 CE) Tamil poet and prince-turned ascetic (Jain?). His *Silappathikaram* is considered 'feminocentric', and is one of the most detailed works about the lives of temple courtesans.

Agarwal, Smita (b. 1958) Writes in English, teaches English literature at Allahabad University.

Ajneya or Agyeya (S.H. Vatsyayan) (1911–87) Hindi poet, fiction writer, playwright, editor, founded 'New Poetry' (Nai Kavita) in Hindi; experimentalist in other forms. According to Lucy Rosenstein, 'Agyeya's writing has pushed back boundaries in big, difficult, passionate subjects.'

Akha (17 CE) Bhakti poet, from a goldsmith's background, writing in Gujarati in the first half of 17 CE. He pioneered the use of satirical poems called *chhappa*.

Akkamahadevi (12 CE) Best-known of the saint-poets writing in Kannada at that time

Alexander, Meena (b. 1951) Poet writing in English and academic.

Ali, Aga Shahid (1949–2001) Poet writing in English, translator, academic.

Amaru (c. 800 CE) Classical Sanskrit poet.

Anapiyya (Seyyitu Anapiyya Pulavar, Tamil translation of Arabic 'Sayyid Hanafiya') (19 CE) Used Tamil devotional form of pillaittamil to write poems in praise of the Prophet Muhammad.

Andal (9 CE) Kannada poet; the only woman poet among the Alvars, worshippers of Vishnu.

Annamacharya/Annamayya (1408–1503) Telugu saint-poet said to 'represent to perfection the Telugu temple poet.'

Arvind (b. 1950) Writes in Dogri.

Asvaghosa (c. 1 CE) Buddhist poet; wrote in Sanskrit.

Aurobindo, Sri (1872–1950) Revolutionary, poet writing in English, aesthetician and seer. While his poetry is not in favour today, he can still be read as a sharp critic.

Auvaiyar (100 BCE–250 CE) Classical Tamil poet; the best-known of the classical women poets. She is represented here by her elegy for Anci, her chieftan.

Bana (7 CE) Sanskrit poet and prose writer. A.L. Basham writes, 'Bana's outlook has more in common with the 20th century than has that of any other early Indian writer.'

Barhat, Essar Das (1538–1618) Rajasthani saint-poet.

Basavanna (1106–1167/68) Kannada saint-poet and social reformer, believed to have founded the Veerashaiva sect, devoted to Siva, tried to simplify religion, disliked ritual, believed in the equality of sexes.

Bhagwat, Shobha (b. 1947) Marathi poet and director of Balbhavan, a recreational centre for children in Pune.

Bhanudatta (16 CE) Sanskrit poet and aesthetician whose patron may have been the Nizam of Ahmadnagar. His descriptions of the heroines and heroes of Sanskrit literature inspired painters from Mewar and Basholi, and celebrated commentators. Translator Sheldon I. Pollock describes the poet as 'probably the most famous Sanskrit poet that no one today has ever heard of.' While many books have covered the same subjects as *Bouquet of Rasa* and *River of Rasa*, no one, Pollock adds, has done so with such 'exquisite and subtle artistry'.

Bharati, Subramania (1882–1921) Though he died young, he achieved a great deal in various spheres and is considered one of India's greatest poets. A militant nationalist, he composed nationalist poems and songs. Though born in an orthodox Brahmin family, he felt strongly about the emancipation of women, and the indignities of the caste system. He edited papers in both Tamil and in English, and is said to have been the first to introduce political cartoons in newspapers.

Bharath Has existed in the tradition of the Dungri Bhils for centuries, kept alive by oral renditions.

Bhattacharya, Hiren (b. 1932) One of the pioneers of modern poetry in Assam.

Bhattacharya, Susmita (b. 1947) Bangla poet and teacher, feminist activist.

Bhattacharya, Sutapa (b. 1942) Poet writing in Bangla; academic.

Bhartrhari (c. 400 CE) Classical Sanskrit poet (possibly grammarian and philosopher as well); wrote some of the best-known verse-sequences, often torn between religious feeling and sensuality.

Bhatti (6 CE) Sanskrit poet who lived in south India. His *The Death of Ravana* is both the story of Rama and an illustrative text of grammar and poetics once codified by the grammarian Panini. This classical epic is considered a bold experiment, a 'rich mix of science and art.' It continues to be widely influential among Sanskritists, and is considered the source text for the Old Javanese Ramayana.

Bhavabhuti (c. 725 CE) Classical Sanskrit poet and dramatist A.L. Basham has written that 'his greatness rests on his deep understanding of sorrow'.

Bilhana (c. 11 CE–12 CE) Kashmiri poet; wrote deeply emotional love poetry in Sanskrit.

Bihari (17 CE) Court poet in Amber considered foremost love poet of Hindi poetry in the Braj dialect of the time.

Birjepatil, Jaysinh (b. 1933) Taught English literature at M. S. University of Baroda.

Bithu, Rangrelo (16 CE) Rajasthani satirical poet who did not hesitate to make fun of his king, Rawal Har of Jaisalmer, who promptly threw him into prison, until another king intervened on his behalf.

Bordoloi, Nirmal Prabha (b. 1933) Assamiya poet, fiction writer, journalist and academic; has written on Assamiya folk culture, and fiction for children.

Borkar, B. B. (1910–84) Konkani poet, wrote poetry, fiction and biography in Marathi, poetry in Konkani and Marathi.

Bose, Buddhadeva (1908–74) Wrote in Bengali and in English, poetry, short stories, plays, literary criticism, translations. He set up the department of comparative literature at Jadavpur University, and in 1935 founded a quarterly dedicated to poetry, *Kabita*, which he edited for about twenty-five years.

Buddha, Gautam (c. 563 BCE–483 BCE) The *Dhammapada*, mainly a work on ethics, is traditionally ascribed to the Buddha himself. The teachings were compiled and written down by his disciples. The Pali version is said to be the most popular, though there are three Sanskrit versions and also versions in other languages.

Cakrabartti, Ma Basanti (writing in Bangla since the 1970s) Head of her own ashram in Kolkota and one of the very few women writing hymns in the Uma and Kali sakta tradition.

Cantirakanti (b. 1961) Writes poetry and short stories in Tamil.

Cellatturai, Arul (mid-20 CE) Tamil (Catholic) poet and engineer; published first book in 1985, in Tamil devotional genre adapted to Baby Jesus.

Cempulappeyanirar (c. 1 CE–3 CE) Classical Tamil poet; the name literally means 'red earth and pouring rain' a reference to the poet's 'signature' line.

Chakravarty, Amiya (1901–86) Bangla poet, Rabindranath Tagore's literary secretary from 1926–33; accompanied him on his travels abroad, including his trips to Iraq and Iran. Also closely associated with Mahatma Gandhi and took part in the Salt March in 1930. He was awarded a DPhil by Oxford University where he was senior research fellow. Taught in various universities in the UK, USA and in India.

Chakravarti Nirendranath (b. 1924) Bangla poet who became known as a major poet in the 1950s, critic, journalist, also writes fiction, writes for children; president of Paschimbangla Akademi.

Chandidas Bangla poet, dates given vary, also identity, as there were at least four poets of that name but is thought to have lived before Chaitanya (1485–1533)

Chandra, G.S. Sharat (1935–2000) Wrote poems and short stories in English, was professor of creative writing at the University of Missouri, Kansas City.

Chattopadhyay, Shakti (1934–95) Wrote in Bangla, a leading member of the 'Hungry' poets.

Chaudhuri, Bahinabai (1880–1951) composed her poems in a mixture of two Marathi dialects spoken in the northern area of Maharashtra where she lived. She used the *ovi* metre of songs sung when grinding grain. Her son wrote down her poems as she was illiterate, and later published them after her death.

Chitre, Dilip (b. 1938) Writes in Marathi and English, poetry, fiction, plays, translations.

Chullikkad, Balachandran (b. 1957) Writes in Malayalam; complete poems published in 2000, and his memoirs the year after. He is also a film and TV actor.

Coda, Naane (12 CE) Telugu poet. His work is said to have disappeared from sight even in medieval times but was re-discovered at the end of the nineteenth century. His translators note that he 'clearly has a conception of a regional, desi, tradition evolving in Telugu, in contrast with Sanskrit.'

Dabral, Mangalesh (b. 1948) Writes in Hindi, journalist, editor, translator.

Dai, Mamang (b. 1959) Writes in English, abandoned a career in the IAS for journalism.

Dalvi, Mustansir (b. 1964) Professor of architecture, associate editor of online poetry workshop *Desert Moon Review* and editor of bi-annual online journal *Crescent Moon*.

Darab, Aziz Bano (1934–2005) Wrote in Urdu.

Daruwalla, Keki N. (b. 1937) A formidable and prolific writer; has published poetry, fiction, essays in English, served in the IPS, and for six months was special assistant to former prime minister Charan Singh. His work contains a wide range of landscapes, inner and outer, and a wide range of textures—irony, compassion, humour. He has a deep interest in history and in the way people lived, but, as he says, he is not interested in facile allegories for the present.

Das, Balaram (16 CE) Oriya poet often persecuted because he dared to write about religious subjects though he was considered a shudra.

Das, Devadurllabha (16 CE) Oriya writer of devotional hymns.

Das, Jibanananda (b. 1899–1954) Considered the most important poet in Bengal after Tagore. As one of his translators, Joe Winter, says, 'He does not limit his vision to the chaotic, the disconnected, the bizarre; but is able to map out the edges of the incompleteness that inhabits us, by taking a full account of beauty too.' Clinton B. Seely has written a biography of the poet called *A Poet Apart* (1990).

Das, J. P. (b. 1936) Oriya poet, playwright, fiction writer, civil servant. He is also a well-known art historian.

Das, Kamala (1934–2009) Wrote in English and Malayalam; produced fiction, autobiography, poetry; the first major woman writer in English and perhaps the most controversial in the post-Independence era.

Das, Markanda (15 CE) Probably the first poet of Oriya literature in its formative period; his poem 'Keshab Koili' is considered the earliest example of cuckoo 'musing' poems. 'Koili' means cuckoo while 'Keshab' refers to Krishna.

Das, Sarala (15 CE) Considered the father of Oriya poetry as he was the first to adapt the Mahabharata, not just by using Oriya but also making interesting deviations such as the Pandavas visiting holy places in Orissa, many references to the landscape and Oriya folklore and customs. He was not a Brahmin and it was considered outrageous/brave for him to have dealt with sacred texts in his writing.

Dasa, Purandara (1480–1564) One of the great saint-poets in Kannada.

Dasgupta, Pranabendu (b. 1937) Writes in Bangla, well-known poet of the 1950s, professor of comparative literature.

Dasimayya, Devara (10 CE) One of the earliest Veerashaiva Kannada saint-poets, dedicated to 'Ramanatha', Rama's lord Shiva. Tradition has it that he stopped his extreme ascetic practices on the advice of Shiva who urged him to be more involved in the world. He became a weaver and a famous teacher.

Datta, Jyotirmoy (b. 1936) Poet, journalist, editor, teacher; writes in Bangla and in English.

Dave, Balmukund (1916–93) wrote in Gujarati; worked for thirty years with the Gandhian publishing house Navjivan, later edited a periodical published by them.

Dave, Harindra (1930–95) Gujarati poet, novelist, critic, and editor of various Gujarati papers and periodicals.

Ded, Lal (c. 1330–84) (sometimes known as Lal Dyad) Kashmiri poet. A Brahmin girl married at the age of twelve into an unsympathetic family, she left to become a wandering ascetic in the Shaivite tradition. Her compact, aphoristic verses in a four-line form called *vakh* use both philosophical terminology and homely metaphors.

Derozio, Henry (1809–32) First Indian poet to write in English, key figure in the Bengal Renaissance. A commentator writes, Derozio 'did more to impart the idea of young India than any other person of his times. A teacher, philosopher and poet, Derozio brought the first waves of European enlightenment into the new education system that was then taking shape.'

Deshika, Vedanta (Venkatanatha) (1268–1369) Described as a theologian, one of the most influential after Ramanuja. 'Mission of the Goose' (*Hamsasandesa*) is a 'messenger poem' which makes the occasional dig at Kalidasa. The note on the title says that the 'ultimate godhead is often pictured as a goose that lives in both worlds—the heavens and the water on earth.' In this poem Rama sends a message to Sita through the goose. In his 'Compassion' he sings his sorrow to the goddess Compassion. A note on the poem says that later Sanskrit poets often wrote 'personal, often iconoclastic modes, using Sanskrit to reflect back on itself and its long tradition.'

de Souza, Eunice (b. 1940) Poet writing in English, novelist, editor, academic.

Dey, Bishnu (1909–87) Bangla poet, academic, translator, has written a book in English on aesthetics entitled *In the Sun and Rain*, and books on the paintings of Jamini Roy and Rabindranath Tagore. Wrote cinema criticism and was involved with IPTA. Influenced both by Marxism and T.S. Eliot's constant references to esoteric myths, books, etc., in his poems. Reacting against Tagore's poetry, he and others associated with a group around the journal *Kallol* that incorporated modern concepts of doubt and conflict.

Dharker, Imtiaz (b. 1954) Poet writing in English, documentary film-maker, artist, describes herself as 'A Scottish Muslim Calvinist, brought up in a Lahori household in Glasgow.' Now travels between the UK, where she lives, and India.

Dharmakirti (c. 700 CE) Buddhist philosopher and poet, born in south India, studied and taught at the Buddhist school of logic at Nalanda.

Some of his verses encapsulate Buddha's teaching against caste and against the dogma of creation. But, as with other scholars and religious figures, his poetry includes themes of ambivalence about love. Love may be a delusion or last for a very brief time, but he still cannot forget the 'gazelle-eyed girl.'

Dhasal, Namdeo (b. 1949) Marathi Dalit poet. His first book of poems, *Golpitha*, is about the red-light area of that name in Mumbai where he was brought up. Dilip Chitre who has translated a selection of his work describes him as a 'Poet of the Underworld.' He founded the Dalit Panthers in 1972, inspired partly by revolutionary movements abroad.

Dhoomil/Dhumil (1935–75) Hindi poet. Taught electrical engineering in Varanasi.

Dhurjati (16 CE) Said to be the first Telugu poet to write what could be called an entirely subjective poem.

Dikshita, Nilakantha (1580–1644) Played an important part as a minister to the king of Madurai, Tirumalai Nayaka, and according to the account given by the publishers and translators, he also 'embodied the new poetic ethos of his time. "Peace" is a mordantly ironic, self-deprecating, and highly introspective work.'

Divate, Hemant (b. 1967) One of the better-known poets writing in Marathi today, runs a publishing house called Abhidhanantar for Marathi books and Poetrywala, for English. Has been editing a poetry quarterly, also called *Abhidhanantar* for several years. Widely translated in Indian and foreign languages.

Doshi, Tishani (b. 1975) Writes in English. She is also a dancer who worked with the choreographer Chandralekha in Chennai. Won the Forward Poetry Prize for best first collection in 2006.

Dutt, Greece Chunder (1833–92) Wrote in English, part of the Dutt family of Bengal.

Dutt, Michael Madhusudan (1824–73) Bangla poet who began by writing in English and then switched to Bangla. Considered one of the great poets of Bengal, he experimented with diction and verse forms and introduced both the sonnet and the blank verse. His most famous work is *Meghanada Badha* written in 1861, and based on a story from the Ramayana.

Dutt, Toru (1856–77) The most well-known of the Dutt family, poet, novelist, translator, wrote in English and in French.

Eknath (1533–99) One of the great saints of Maharashtra, poet, commentator on religious texts. Born in Paithan, a centre of Sanskrit learning and Brahmin orthodoxy, he became a reformist who rejected untouchability, and taught in Marathi.

Ezekiel, Nissim (1924–2004) Leading post-Independence poet writing in English, academic, also wrote plays, art and literary criticism. 'I cannot leave the island/I was born here and belong,' he writes in 'Island'. Gieve Patel, who wrote the introduction to the collected poems, writes, 'For all the poet's stated aim to write clear and direct verse, in many of the best poems there are finely shaded inner movements, requiring an acutely tuned register to pick them up'.

Ezhuthacchan (c. 16 CE) Wrote in Malayalam, a 'father-figure in modern Malayalam' because he standardized the language which he felt was too influenced by both Sanskrit and Tamil.

Faiz, Ahmad Faiz (1911–84) Urdu poet who moved to Pakistan after Independence/Partition. His work has been described as 'the high point of progressive literature in Urdu'.

Farid, Sheikh (1173–1265) Punjabi Sufi poet.

Fazli, Nida (b. 1938) Urdu poet, novelist, critic, translator, film lyricist.

Gadhvi, Pravin (b. 1951) Writes in Gujarati, an IAS official, Dalit poet.

Gandhi, Leela (b. 1966) Poet writing in English, academic.

Gangopadhyay, Sunil (b. 1934) Bangla poet, fiction writer, playwright, translator.

Ghalib, Mirza Asadullah Khan (1797–1869) Generally considered the greatest Urdu poet.

Ghose, Manmohan (1869–1924) Poet writing in English.

Gill, Gagan (b. 1959) Gave up being literary editor in various papers to be a full-time writer, essayist, translator. Lucy Rosenstein writes that Gill 'focuses on the gamut of female experience', but she also writes about pain as part of the human experience, death and occasionally on politics.

Gnanakoothan (b. 1938) Tamil poet and critic.

Gorakhpuri, Firaq (1896–1982) Best known as a poet of the classical ghazal in Urdu, though he was also an innovator who took Urdu poetry in new directions; taught English literature at Allahabad University. Also a freedom fighter.

Goswami, Joy (b. 1954) Bangla poet and journalist.

Harihara A Veerashaiva poet who wrote in Kannada, dominated the second half of the medieval period, and is said to have broken with tradition and written simple poems for the common man.

Harsha/Harshavardhan (590 CE–657 CE) One of the great kings of India. He became a Buddhist, a patron of literature. He wrote three plays in Sanskrit of which *Ratnavali* is one.

Hasan, Bilqees Zafirul (b. 1938) Urdu poet, short-story writer, playwright.

Hasan, Anjum (b. 1972) Writes poetry and fiction in English.

Honnalgere, Gopal (1942–2003) Wrote in English, taught art and writing in various schools.

Hoskote, Ranjit (b. 1969) Poet, critic and cultural theorist.

Husain, Shah 'Madho Lal' (1539–93) Wrote in Punjabi, described as an 'ecstatic sufi who made few concessions to mainstream religion or society.'

Ibopishak, Thangjam (b. 1948) Manipuri writer, teaches Manipuri.

Akbar Ilahabadi (1846–1921) Urdu poet known for his satirical verse, district judge in Allahabad.

Iman, Akhtar-ul (1915–96) Urdu poet, Persian scholar, film director and scriptwriter, part of the Progressive Writers' Movement.

Islam, Kazi Nazrul (1899–1976) Bangla poet, wrote politicized poems with a nationalist flavour addressed to the goddesses of Bengal, goddesses not named but their functions assumed by Mother India.

Iqbal, Mohammad (1873–1938) Wrote in Urdu and Persian and is regarded as one of the greatest Urdu poets, and one of the founding fathers of Pakistan.

Jabeen, Mahe (b. 1961) Telugu poet and social scientist.

Jafri, Ali Sardar (1912–2000) Urdu poet and short-story writer, editor, documentary film-maker, freedom fighter, radical activist, member of the Progressive Writers' Movement.

Jayadeva (12 CE) Sanskrit poet, famous for his *Gita Govinda* which is an erotically charged series of songs about Krishna, Radha and the milkmaids.

Joshi, Umashankar (1911–88) Wrote poetry, fiction and plays in Gujarati; academic and vice-chancellor of the University of Gujarat.

Janabai (c. 1298–1350) Marathi Bhakti saint-poet.

Janna (1163 CE) Jain poet. Chief poet at the court of Hoysala King Veeraballala and a major classical Kannada poet. Called 'Emperor among poets' by the King.

Jayavallabha (c. 8 CE) Jain monk from the svetambara sect. Compiler of the *Vajjalagam*, a collection of independent verses in Prakrit.

Jha, Govindadas (1570–1640) Considered one of the three great writers in medieval Maithili.

Jnanadeva (1275–96) Marathi bhakti poet, considered the greatest saint of Maharashtra. At fifteen, he composed the *Jnaneshwari*, a commentary on the Bhagvad Gita. His sister Muktabai was also a saint-poet as were two of his brothers. They had a difficult childhood: their father who had renounced life at home later returned to married life. The Brahmin community to which they belonged ostracized the whole family.

Joseph, S. (b. 1965) Malayalam poet with four books of poems. He received the Kanaka Sree Award from the Kerala Sahitya Akademi.

Jussawalla, Adil (b. 1940) Writes in English, edited *New Writing in India* for Penguin UK in 1974, a major literary figure based in Mumbai and one of the founders of the poet's publishing cooperative Clearing House.

Kabir (c. 1398–1448) Saint-poet; all information uncertain including attribution of some poems. Wrote in Bhojpuri, a dialect of Hindi; he was a Muslim weaver but his poems harmonize Ram and Rahim and are impatient with ritual.

Kalia, Mamta (b. 1940) Writes poetry in Hindi and in English, fiction in Hindi. Was principal of a women's college in Allahabad.

Kalidasa (c. 5 CE–6 CE) Considered the greatest poet and dramatist in Sanskrit, his name virtually synonymous with literature. Academics like to call him the 'Shakespeare of India'.

Kambar, Chandrashekhar (b. 1937) Kannada poet, playwright, novelist, folklorist, film director.

Kamble, Arun (b. 1953) Dalit poet writing in Marathi, one of the founder members of Dalit Panthers, teaches in the department of Marathi, Mumbai University.

Kampan (1180–1250) Tamil epic poet during the reign of the great Cholas, wrote the Ramayana which he called the *Iramavataram*; according to his translators the quality of his work and its influence earned him the title 'Universal Monarch of Poets'.

Kanakadasa (1509–1609) Poet, philosopher, musician and social reformer writing in Kanada.

Kandasamy, Meena (b. 1984) Editor of *The Dalit* magazine for a year and translator, writes in English.

Kapilar   Classical Tamil poet, a friend of his chieftain Pari who withstood the sieges of three powerful kings. After his death Kapilar wrote a lament; also found husbands for Pari's daughters. Rough dates of the Ettuttokai anthologies in which he is represented are c. 300 BC–AD 200.

Karandikar, Vinda (b. 1918) Marathi poet, academic.

Karmakar, Jyotsna (b. 1950) Bangla poet and child development project officer.

Khair, Tabish (b. 1966) Poet and novelist writing in English and academic, teaches in Denmark.

Khatoon, Habba (16 CE) Kashmiri, broke away from mystic poetry, flourished in the court of Sultan Yusuf Shah.

Khilani, Lakhmi (b. 1935) Writes in Sindhi, short-story writer, translator, playwright.

Khusrau, Amir (1253–1325) Sufi poet, musician, scholar.

Kolatkar, Arun (1932–2004) wrote in Marathi and in English, graphic artist, founder member of the poets' publishing cooperative Clearing House.

Komal, Balraj (b. 1928) One of the New Wave poets in Urdu prominent in the 1960s, critic, academic, short-story writer.

Ksetrayya (17 CE) Writer of devotional songs in Telugu in which he uses the persona of a courtesan.

Kurup, O.N.V. (b. 1931) A prolific poet who has published over twenty-three volumes of poetry in a variety of styles in Malayalam. Known particularly for his social-concern poems.

Kanaka, Ha. Ma. (b. 1964) Writes in Kannada, theatre actor, journalist, translator.

Latif, Shah Abdul (1689–1752) Major Sindhi mystic poet.

Madarasa, Sakalesha (12 CE) Kannada saint-poet whose poems, like those of Basavanna, Devara Dasimayya, Mahadeviyakka, Allama Prabhu and others are called *vacanas*. Vacanas are bhakti poems. All these poets reject ritual, attempts to manipulate God, polytheism, animal sacrifice and caste distinctions. For them, as A.K. Ramanujan observes, 'All true experience of god is *krpa*, grace that cannot be called, recalled or commanded.'

Madeshwara (15 CE) Veerashaiva saint, Kannada composer of oral epics. One of the special qualities of the epic chosen is that there is real concern about the plight of women and the ordeals they have to undergo. This is said to be characteristic of Kannada folk epics. In the extract chosen, Sankamma is a strong character who refuses to swear an oath of fidelity to her husband as she considers it demeaning.

Mahadeviyakka (12 CE) Kannada saint poet; said to have died in her twenties.

Mahapatra, Anuradha (b. 1957) Bangla poet and social activist, works with Uprooted Tillers' Rights Association, teaches street children.

Mahapatra, Jayanta (b. 1928) Writes in English; Oriya academic, translator, editor.

Mahapatra, Sitakant (b. 1937) Writes in Oriya. Specialist in tribal literature, particularly that of the Santhals.

Majumdar, Harinath (1833–96) journalist, composer of Baul hymns, wrote prose narratives in Bangla.

Male Madeshwara (c. 14 CE) Narrates the story of Madeshwara, a young Veerashaiva saint. He was a historical figure who probably lived in the fourteenth century.

Malik, Keshav (b. 1924) Writes in English, art critic, curator.

Mansuri, Adil (b. 1936) Gujarati poet, journalist.

Mardhekar, Bal Sitaram (1909–56) Pioneer of modernism in Marathi poetry, also wrote fiction.

Mathur, Shakunt (b. 1920) Regarded as the forerunner of feminism in Hindi poetry.

Mehrotra, Arvind Krishna (b. 1947) Poet, editor, translator, academic, critic, founder member of the poets' publishing cooperative Clearing House.

Mehta, Jaya (b. 1932) Writes in Gujarati, academic, editor, translator, literary critic.

Mehta, Narsinh (1408–80) Bhakti poet, regarded as father of Gujarati poetry.

Menon, Siddhartha (b. 1967) Teaches at Rishi Valley School in Andhra Pradesh.

Mirabai (1498–1546) Rajasthani princess who scandalized Rajasthan by singing and dancing in public in her choice of vocation as saint-poet.

Mir Taqi Mir (1722–1810) One of the most important poets of the eighteenth century, noted for his melancholy, a formative influence in Urdu, known for his ghazals. Ghalib wrote more than one couplet in praise of him.

Miranda, Fr. Joaquim Born in Goa. Dates not known but his most celebrated poem 'Riglo Jesu Molleantu' (Jesus Entered the Garden) was written in Konkani between 1763–83.

Mitra, Debarati (b. 1946) Bangla poet and lecturer at Jadhavpur University.

Mohamad, Sheikh (16 CE) Wrote Marathi hymns in praise of Lord Krishna.

Mohiuddin, Khadar (b. 1955) Writes in Telugu; represented here by a section of his best-known poem, 'Birthmark', about the bitter experience of being a Muslim in India, but he participates in Ugadi Sammelans, Telugu New Year poetry readings which now include poems by women and by Dalits, Hindus and Muslims.

Moraes, Dom (1938–2004) Wrote poetry and non-fiction in English. His first book of poems, written at nineteen, won him the Hawthornden Prize.

Mukerji, Dhan Gopal (1890–1937) Wrote poetry and non-fiction in English, and was one of the early 'translators' of Indian culture in the US.

Muktabai (13 CE) Bhakti poet, wrote in Marathi, sister of Jnanadeva.

Muktibodh, Gajanan Madhav (1917–69) Hindi poet considered a bridge between the Progressive movement and New Poetry movement, also called the modern movement. Wrote fiction, criticism journalism, was also a broadcaster and teacher.

Nagra, Daljit (b. 1966) Lives in the UK. Won the Forward Prize both for his first poem and his first book, *Look We Have Coming to Dover*, published by Faber and Faber in 2007. Continues to teach English in schools much to the amazement of his students.

Naidu, Sarojini (1879–1949) Poet in English and political activist.

Nair, Rukmini Bhaya (b. 1952) Poet writing in English, academic.

Nambiar, Kunchan (1700–70) Malayalam poet, belonged to a sub-sect specializing in temple art forms such as the 'Kothu' described as a dramatic narration, a mix of puranic mythology and contemporary satire.

Nambisan, Vijay (b. 1963) Writes poetry and non-fiction in English, translator.

Nambudiri, Punam (c. 16 CE) Wrote in Malayalam. The Nambudiris, who were Brahmins, are said to have introduced Sanskrit into the local language.

Namdev (1220–1350) Bhakti saint-poet in Marathi, travelled widely in India to spread the idea of bhakti.

Nammalvar (9 CE) Tamil poet, most important of the twelve alvars dedicated to Vishnu, and among the earliest bhakti poets.

Nanak, Guru (1469–1539) Founder of Sikhism, saint-poet.

Nanmullai, Allur (c. 1 CE–2 CE) Classical Tamil poet.

Nara (b. 1932) Pen name of Velcheru Narayana Rao, scholar and translator of several Telugu texts, academic.

Narain, Kunwar (b. 1927) Writes in Hindi and his work has been described as deeply humanist. He is also a short-story writer, editor, translator, and is involved in music and theatre.

Narayana (12 CE) Sanskrit poet; wrote *Hitopadesa*, one of the most popular versions of the *Panchatantra* stories.

Ngangom, Robin (b. 1959) Writes in English and in Manipuri.

Nirala (Suryakant Tripathi) (1899–1961) A leading member of various movements in Hindi poetry. Poet, novelist, essayist.

Nongkynrih, Kynpham Sing (b. 1964) Writes poems and fiction in both Khasi and English. His poems have been translated into several languages including Welsh and Swedish. He received the first North-East Poetry Award in 2004 from North-East India Poetry Council, Tripura.

Nur Jehan, Empress (1577–1645) Favourite wife of Emperor Jehangir.

Padgaonkar, Mangesh (b. 1929) Marathi poet, essayist, academic, editor.

Pakalikkuttar (dates uncertain, possibly born mid-14 CE and died sometimes in the first quarter of the 15 CE) It is said that the Tamil devotional form, the pillaittamil, began to flourish with his compositions.

Pande, Mrinal (b. 1946) Writes fiction and plays in Hindi.

Pandit, R.V. (1917–90) Wrote in Konkani was involved in the Goa Liberation Movement.

Pandya, Natwarlal 'Ushnas' (1920–2011) Gujarati poet and one-time principal of Arts College, Valsad, literary critic and essayist.

Paniker, K. Ayyappa (b. 1930) Malayalam poet, critic, academic, translator.

Parikh, Vipin (b. 1930) Writes poems and essays in Gujarati.

Parthasarthy, R. (b. 1934) Writes in English and Tamil. Editor, translator, academic.

Pash (1950–88) Best-known of the left and progressive poets, opposed Sikh nationalist violence, shot dead by a Khalistani militant. Edited a literary magazine called *Siarh*.

Patel, Gieve (b. 1940) Poet, painter, playwright, translator, doctor of medicine. Founder member of poets' publishing cooperative Clearing House.

Patel, Ravji (1939–68) Gujarati novelist, short-story writer, poet.

Patil, Chandrashekara (b. 1939) Poet and playwright in Kannada, academic.

Periyalvar/Periyazhwar/Vishnuchittan (9 CE) Tamil poet wrote poems in praise of Krishna's pranks as a child, inspired the pillaittamil verse form in which the poet adopts the voice of a mother and god is worshipped as an extraordinary child.

Perunkatunko, Palai Patita Classical Tamil poet dates uncertain, anywhere from c. 300 BCE to 200 CE.

Phookan/Phukan, Nilmani (b. 1933) Assamiya poet, academic, translator. Considered one of Assam's most important poets.

Pinto, Jerry (b. 1966) Writes in English, journalist, and editor of several anthologies; recently published his much-acclaimed first novel.

Prabhu, Allama (c. 12 CE) Kannada saint-poet. As with other Veerasaiva saints he rejected external ritual. Other well-known saints such as Basavanna and others regarded him as the Master.

Prasad, G. J. V. (b. 1955) Poet, novelist and critic. Won the Katha Award for his translations from Tamil into English.

Pritam, Amrita (1919–2005) First prominent Punjabi woman poet, novelist and short-story writer.

Purandara Dasa (1485–1565) Kannada saint-poet. William J. Jackson tells us that 'Purandaradasa was in the prime of his life during the heyday of the Vijayanagar empire.' The fall of this empire in 1565 'led to many problems in society, and some of Purandaradasa's songs reflect the loss and bewilderment of a turbulent land crying out for help'.

Ramaiya, Nita (b. 1941) Academic, writes in Gujarati.

Ramakrishnan, Kadammanitta (b. 1935) Malayalam poet and translator, described as a 'progressive modernist'.

Ramanujan, A. K. (1929–93) Wrote in English and Kannada. Significant poet, translator, folklorist, philologist; taught at the University of Chicago.

Rasananda (17 CE) Oriya saint-poet.

Rath, Ramakanta (b. 1934) Oriya poet and civil servant; President of the Sahitya Akademi from 1998–2002. J.M. Mohanty writes, 'Rath provided a deep troubled voice to modern Oriya poetry, troubled because of its intense awareness of futility'.

Rath, Baladev (1789–1845) One of the major Oriya Vaishnav poets dedicated to Krishna, particularly known for his *champu* poems which are arranged alphabetically, using Oriya consonants from *ka* to *ksha*. These poems are used both as song and dance. Said to be the only Oriya poet to use Persian words.

Ravidas (c. 14 CE–15 CE) Contemporary of Guru Nanak. A saint-poet who felt that God redeemed 'even tanners of hides'—a reference to the family trade. Some of his poems are included in the *Adi Granth*, the Sikh scripture.

Rayaprol, Srinivas (1925–98) Wrote in English, founded and edited the journal *East and West* from 1956–61.

Revathi, Kutti (b. 1974) Writes in Tamil, working on a doctorate in medical anthropology.

Rituraj (b. 1940) Writes in Hindi; teaches.

Rodrigues, Santan (1948–2008) Poet in English, founder of eight *Kan*, a poetry magazine in the 1970s, founder member of New Grand poets' cooperative.

Sarosh, Minal (b. 1960) *Mitosis and Other Poems* was published by Writers Workshop, Kolkata, 1992.

Sachdev, Padma (b. 1940) Dogri poet, prose writer, broadcaster.

Sahay, Raghuvir (1929–90) Hindi poet, journalist, translator, essayist, fiction writer.

Salabega (b. 16 CE) A Muslim, he was devoted to Lord Jaganath to whom he addressed his hymns which are widely popular in Orissa and influential in Oriya literature.

Sami (1743–1850) Sindhi religious poet, interpreted Vedantic thought in his work.

Sankaracarya (c. 8 CE–9 CE) Considered the greatest philosopher India has produced. Wrote devotional hymns in Sanskrit.

Sant, Indira (1914–2000) Wrote fiction and poetry in Marathi, considered one of the most intense lyrical voices in Marathi.

Sarangapani (18 CE) Telugu temple poet, wrote 'courtesan' songs.

Sastri, Chellapilla Venkata (1870–1950) Telugu poet.

Satchidanandan, K. (b. 1946) Writes in Malayalam; for several years Secretary of the Sahitya Akademi; earlier was a professor of English.

Sauda, Mirza Mohamed Rafi (1713–80) Urdu satirical poet.

Saxena, Sarveshwar Dayal (1927–83) Hindi poet, playwright, short-story writer.

Satavahana Hala (2 CE) Is said to have compiled the *Gathasaptasati*, possibly the oldest extant anthology of poetry from South Asia.

Sen, Ramprasad (1718–75) Bangla poet requested by Nadia zamindar to stay at his court and compose hymns to Kali/Uma.

Seth, Vikram (b. 1952) Poet and novelist writing in English. Best known for his verse novel *The Golden Gate* and his novel *A Suitable Boy*.

Shah, Bullah (1680–1759) Punjabi Sufi poet.

Shah, Waris (18 CE) Punjabi writer considered the greatest of the romance writers.

Sharma, B. C. Ramchandra (1925–2005) Writes in Kannada and in English, poet and translator.

Shetty, Manohar (b. 1953) Poet writing in English, editor of anthologies in English translation.

Shivarudrappa, G. S. (b. 1926) Kannada poet and academic.

Shukla, Vinod Kumar (b. 1937) Hindi poet, fiction-writer.

Siddalingaiah (b. 1954) Poet-playwright writing in Kannada, activist pioneer of Dalit-Bandaya movement in Kannada.

Siddaramayya (12 CE) Kannada Veerashaiva poet, contemporary of and influenced by Basavanna, and believed like him that one could combine life in the world with both devotion to Siva and a spirit of renunciation. The egalitarian vision of the Veerashaiva poets won them thousands of followers.

Silgardo, Melanie (b. 1956) Writes in English, co-founder of Newground, a poets' publishing cooperative; later worked with Virago.

Singh, Kedarnath (b. 1934) Hindi poet, literary critic, translator, editor of two anthologies of Hindi poetry, and the journal *Shabd*.

Soma (5 BCE) Buddhist nun, Pali.

Sri Sri (1910–83) Telugu poet, journalist, critic, playwright, revolutionary.

Sriharsha (12 CE) Epic poet whose *Naiadhiyacarita*, or *Naiadha*, is among the most popular mahakavyas in Sanskrit literature.

Subbiah, Shanmuga (b. 1924) Writes in Tamil.

Subramaniam, Arundhathi (b. 1967) Writes in English, editor of the India domain, Poetry International Web.

Sunani, Basudev (b. 1962) Dalit poet, writes in Oriya.

Surendran, C.P. (b. 1959) Poet writing in English, novelist, journalist, editor.

Suri, Hemacandra (12 CE) Jain scholar writing in Prakrit/Apabhramsa.

Suri, Tenneti (1911–58) Telugu poet, playwright, journalist.

Surve, Narayan (c. 1926) Marathi Dalit poet, teacher, activist.

Tagore, Rabindranath (1866–1941) Bangla poet and writer of fiction, plays, songs. He was also a painter, musician, educator, and, inspired partly by experiences abroad, reshaped Bangla literature, music and the arts. Received Nobel Prize for Literature in 1913.

Thakore, Anand (b. 1971) Writes poetry in English; Hindustani classical singer.

Thayil, Jeet (b. 1959) Writes in English, poet, musician, songwriter. Editor of *60 Poets*, an anthology of Indian poetry in English by writers living in India and abroad.

Trilochan (1917–2007) Hindi Progressive poet who wrote about ordinary people, introduced the sonnet form in Hindi.

Tukaram (b. 1608) Vanished without trace in 1649. A bhakti poet, considered the greatest of the Marathi poets.

Tulsidas (1532–1623) Poet and philosopher regarded as the greatest Hindi poet, dedicated his life to Ram. *Ram Charit Manas* is his major work.

Tyagaraja (1767–1847) The most famous South Indian saint-poet/musician, wrote in Telugu.

Usha, S. A. (b. 1954) Kannada poet and academic.

Vajpeyi, Kailash (b. 1936) Prolific Hindi poet, awarded the Sahitya Akademi Award 2009.

Vallana (c. 900 CE–1100 CE) Sanskrit poet.

Vallathol (Vallathol Narayana Menon) (1878–1958) Poet, translator, freedom fighter, revived Kathakali, founded the Kerala Kalamandalam as part of this revival. Considered the greatest Malayalam poet.

Valmiki (c. 400 BCE–250 CE) The 'first poet of Hinduism,' post-Vedic but dates vary; created the first Indian verse form.

Vanparanar (c. 100 CE–250 CE) Classical Tamil poet.

Varma, Attoor Ravi (b. 1931) Malayalam, poet, critic, academic.

Varma, Shrikant (1931–86) Hindi poet, fiction writer, parliamentarian.

Vemana (c. 17 CE–18 CE) Telugu poet-philosopher, his poems are critical of caste, rituals, and externals; among the favourites of Telugu readers.

Verma, Mahadevi (1907–87) Described as the first woman to become a leading Hindi writer, helped to create the Chhayavad Movement.

Vidyapati (15 CE) Maithili and Sanskrit scholar and poet.

Vijayalakshmi (b. 1960) Writes in Malayalam.

Yashaschandra, Sitanshu (b. 1941) Poet and playwright in Gujarati.

Zote, Mona (b. 1973) Lives in Mizoram, writes in English, employed in government service.

While every effort has been made to find information about the poets, this has not been possible in all cases; any omissions brought to our attention will be remedied in future editions.

Notes on the Translators*

Acharya, Pradip   Teaches English literature in Guwahati, literary critic, translator of writing from Assam, translation theorist.

Adarkar, Priya   Retired regional manager, Longman's, translates from Marathi.

Amur, G.S.   Professor of literature, considered a leading writer and critic in Kannada.

Anamika   Hindi poet, novelist, critic, translator, lectures on English literature at Satyawati College.

Annamalai, E.   Linguist specializing in Tamil grammar, has taught at various universities in Europe, and the University of Chicago, published several books in the area.

Ashokamitran   Influential novelist, critic in post-Independence Tamil literature.

Atkins, A.G.   Protestant missionary in India whose rhyming-verse translation of Tulsidas is considered poetically sensitive to the music of Tulsidas.

Avalon, Arthur   (1865–1936) Pseudonym for Sir John Woodroffe, British Orientalist with a deep interest in Hindu philosophy and yogic practice, a leading authority on Shaktic and Tantric thought. Reader in

*In instances where translators are also poets whose work is included in this collection, please look at 'Notes on the Poets' for biographical informaion.

Indian Law at the University of Oxford, translated more than twenty Sanskrit texts.

Bahadur, Krishna P.   Served the Uttar Pradesh government in various administrative assignments and retired as commissioner, has written on Indian philosophy, culture, sociology, Sufi mysticism, and edited a volume of Bharati's *Satasai*.

Bakht, Baidar   Adjunct professor of civil engineering at the Universities of Toronto and Manitoba; translates modern Urdu poetry in collaboration with Canadian poets and scholars.

Basham, A. L. (1912–86) Professor of Asian studies, Australian National University.

Bezboruah, D.N.   Taught English and linguistics for two decades before starting an English newspaper, *The Sentinel*, from Guwahati.

Bhagat, Niranjan   Poet, professor of English literature, critic.

Bhagwat, Durga (1910–2002) Studied Sanskrit and Buddhist literature, spent time researching tribes in Madhya Pradesh, writer in Marathi.

Bhatia, Manjit Kaur   Hindi writer and translator, in the publication department of the Sahitya Akademi, Delhi.

Brasch, Charles (1909–73) New Zealand poet, founded literary journal *Landfall*, arts patron.

Bronner, Yigal   Assistant professor of Sanskrit language and literature, department of South Asian Languages and Civilizations, University of Chicago.

Brough, John (1917–84) Professor of Sanskrit at SOAS and then at Cambridge.

Brown, Carolyn B.   Taught courses in American and British literature at the University of Iowa; translation co-ordinator and editor of the International Writing Program; translates from the Bangla and several other languages.

Bryce, Winifred   Sociologist, educationist, former principal of Indore Christian College, later head of Indore School of Social Work; retired and died in Canada in 1967.

Chattarji, Sampurna   Mumbai-based poet, novelist, translator.

Chaudhuri, Sukanta   Taught at Jadhavpur University, specialist in Renaissance studies, has translated from the Bangla, also lectures and writes on textual theory and criticism.

Dharwadker, Vinay   Poet, professor, department of languages and cultures of Asia, University of Wisconsin–Madison.

Doniger, Wendy   Professor of the history of religions and Indian studies at the University of Chicago.

Doraiswamy, T. K. (1921–2007) Pen name 'Nakulan,' Poet, novelist, professor of English, translator.

D'Souza, Priya   Project co-ordinator for SPARROW, which collects and stores material about women; photographer.

Dube, S. C. (1922–96) Anthropologist, wrote on tribals and rural India, academic connected with various universities, among them Osmania University in Hyderabad.

Duggal, K. S.   Writes in Hindi, Punjabi, Urdu, English; writes on Sikhs and Sikhism, and Punjabi mystic poets.

Dutt, Romesh C. (1848–1909) Indian civil service, economic historian, translator, lecturer in University College, London, Dewan of Baroda State.

Dyson, Ketaki Kushari   Has published poetry, fiction, drama and criticism, in Bangla and in English.

Elwin, Verrier (1902–1964) Christian missionary who came to India, anthropologist, worked with the Gond tribals of Central India (now Madhya Pradesh).

Fallon, Oliver   American Sanskrit scholar.

Farooqi, Mehr Afshan   Professor of South Asian Literature at the University of Virginia.

Faruqui, Shamsher Rahman   Urdu writer and critic, has published the literary journal *Shabkhoon* from Allahabad for forty years.

Gay, Thomas   ICS member who made India his home. Educated at Oxford, published extensively in journals and periodicals.

Gohain, Hiren   Department of English, Guwahati University, has written on the Vaishnavite movement in Assam, visiting professor at Delhi and at the Indian Institute of Advanced Studies, Shimla.

Gombrich, Richard   British Indologist, scholar of Sanskrit, Pali and Buddhist Studies, retired Boden professor of Sanskrit at the University of Oxford.

Gomes, Olvinho   Konkani writer, and former head of department of Konkani, Goa University.

Griffith, Ralph T.H. (1826–1906) Scholar of Indology and Sanskrit translator.

Haksar, A.N.D.   Indian foreign service, served as high commissioner or ambassador in various places, concentrated on writing and translating after his retirement.

Hart, George L.   Professor in the Department of South East Asian Studies at University of California, Berkeley.

Hasan, Noorul   Retired professor of English from the North Eastern Hill University, Shillong.

Hawley, J. S.   Professor of Religion, Barnard College, writes and has edited books on Hinduism.

Heifetz, Hank   Novelist, poet, journalist, doctorate in South and South East Asian Studies, taught at University of Wisconsin and at the City University of New York.

Hivale, Shamrao (1903–84) Worked among tribals with Verrier Elwin, but also started various welfare measures for them on his own; collected their songs.

Hooper, J.S.M. (1837–1922) Missionary, pilot of the Methodist Union Movement in South India; translated one of the earliest books in the Heritage of India Series sponsored by YMCA Publishing House in Calcutta, which was also one of the earliest books on the Alvars.

Hyder, Qurratulain (1928–2007) Urdu novelist, short-story writer, academic, journalist.

Isherwood, Christopher (1904–86) British writer/later American of fiction, drama, film, travel, autobiography; became interested in Hindu teaching and collaborated with Swami Prabhavananda on the translation of the Bhagvad Gita.

Jackson, William J.   Professor in the department of religious studies at Indiana University, Purdue.

Jaeger, Kathleen Grant   Canadian poet, and translator from Urdu.

Jahangirdas, Chandrashekhar   Marathi writer and critic, concerned with effects of Modernism on Marathi poetry, has written on folk literature, professor at Shivaji University, Kolhapur.

Juergensmeyer, Mark   Director, Orfalea Centre for Global and International Studies, University of California, Santa Barbara.

Kanda, K.C.   Taught English literature in universities in Punjab and Delhi, translates extensively from the Urdu, and edits university anthologies.

Karandikar, G.V.   Translator from the Marathi.

Kewlani, Madhu   Professional translator from the Sindhi.

Khandwalla, Pradip N.   Organization theorist, poet, translator from the Gujarati, editor.

Khare, Vishnu   Hindi poet, has translated from various Indian and European languages, journalist.

Kothari, Rita   Teaches at St Xavier's College, Ahmedabad, runs a research centre on behalf of Katha.

Kurup, P. Narayana   Malayalam poet and literary critic, writes for children.

Lal, P. (1929–2010) Professor of English at St Xavier's College, Kolkata, poet, translator, best known for starting Writers Workshop, a publishing house, frequently visited American universities as visiting professor.

Levertov, Denise (1923–97) British poet, later naturalized American, praised as an avant garde American poet.

Losensky, Paul   Associate professor, Central Eurasian Studies, Indiana University. Special interest in literatures of Iran, India and Central Asia.

Maddern, Marian   Lectures on creative writing in Melbourne; doctoral thesis on linguistic comparison between Bangla and English.

Mascaro, Juan   Eminent Sanskrit scholar, taught at Oxford University and elsewhere.

McDermott, Rachel Fell   Assistant professor of Asian and Middle Eastern Cultures at Barnard College. She is the author/editor of books on Bangla poetry.

Maini, Darshan Singh   Ex-head, department of English, Punjab University, Patiala, writes on Punjabi poetry.

Masson, J. Moussaieff   Taught Sanskrit and Indian Studies at Berkeley and other universities.

Mathers, E. Powys (1892–1939) English translator and poet often ranked with Arthur Waley and Ezra Pound.

Merrill, Christi   Associate chair, Centre for South Asian Studies, University of Michigan, associate professor of comparative literature.

Merwin, W. S.   Poet Laureate and Library of Congress consultant.

Mohanty, Sacidanand   Professor of English, Hyderabad, has written on early Oriya women writers, and cross-cultural issues.

Mohanty, Smita   Critic, has written on Vikram Seth.

Moorty, J. S. R. L. Narayana   Teaches western and eastern philosophy, Monterey Peninsula College, has written on Krishnamurthy, translates from the Telugu.

Mukhopadhyay, Sarat Kumar   Bangla poet and writer, translates poetry and fiction from English into Bengali.

Muller, F. Max (1823–1900) German scholar of comparative language, religion, mythology with a special interest in Sanskrit philology and the religions of India.

Munawar, Naji   Head, department of Kashmiri, Kashmir University, particularly noted for his writing for children.

Murthy, K. Narasimha   Taught English literature, Mysore University, later joined the IAS, poet, critic and editor of English quarterlies of Sahitya Akademi.

Mutalik, Keshav M.   Retired as principal of Sydenham College of Commerce and Economics, translates from the Kannada.

Nabar, Vrinda   Taught at University of Mumbai, co-translated with Nissim Ezekiel from the Marathi.

Nadig, Sumatheendra   Poet, short-story writer, translator, close associate of Adiga, and important poet of the 1960s.

Nandkumar, Prema   Specializes in Aurobindo studies.

Narain, Apurva   Literature is his 'abiding interest' but also works in the ecology-development area.

Nayak, Lipipuspa   Teaches English and has published eight books, including translations from the Oriya. She was awarded the Government of India National Culture Fellowship (2003–05), and was shortlisted for Fulbright Fellowship.

Neki, J. S.   Poet, medical doctor, writes on Sikhs and Sikh history and culture.

Pati, Madhusudan   Lectures at Sambhalpur University, has written on Sanskrit texts and Oriya poets.

Patel, Madhubhai   Grew up in the region of South Gujarat from which he collected folk songs for the Indian Musicological Society, ex-principal, Commerce College, Mehsana.

Pattanaik, D. B.   Writes on Hindu myth.

Paz, Octavio (1914–98) Mexican diplomat, writer, poet, taught at Cambridge and Harvard, Nobel Prize for Literature 1990.

Petievich, Carla   Doctoral degree in Urdu, teaches History and directs the Women's Studies Programme at Montclair State University.

Pollock, Sheldon   Ransford Professor of Sanskrit and Indian Studies, Columbia University, New York; General editor, Murty Classical Library of India, Harvard University Press.

Prabhavananda, Swami (1893–1976) Indian philosopher, monk of the Ramakrishna order, religious teacher.

Raman, N. Kalyan   Translator of contemporary Tamil fiction and poetry.

Ramanathan, Suguna   Retired head of department of English, St Xavier's College, Ahmedabad, translates from the Gujarati, writes fiction under the name Suguna Nair.

Rao, H.V. Nagaraja   Formerly senior Sanskrit research scholar, specializing in Sanskrit grammar and poetics at Oriental Research Institute, Mysore; visiting fellow to Chicago University and Jerusalem.

Ray, David   Author of twenty-two books including *After Tagore: Poems Inspired by Rabindranath Tagore*, lives in Tucson where he continues to write poetry, fiction, essays.

Rao, Velcheru Narayana   Krishnadevaraja Professor of Language and Culture of Asia at the University of Wisconsin–Madison, USA.

Rhys-Davids, C.A.F. (1857–1942) President of the Pali Text Society, 1923–42.

Richman, Paula   William H. Danforth Professor of South Asian religions, USA.

Roberts, Elliot   Teaches world literature and creative writing at Monterey Peninsula College, translates from the Telugu.

Rosenstein, Lucy   Studied Hindi in Sofia, Bulgaria, where she grew up. MA and PhD in Hindi from SOAS, University of London, where she teaches.

Rubin, David   Has been visiting professor, Columbia University. Translates from Hindi prose and poetry, and is also a writer of fiction.

Russell, Ralph (1918–2008) Considered the leading western scholar of Urdu of his generation; head of Urdu, SOAS, 1949–81.

Schiffman, H.   Writes on linguistic culture and language policy.

Seely, Clinton B.   Department of South Asian languages and civilizations, University of Chicago, scholar of Bangla language and literature.

Selby, Martha Ann   Associate professor of South Asian studies, University of Texas at Austin.

Sharma, Padma   With Ramachandran, C.N. has translated from the Kannada.

Sharma, Sunil (b. 1964) Professor of Persian and Indian Literatures at Boston University.

Sharma, T.R.S.   Has taught English literature in universities in India and abroad, edited three volumes of Ancient Indian Literature for the Sahitya Akademi.

Shauq, Shafi   Professor and head of the post-graduate department of Kashmiri at the University of Kashmir.

Shivanath   Dogri writer, scholar, translator, on Sahitya Akademi advisory board for Dogri.

Shulman, David   Poet in Hebrew, and professor of South Asian studies and comparative religion at Hebrew University, Jerusalem.

Siegel, Lee   New York writer and cultural critic.

Singh, Gurcharan   Educationist and writer, retired as vice chairman of the Punjab School Education Board.

Singh, Kesri   Rajasthani poet, edited an anthology of Rajasthani poetry translated into English.

Singh, Khushwant   Novelist, columnist, translator.

Sitesh, Aruna   Principal, Indraprastha College, Delhi, writes fiction in Hindi, co-edits quarterly *Pratibh India*.

Sivadasan, C.P. (1940–2010) Kannur University, member of Kerala Sahitya Akademi, wrote criticism on Malayalam and English literature.

Sorley, H. T. (19 CE–20 CE) British officer with the Indian civil service, posted in Sindh, learned Sindhi to translate and write on Shah Abdul Latif.

Sundaram, P. S.   Professor of English at various universities in India, translates from the Tamil.

Swain, Rabindra K.   Poet writing in English, translates from the Oriya.

Swami Mahadevananda (Roger Timms) An actor on the British stage, he came to India to study Indian dance and drama, later took sannyasa at Rishikesh; president of Sivananda Yoga-Vedanta Centres International.

Swamy, Nagabhushana O.L.   Lecturer in English, Kannada critic, columnist, translator.

Thomas, A. J.   Poet writing in English, translates fiction and poetry from the Malayalam.

Trivedi, Harish   Professor in department of English, Delhi University.

Usborne, C. F. (1874–1919) Indian civil service. His translation of Waris Shah's *Heer and Ranjha* is regarded as a classic.

Vajpeyi, Ananya   Teaches in the history department of University of Massachusetts, Boston.

Vaudeville, Charlotte   French Indology scholar, specializing in bhakti/devotional literature.

Warder, A. K.   Indology scholar, mainly in Buddhist Studies, Pali and Sanskrit, Professor Emeritus of Sanskrit at the University of Toronto.

Weissbort, Daniel   Professor of English and comparative literature at the University of Iowa; with the poet Ted Hughes he founded the magazine *Modern Poetry in Translation* in 1965; has translated Russian poetry, edited an anthology of post-war poets of eastern and central Europe; has published four volumes of his own poetry.

Winter, Joe   Teacher in England, poet, lived in Kolkata for a while, translated Tagore and Jibananda Das from the Bangla.

Zide, Arlene   New York-based poet and translator from Hindi and Urdu.

While every effort has been made to find information about the translators, this has not been possible in all cases; any omissions brought to our attention will be remedied in future editions.

Copyright Acknowledgements

Grateful acknowledgement is made to the following for permission to reprint copyright material:

'Which Language Should I Speak?', Arun Kamble, trans. Priya Adarkar, *Poisoned Bread*, ed. Arjun Dangle, Orient Longman Ltd, Mumbai, 1992.

'Is Poetry Always Worthy When It's Old?', Kalidasa, trans. John Brough, *Poems from the Sanskrit*, ed. John Brough, PUK, London, 1968.

'Sreeramayana That Runs into a Hundred Crores', from *Adhyatma Ramayana*, Ezhuthaccan, trans. K. Satchidanandan, *Sahitya Akademi Medieval Indian Literature (Vol. 3)*, ed. K. Ayyappa Paniker, Sahitya Akademi, Delhi, 1999.

'Poet, Lover, Birdwatcher', Nissim Ezekiel, *Collected Poems*, OUP, Delhi, 1989.

'Banglabasha', Michael Madhusudhan Dutt, trans. Clinton B. Seely, *Madhusudhan Rachanabali*, ed. Ksetra Gupta, Sahitya Samsad, Kolkata, 1967.

'In Arabic', Agha Shahid Ali, *Call Me Ishmael Tonight*, The Agha Shahid Ali Trust, 2003.

'The Character I Created', Chandrasekhar Kambar, trans. O.L. Nagabhushana Swamy, *Rocks of Hampi*, Sahitya Akademi, Delhi, 2006.

'The Average Temperature of a Word Required for It to Be Used in a Line of Poetry?', Hemant Divate, trans. Dilip Chitre, *Virus Alert*, Poetrywala Mumbai, 2003.

'White Paper', Nara, trans. Velcheru Narayana Rao, *The Oxford Book of Modern Indian Poetry*, ed. Vinay Dharwadker and A.K. Ramanujan, Chicago Review/OUP, Delhi, 1994.

'Gandhi and Poetry', K. Satchidanandan, *Signatures*, NBT, Delhi, 2003.

'Alphabet', Debarati Mitra, trans. Marian Maddern, *When Poetry Comes*, ed. Marian Maddern, Sahitya Akademi, Kolkata, 1999.

From *On Poetry in Telugu*, Naane Coda, trans. David Shulman and Velcheru Narayana Rao, *Classic Telugu Poetry*, OUP, Delhi, 2002.

'If Learned Critics Publicly Deride', Bhavabhuti, trans. John Brough, *Poems from the Sankrit*, ed. John Brough, PUK, London, 1968.

'Mulligatawny Dreams', Meena Kandasamy, *Touch*, Peacock Books, Mumbai, 2006.

From *Prologue to The Progress to the Palace*, Kunchan Nambiar, trans. G. Kumara Pillai, *Sahitya Akademi Medieval Indian Literature (Vols. 3)*, ed. K. Ayyappa Paniker, Delhi, 1999.

'I Was Born for Poetry', Chellapilla Venkata Shastry, trans. Velcheru Narayana Rao, *Twentieth Century Telugu Poetry*, ed. Velcheru Narayana Rao, OUP, Delhi, 2002.

'What Poetry Means to Ernestina in Peril', Mona Zote, Poetry International Web, India, india.poetryinternational.org, ed. Arundhati Subramaniam, 2005.

'These My Words', Hiren Bhattacharya, trans. D.N. Bezboruah, *Another India*, ed. Meenakshi Mukherjee and Nissim Ezekiel, PBI, Delhi, 1990.

'After Gujarat', J.P. Das, *Poems*, Grassroots, Bhubaneswar, 2004.

'First Poem', Arvind, trans. Shivnath, *A Selection of Contemporary Dogri Poetry*, ed. Shivanath, Sahitya Akademi, Delhi, 2006.

'Homage to Jayadeva', Govindadas Jha, trans. Jagdish Prasad Karna, *Sahitya Akademi Medieval Indian Literature (Vol. 3)*, ed. K. Ayyappa Paniker, Delhi, 1999.

From *My Explanation*, Kazi Nazrul Islam, trans. Badusha Chakravarty, *The Rebel and Other Poems*, Sahitya Akademi, Delhi, 1998.

'Poets', Rituraj, trans. Manjit Kaur Bhatia, Christi Merrill, Daniel Weissbort and Nalini Taneja, *Survival*, ed. Daniel Weissbort and Girdhar Rathi, Sahitya Akademi, Delhi, 1994.

From *Faith and Erudition*, Vallathol Narayana Menon, trans. Vijay Nambisan, *Puntanam and Melpattur*, ed. Vijay Nambisan, PBI, Delhi, 2009.

'Poetry is for Those Who Wouldn't Read It', Nilmani Phookan, trans. Pradip Acharya, *Selected Poems*, Lawyers' Book Stall, Guwahati, 1994.

'If There Are No Flowers', Firaq Gorakhpuri, trans. Noorul Hasan, *The Selected Poetry of Firaq Gorakhpuri*, ed. Noorul Hasan, Sahitya Akademi, Delhi, 2008.

'Daywatch in the Scriptorium', Smita Agarwal, *Wish Granting Words*, Ravi Dayal Publishers, Delhi, 2002.

'City of Memories', Sunil Gangopadhyay trans. Kaalyan Roy and Bonnie MacDougall, *Signatures*, NBT, Delhi, 2003.

'Her Face Is Not the Moon nor Are Her Eyes', Bhartrhari, trans. John Brough, *Poems from the Sanskrit*, ed. John Brough, PUK, Harmondsworth, 1968.

'Evenings in Iowa City, Iowa', Dilip Chitre, *India: An Anthology of Contemporary Writing*, ed. David Ray and Amritjit Singh, University of Missouri, Kansas City, 1982.

'Poem', Thangjam Ibopishak, trans. Robin Ngangom, *Gestures*, ed. K. Satchidanandan, Sahitya Akademi, Delhi, 1996.

'Outside', Mangalesh Dabral, *Signatures*, NBT, Delhi, 2003.

From Jayavallabha's *Vajjalagam*, trans. H.V. Nagaraja Rao and T.R.S. Sharma, *Ancient Indian Literature*, Sahitya Akademi, Delhi.

'For my Forty-eighth Winter:2', Buddhadeva Bose, trans. Ketaki Kushari Dyson, *Selected Poems of Buddhadeva Bose*, trans. & intro. by Ketaki Kushari Dyson, OUP, Delhi 2000.

'An Old Tale from China', B.C. Ramchandra Sharma (trans.), *The Seven-Walled Fort*, Sahitya Akademi, Delhi 2001.

'On Reading a Love Poem', Kedarnath Singh, trans. Vinay Dharwadker,

The Oxford Anthology of Modern Indian Poetry ed. Vinay Dharwadkeer & A.K. Ramanujan, OUP, Delhi, 1994.

'Creation Hymn' from the Rig Veda, trans. Wendy Doniger, *The Rig Veda*, PBI, Delhi, 2005.

'Creation Myth' from the oral Kannada epic *Halumatha Mahakavya*, Anon, trans. C.N. Ramachandran and Padma Sharma, *Strings and Cymbals*, Prasaranga Kannada University, Hampi, 2007.

'Creation', Akhtar-ul-Iman, trans. Kathleen Grant Jaeger and Baidar Bakht, *Gestures*, ed. K. Satchidanandan, Sahitya Akademi, Delhi, 1996.

'The Summer Sun', Harihara, trans. K. Narasimha Murthy, *Sahitya Akademi Medieval Indian Literature* (Vol. 2), ed. K. Ayyappa Paniker, Sahitya Akademi, Delhi, 1997.

'Calcutta', Amiya Chakravarty, trans. Carolyn B. Brown and Sarat Kumar Mukhopadhyay, *Another Shore*, Sahitya Akademi, Delhi, 2001.

'My Goa', R.V. Pandit, trans. Thomas Gay, *My Goa and Other Poems*, Antonio Caetano Fernandes, Panaji, 1971.

'Rain of the World', Anon, trans. Madhubhai Patel, *Folksongs of South Gujarat*, compiled by Madhubhai Patel, Indian Musicological Society, Mumbai and Baroda, 1974.

'Crabs on the Beach', Jyotirmoy Datta, *An Anthology of Bengali Writing*, ed. Buddhadeva Bose, Macmillan, Mumbai, 1971.

'Flash', Vikram Seth, *The Rivered Earth*, HH/PBI, 2011.

'A Single Shooting Star', Gajanan Madhav Muktibodh, trans. James Mauch, *India: An Anthology of Contemporary Writing*, ed. David Ray and Amritjit Singh, University of Missouri, Kansas City, 1982.

'Water Fowl', Greece Chunder Dutt, *Cherry Blossoms*, T. Fisher Unwin, London and Thacker, Spink and Co., Kolkata, 1887.

'From Rtusamtaram', Canto III, verses 13–24, Kalidasa, trans. Chandra Rajan, *Loom of Time*, PBI, Delhi, 1989.

'The Tiger and the Deer', Sri Aurobindo, *Collected Poems*, Sri Aurobindo Ashram, Pondicherry, 1972.

'A Stallion Wakes from His Sleep', Bana, trans. A.L. Basham, *The Wonder That Was India*, Picador, Basingvoke & Oxford, 2004.

'Lullaby', Anon, trans. C.F. Usborne, *Panjabi Lyrics and Proverbs*, Civil and Military Gazette Press, Lahore, 1905.

'Erok Sim Bonga', Anon, trans. Sitakant Mahapatra, *Bankhen*, Prakashan Prachi, Delhi, 1979.

'The Bird Sanctuary', Sarojini Naidu, *The Feather of the Dawn*, ed. Padmaja Naidu, Asia Publishing House, 1961.

'Summer' from *Vajjalagam*, trans. Martha Ann Selby, *The Circle of Six Seasons*, ed. Martha Ann Selby, PBI, Delhi, 2003.

'From *Anubhavamrita*', Sri Jnanadeva, trans. Dilip Chitre, *Chandrabhaga* No. 3, Chandrabhaga, Cuttack, 1980.

'From *Gitanjali*, 100', Rabindranath Tagore, trans. Joe Winter, Writers Workshop, Kolkata, 1998.

'Wind, 9', Subramania Bharati, trans. A.K. Ramanujan, *The Oxford Anthology of Modern Indian Poetry*, OUP, Delhi, 1994.

'A Hymn to Night for Protection and Prosperity', trans. Ralph T.H. Griffith, *The Hymns of the Atharva Veda*, F.J. Lazarus and Co., Benares, 1917.

'From the *Isa Upanishads*' *The Upanishads*, trans. by Valerie J. Roebuck, PBI, 2000.

'Miles upon Miles', Umashankar Joshi, trans. Suguna Ramanathan and Rita Kothari, *Modern Gujarati Poetry*, ed. Suguna Ramanathan and Rita Kothari, Sahitya Akademi, Ahmedabad, 1998.

'From the Bhagvad Gita, Section VIII, Section XII, Section XV', Vyasa, trans. Swami Prabhavananda and Christopher Isherwood, The Vedanta Society of Southern California, 1944.

'Learn from the Almond Leaf', Eunice de Souza, unpublished.

'The Earthworm's Story', Melanie Silgardo, *Three Poets*, Newground, Mumbai, 1978.

'Beetles', Siddhartha Menon, *Woodpecker*, Siddhartha Menon, Sahitya Akademi, Delhi, 2010.

'The Hang', Santan Rodrigues, 'I Exist,' Writers Workshop, Kolkata, 1976.

'Tusker Kills Mahout at Religious Ceremony', Anand Thakore, *Elephant Bathing*, Poetrywala, Mumbai, 2012.

'From *Sivahandakahari*', Sankaracarya, trans. P.S. Sundaram, *Ancient Indian Literature*, ed. T.R.S. Sharma, Sahitya Akademi, Delhi, 1999.

'Many Many Aeons', Rasananda, trans. Sachidananda Mohanty and Smita Mohanty, *Sahitya Akademi Medieval Indian Literature* (Vol. 3), ed. K. Ayyappa Paniker, Sahitya Akademi, Delhi, 1999.

'Love's Messengers (2),' Naamalvar, *Hymns for the Drowning*, trans. A.K. Ramanujan, PBI, Delhi, 1993.

'Imaginary Re-Union 2', Vidyapati, trans. Ajit Kumar Ghosh, Sahitya Akademi, Vol. 3, Delhi, 1999.

'From *Hush-a-bye Baby*', Periyazhwar (Vishnuchittan), trans. P.S. Sundaram, *The Azhwars*, PBI, Delhi, 1996.

'Like an Elephant, Caught', Akkamahadevi, trans. B.C. Ramchandra Sharma, *Sahitya Akademi Medieval Indian Literature*, Vol. 2, 1994, ed. K. Ayyappa Paniker, Sahitya Akademi, Delhi.

'Yeshwant Rao', Arun Kolatkar, *Jejuri*, Clearing House, Mumbai, 1976.

'Little House (6)', Arul Cellatturai, trans. Paula Richman, *Extraordinary Child*, PBI, Delhi, 2008.

'Open the Wattle-door O Jnaneshwar!', Muktabai, trans. Pradeep Gopal Deshpande, *Sahitya Akademi Medieval Indian Literature*, Vol. 3, ed. K. Ayyappa Paniker, Sahitya Akademi, 1999.

'Let the Pot with Just Water in it', Eesar Das Barhat, trans. Kesri Singh, *Sahitya Akademi Medieval Indian Literature (Vol. 4)*, ed. K. Ayyappa Paniker, Sahitya Akademi, Delhi, 2000.

'Saku Saku', Kanakadasa, trans. William J. Jackson, *Songs of Three Great South Indian Saints*, OUP, Delhi, 1998.

'It's Dark above the Clutching Hand', Allama Prabhu, trans. A.K. Ramanujan, *Speaking of Siva*, PBI, Delhi, 1973.

'From *Bahinabai's Life and Thinking*', Bahninabai Chaudhuri, trans. Chandrashekhar Jahagirdar and Justin E. Abbott, *Sahitya Akademi Medieval Indian Literature (Vol. 3)*, ed. K. Ayyappa Paniker, Sahitya Akademi, Delhi, 1999.

'The Dove of Death', from the Rig Veda, trans. Wendy Doniger, *The Rig Veda*, PBI, 2005.

'Chet (March–April)', Guru Nanak, trans. Khushwant Singh, *Hymns of the Gurus*, PBI, Delhi, 2003.

'Like a Monkey on a Tree', Basavanna, trans. A.K. Ramanujan, *Speaking of Siva*, PBI, Delhi, 1973.

'From *Rahasya Manjari*', Devadurllabha Das, trans. Rajendra Prasad Das, *Sahitya Akademi Medieval Indian Literature* (Vol. 3), ed. K. Ayyappa Paniker, Sahitya Akademi, Delhi, 1999.

'God My Darling', Janabai, trans. Arun Kolatkar, *The Boatride and Other Poems*, Pras, Mumbai, 2009.

'Strange Are the Times', Bullah Shah, trans. K.S. Duggal, *Sahitya Akademi Medieval Indian Literature (Vol. 3)*, ed. K. Ayyappa Paniker, Sahitya Akademi, Delhi, 1999.

'Ghazal 257: Poverty Is More Pleasant Than Majesty', Amir Khusrau, trans. Paul E. Losensky, *In the Bazaar of Love*, PBI, Delhi, 2011.

'So It is Done by God Gopal', Sheikh Mohamad, trans. Pradeep Gopal Deshpande, *Sahitya Akademi Medieval Indian Literature* (Vol. 3), ed. K. Ayyappa Paniker, Sahitya Akademi, Delhi, 1999.

From *Returning from the Pilgrimage*, Namdev, trans. Pradeep Gopal Deshpande, *Sahitya Akademi Medieval Indian Literature* (Vol. 3), ed. K. Ayyappa Paniker, Sahitya Akademi, Delhi, 1999.

'Jaya', Harinath Majumdar, trans. Rachel Fell McDermott, *Singing to the Goddess*, OUP, New York, 2001.

From *Eight Poems*, Sheikh Farid, trans. J.S. Neki, *Sahitya Akademi Medieval Indian Literature* (Vol. 3), ed. K. Ayyappa Paniker, Sahitya Akademi, Delhi, 2000.

Copyright Acknowledgements

'I Want a God', Vipin Parikh, trans. Pradip N. Khandwalla, *Beyond The Beaten Track*, Gujarat Sahitya Parishad, Ahmedabad, 2008.

'Who Shall Deliver Me from the Body of This Death?', Periyalvar, from *Hymns to the Alvars* (trans. J.S.M. Hooper), *Hymns of the Alvars*, Calcutta Association Press, Kolkata, 1929.

'Man and God', Mohammad Iqbal, trans. Khushwant Singh, *Celebrating the Best of Urdu Poetry*, PBI, Delhi, 2007.

'Wonder of Wonders', Eknath, trans. Arun Kolatkar, *The Boatride and Other Poems*, Pras Prakashan, Mumbai, 2009.

'From *Sivamahimnahstava*', Puspadanta, trans. Arthur Avalon, Luzac and Co., London, 1917.

'Vaishnav Struts about Town', Akha, trans. Gieve Patel, *The Little Magazine*.

'Ma, if You Wore a Benarasi Sari', Ma Basanti Cakrabartti, trans. Rachel Fell McDermott, *Singing to the Goddess*, OUP, New York, 2001.

From *Jesus Entered the Garden*, Joaquim Miranda, trans. Olivinho Gomes and Jose Pereira, *Sahitya Akademi Medieval Indian Literature* (Vol. 1), ed. K. Ayyappa Paniker, Delhi, 1997.

'Imagine That I Wasn't Here', Annamayya, trans. David Shulman, *The Wisdom of Poets*, OUP, Delhi, 2001.

'If You Abuse Me with Your Language', Narsinh Mehta, trans. Swami Mahadevananda, *Devotional Songs of Narsi Mehta*, Motilal Banarasidas Publications, Delhi, 1985.

'Come So I Can Bedeck with Anklets and Bells', Anapiyya, trans. Paula Richman, *Extraordinary Child*, PBI, Delhi, 2008.

'He Bartered, My Heart', Mahadeviyakka, trans. A.K. Ramanujan, *Speaking of Siva*, PBI, Delhi, 1973.

'A Courtesan to Her Lover', Ksetrayya, trans. A.K. Ramanujan, A.K. Ramanujan, David Shulman and Velcheru Narayana Rao, *When God Is a Customer*, University of California Press (Berkeley and Los Angeles), 1994.

'This Pain Has Driven Me Mad', Mirabai, trans. (for this anthology) Ranjit Hostoke, *Mirabai ki Padavali*, Hindi Sahitya Sammelan, Allahabad/Prayag 1973.

From *Tiruccentur Pillaittamil (Little House Poem 4)*, Palalikkuttar, trans. Paula Richman, *Extraordinary Child*, PBI, Delhi, 2008.

'Let's Be Girls, Ma', Nazrul Islam, trans. Rachel Fell McDermott, *Singing to the Goddess*, OUP, New York, 2001.

'Both of Us Are Tired', Sakalesha Madarasa, trans. B.C. Ramchandra Sharma, *Sahitya Akademi Medieval Indian Literature* (Vol. 2), ed. K. Ayyappa Paniker, Sahitya Akademi, Delhi, 1997.

'God's Own Dog: VI', Tukaram, trans. Dilip Chitre, *Says Tuka*, PBI, Delhi, 1991

'O Sakhi, the Flute Plays in the Grove', Salabega, trans. Sachidananda Mohanty and Smita Mohanty, *Sahitya Akademi Medieval Indian Literature (Vol. 3)*, ed. K. Ayyappa Paniker, Sahitya Akademi, Delhi, 1999.

'What a Joke!', Ramprasad Sen, trans. Rachel Fell McDermott, *Singing to the Goddess*, OUP, New York, 2001.

'Tell Me Why This Bad Mood Now', Tyagaraja, trans. William J. Jackson, *Tyagaraja: Life and Lyrics*, OUP, Delhi, 1991.

'I Swear', Purandara Dasa, trans. Keshav M. Mutalik, *Songs of Divinity*, ed. Keshav M. Mutalik, Popular Prakashan, Mumbai, 1995.

From *Tiruppavai*, Andal, trans. P.S. Sundaram, *The Poems of Andal*, Ananthacarya Indological Research Institute, Mumbai, 1987.

'Krishna the Omnipresent', Subramania Bharati, trans. Prema Nandkumar, *Poems of Subramania Bharati*, Sahitya Akademi, Delhi, 1977, 2004.

'My Sister's Bible', S. Joseph, trans. K. Satchidanandan, *No Alphabet in Sight*, ed. & intro. K. Satyanarayana & Susie Tharu, PBI, Delhi, 2011.

'Momin', Kailash Vajpeyi, trans. Ananya Vajpeyi, *An Anthology of Modern Hindi Poetry*, Rupa & Co., Delhi, 2000.

'On the Loft', Minal Sarosh, *Mitosis & Other Poems*, Writers Workshop, Kolkata, 1992.

'Whirlwind', Ravji Patel, trans. Hansa Jhaveri, *Indian Poetry Today*, ICCR, Delhi.

'The City, Evening, and an Old Man: Me', Dhoomil, trans. Arvind Krishna Mehrotra, *New Writing in India*, PUK, Harmondsworth, 1974.

From *Peace*, Nilakantha Dikshita, trans. David Shulman and Yigal Bronner, *Southern Poetry Volume*, New York University Press and JJC Foundation/Clay Sanskrit Library, New York, 2009.

'The Abandoned British Cemetery at Balasore, India', Jayanta Mahapatra, *The False Start*, Clearing House, Mumbai, 1980.

'No Matter the Way Be Unknown', Mahadevi Verma, trans. Vinay Dharwadker, *Another India*, ed. Meenakshi Mukherjee and Nissim Ezekiel, PBI, Delhi, 1990.

'Background, Casually', Nissim Ezekiel, *Collected Poems*, OUP, Delhi, 1989.

'When a Stone Is in One's Hands', Jaya Mehta, trans. Pradip N. Khandwalla, *Beyond the Beaten Track*, ed. Pradip N. Khandwalla, Gujarat Sahitya Parishad, Ahmedabad, 2008.

'Old Age', Nirendranath Chakravarti, trans. Sukanta Chaudhuri, *The King Without Clothes*, Sahitya Akademi, Delhi, 1989.

'Annihilate the Stillness of the Evening', Firaq Gorakhpuri, trans. Noorul Hasan, *The Selected Poetry of Firaq Gorakhpuri*, ed. Noorul Hasan, Sahitya Akademi, Delhi, 2008.

'On Hunger' from *Hitopadesa*, Narayana, trans. A.N.D. Haskar, 'Hitopadesa' in *A Treasury of Sanskrit Poetry*, ICCR, Delhi, 2002.

'Those That Will Never Come to My Home', Vinod Kumar Shukla, trans. Dilip Chitre and Daniel Weissbort, *Gestures*, ed. K. Satchidanandan, Sahitya Akademi, Delhi, 1996.

'Between', Melanie Silgardo, unpublished.

'Lamp', Mangesh Padgaonkar, trans. Vinay Dharwadker, *Another India*, ed. Meenakshi Mukherjee and Nissim Ezekiel, PBI, Delhi, 1990.

'Satyabhama', Basudev Sunani, trans. Rabindra K. Swain, *Karadi*

Haata, Eeshan Ankit Prakashani, Nuapada, 2005, English trans. by Rabindra K. Swain on India: Poetry International Web, India, 2006.

'Taj Mahal', R. Parthasarthy, *London Magazine* (Aug–Sept 1997), London, 1997.

'Salutations', Shanmuga Subbiah, trans. T.K. Doraiswamy.

'In Bedlam', Dhan Gopal Mukerji, *This Strange Adventure,* ed. Fredoon Kabraji, New India Publishing Company, London, 1947.

'Rumour', Manohar Shetty *Personal Effects*, Doosra Press, Dona Paula, Goa, 2010.

'Sitting', trans. R. Viswanathan, Attoor Ravi Varma, *Malayalam Poetry Today*, ed. Prof. K.M. Tharakan, Kerala Sahitya Akademi, Thrissur, 1984.

'Anxiety', A.K. Ramanujan, *Collected Poems*, OUP, Delhi, 1995.

'Ghazals', Aziz Bano Darab, trans. Qurratulain Hyder and Arlene Zide, *In Their Own Voice*, ed. Arlene Zide, PBI, Delhi, 1993.

'Day by Day', Kunwar Narain, trans. Lucy Rosenstein, *Poetry in Hindi*, ed. Lucy Rosenstein, Permanent Black, Delhi, 2003.

'This Is the Order', Bal Sitaram Mardheker, trans. Dilip Chitre, *An Anthology of Marathi Poetry*, ed. Dilip Chitre, Nirmala Sadanand Publishers, Mumbai, 1967.

'Homecoming', Tishani Doshi, *60 Indian Poets*, ed. Jeet Thayil, PBI, Delhi, 2008.

'Sun', Padma Sachdev, trans. Shivaanath, *A Handful of Sun and Other Poems*, Sahitya Akademi, Delhi, 2000.

'Window', Jerry Pinto, *60 Indian Poets*, ed. Jeet Thayil, PBI, Delhi, 2008.

'On the Tomb of Us Poor People', The Empress Nur Jahan, trans. Barakat Ullah, *Poems by Indian Women*, ed. Margaret Macnicol, Association Press YMCA, Kolkata, 1928.

'Breasts', Kutti Revathi, trans. N. Kalyan Raman, Poetry International Web, India, for English trans; Mulaigal Thamizhini, Chennai, 2002.

'To Grandmother, Long After', Jyotsna Karmakar, trans. Marian Maddern, *When Poetry Comes*, Sahitya Akademi, Kolkata, 1999.

'Fern', Ranjit Hoskote, *Both Sides of the Sky*, ed. Eunice de Souza, NBT, Delhi, 2008.

'The City', Adil Mansuri, trans. Suguna Ramanathan and Rita Kothari, *Modern Gujarati Poetry*, ed. Suguna Ramanathan and Rita Kothari, Sahitya Akademi, Ahmedabad, 1998.

'Time Does Not Fly', Sitakant Mahapatra, trans. by the poet, *The Sky of Words and Other Poems*, Sahitya Akademi, Delhi, 1996.

'A Labourer's Laughter II', Balachandran Chullikkad, trans. A.J. Thomas, *Signatures*, ed. K. Satchidanandan, NBT, Delhi, 2003.

'Spiritus Mundi', Jeet Thayil, *60 Indian Poets*, ed. Jeet Thayi, PBI, 2008.

'Solar', Sitanshu Yashashchandra, trans. Suguna Ramanathan and Rita Kothari, *Modern Gujarati Poetry*, ed. Suguna Ramanathan and Rita Kothari, Sahitya Akademi, Ahmedabad, 1998.

'Five Acts', Susmita Bhattacharya, trans. Joe Winter, *Dark*, Sanbun, Delhi, 2004.

'Map-maker', Keki Daruwalla, Ravi Dayal Publishers, Delhi, 2002.

I Lalla: The Poems of Lal Ded, trans. Ranjit Hoskote, PBI, Delhi, 2011.

'Shadow' Pravin Gadhvi, trans. Pradip N. Khandwalla, *Beyond the Beaten Track*, ed. Pradip N. Khandwalla, Gujarati Sahitya Parishad, Ahmedabad, 2008.

'Two Women Knitting', Mrinal Pande, trans. Mrinal Pande and Arlene Zide, *In Their Own Voice*, ed. Arlene Zide, PBI, Delhi, 1993.

'A Child-Husband', Anon, trans. Winifred Bryce, *Women's Folksongs from Rajputana*, compiled by Winifred Bryce, Publications Department, Ministry of Information and Broadcasting, Delhi, 1961.

'The Ambiguous Fate of Gieve Patel, He Being Neither Muslim nor Hindu in India', Gieve Patel, *How Do You Withstand, Body*, Clearing House, Mumbai, 1976.

'The Girl's Desire Moves among Her Bangles', Gagan Gill, trans. Mrinal Pande and Arlene Zide, *The Oxford Book of Modern Indian Poetry*, OUP, Delhi, 1994.

'A Poem', Ali Sardar Jafri, trans. Baidar Bakht and Kathleen Grant Jaeger, *Signatures*, ed. K. Satchidanandan, NBT, Delhi, 2003.

'Sita's Disgrace' from *The Ramayana of Valmiki*, Book VI, Canto CXVII, Valmiki, trans. Ralph T.H. Griffith, F.J. Lazarus and Co., Benaras, 1895.

'Lanka' from *The Ramayana of Valmiki*, Valmiki, trans. Ralph T.H. Griffith, F.J. Lazarus and Co., Benaras, 1895.

'On Drinking', Ghalib, trans. Khushwant Singh, *Celebrating the Best of Urdu Poetry*, PBI, Delhi, 2007.

'Lament of Old Age', Ghalib, trans. Khushwant Singh, *Celebrating the Best of Urdu Poetry*, PBI, Delhi, 2007.

'The Moon Rise' from *Ramayana Campu*, Punam Nambudiri, trans. V.R. Prabodhchandran Nayar, *Sahtiya Akademi Medival Indian Literature (Vol. 3)*, ed. K. Ayyappa Paniker, Sahitya Akademi, Delhi, 1999.

'I Will Seek You Down the Wandering Brooks', Habba Khatoon, trans. Triloknath Raina, *Sahitya Akademi Medival Indian Literature (Vol. 2)*, ed. K. Ayyappa Paniker, Sahitya Akademi, Delhi, 1997.

'A Love Poem', Mahe Jabeen, trans. Velcheru Narayana Rao, *Twentieth Century Telugu Poetry*, ed. Velcheru Narayana Rao, OUP, Delhi, 2002.

'Oh, Pardon Me', Baldev Rath, trans. Saubhagya Kumar Misra, *Sahitya Akademi Medieval Indian Literature*, Vol. 3, ed. K. Ayyappa Paniker, Sahitya Akademi, Delhi, 1999.

'She Neither Turned Away, Nor Yet Began', Amaru, trans. John Brough, *Poems from the Sanskrit*, ed. John Brough, PUK, Harmondsworth, 1968.

'There Are Good Omens: The House-Lizard Chips', Palai Patiya Perunkatunko, trans. E. Annamalai and H. Schiffman, *Ancient Indian Literature*, ed. T.R.S. Sharma, Sahitya Akademi, Delhi, 2000.

'From the *Prologue of Mission of the Goose*', Vedanta Deshika, trans. David Shulman and Yigal Bronner, *Southern Poetry Volume*, New York University Press and JJC Foundation, New York, 2009.

'Noun', Leela Gandhi, *60 Indian Poets*, ed. Jeet Thayil, PBI, Delhi, 2008.

'From Heer-Ranjha', Waris Shah, trans. K.C. Kanda, *Sahitya Akademi Medieval Indian Literature (Vol. 3)*, ed. K. Ayyappa Paniker, Sahitya Akademi, Delhi, 1999.

'Peabody', Mustansir Dalvi, *Desert Moon Review*, 2002.

'The Jewel Knight' Anon, trans. Winifred Bryce, Publications Department, Ministry of Information and Broadcasting, Delhi.

From *Fifty Stanzas of a Thief*, Bilhana, trans. Richard Gombrich, *Love Lyrics* by Amaru and Bhartihari, Clay Sanskrit Library and New York University Press, New York, 2005.

'Complaints', Anon, trans. S.C. Dube, *Field Songs of Chattisgarh*, ed. S.C. Dube, The Universal Publishers, Lucknow, 1947.

'The Ballad of Laila', Anon, trans. C.F. Usborne, *Panjabi Lyrics and Proverbs*, Printed at the Civil and Military Gazette Press, Lahore, 1905.

'The First Stage of Radha's Love', Chandidas, trans. Ujjwal Majumdar, Sahitya Akademi Medieval Indian Literature, ed. K. Ayyappa Paniker, Sahitya Akademi, Delhi.

'Open the Book, Brother Brahmin', Shah 'Madho Lal' Husain, trans. Carla Petievich, *When Men Speak as Women*, ed. Carla Petievich, OUP, Delhi, 2007.

From *Gita Govinda*, Jayadeva, trans. Lee Siegel, *Gita Govinda: Love Songs of Radha and Krishna*, New York University Press and Clay Sanskrit Library, New York, 2009.

'Let's Go to the Upland Woods, My Friend', Habba Khatoon, trans. Trilokinath Raina, *Sahitya Akademi Medieval Indian Literature*, Vol. 2, ed. K. Ayyappa Paniker, Sahitya Akademi, Delhi, 1997.

'I've Brought this Summer Just for You', Kutti Revathi, trans. N. Kalyan Raman, Poetry International Web, India, ed. Arundhati Subramaniam, Kumudan Theeramathi, Chennai, 2002.

'Asleep', Dom Moraes, *60 Indian Poets*, ed. Jeet Thayil, PBI, Delhi, 2008.

From *Ratnavali*, Harsha, trans. David Shulman, *The Wisdom of Poets*, OUP, Delhi, 2002.

'On the Banks of a Lake', Anon, trans. Olivinho Gomes, *Sahitya Akademi Medieval Indian Literature (Vol. 3)*, ed. K. Ayyappa Paniker, Sahitya Akademi, Delhi, 1999.

'The Song of Praise', trans. R. Parthasarahty, PBI, Delhi, 2004.

The Dalliance of the Leopards, Anon, trans. E. Powys Mathers, *Clinging to a Lost Learning*, The Pushkin Press, London, 1944.

'Love Song', Anon, trans. Shamrao Hivale and Verrier Elwin, *Songs of the Forest*, ed. *The Clilapattikeram*, Shamrao Hivale and Verrier Elwin, George Alien and Unwin Ltd, London, 1935.

'Distance Destroys Love', Anon, trans. Arvind Krishna Mehrotra, *The Absent Traveller*, Ravi Dayal Publishers, Delhi, 1991.

'The Song of Phatmal', Anon, trans. Kesri Singh, *Sahitya Akademi Medieval Indian Literature (Vol. 4)*, ed. K. Ayyappa Paniker, Sahitya Akademi, Delhi, 2000.

'From *The Tale of the Glory-Bearer*', Janna, trans. T.R.S. Sharma, *From the Tale of the Glory-Bearer*, PBI, Delhi, 1994.

'What He Said', Cempulappenyanirar, trans. A.K. Ramanujan, *The Interior Landscape*, OUP, Delhi, 1994.

'What She Said', Allur Nanmullai, trans. A.K. Ramanujan, *The Interior Landscape*, OUP, Delhi, 1994.

'Song', Anon, trans. E. Powys Mathers, *Love Songs of Asia*, The Pushkin Press, London, 1944.

'A Woman Talking to Herself', Annamaya, trans. A.K. Ramanujan, David Shulman and Velchuru Narayana Rao, *When God Is a Customer*, University of California Press Berkeley and Los Angeles, 1994.

'The Wayward Heart', Shah Abdul Latif, trans. H.T. Sorley, *Shah Abdul Lalit of Bhit: His Poetry, Life and Times*, Oxford University Press, London, and Humphrey Milford, 1940.

'His Infatuates Complain', Muttollayiram, trans. M.L. Thangappa, *Red Lilies and Frightened Birds*, PBI, Delhi, 2011.

'The Miracle of Wine', Mir Taqi Mir, trans. Khushwant Singh, *Celebrating the Best of Urdu Poetry*, PBI, Delhi, 2007.

'Daily Wages', Amrita Pritam, trans. Charles Brasch and Amrita Pritam, *The Penguin Book of Women Poets*, PUK, Harmondsworth, 1978.

'Saba's Hands Wear a Bridal Henna Tint Now', Balraj Komal, *A Sky Full of Birds*, Sahitya Akademi, Delhi, 1992.

From *Bouquet of Rasa*, Bhanudatta, trans. Sheldon I. Pollock, New York University Press, New York, 2009.

From *Lakshmi Purana*, Balaram Das, trans. Lipipuspa Nayak, Grassroots, Bhubaneshwar, 2008.

'Draupadi', Supta Bhattacharya, trans. Marian Maddern, *When Poetry Comes*, Sahitya Akademi, Calcutta, 1999.

'The Stone Age', Kamala Das, *Only the Soul Knows How to Sing*, DC, Books, Kottayam, 1996.

'Wanted: A Broom', Cantirakanti, trans. Martha Ann Selby and K. Paramasivan, *In Their Own Voice*, ed. Arlene Zide, PBI, Delhi, 1993.

'Champa Doesn't Know Her Alphabet', Trilochan, trans. Anamika and Arlene Zide, *Sahitya Akademi Journal: Indian Literature Sept.–Oct. 2008*.

'Tree', Arundhati Subramaniam, *The Way I Live: New & Selected Poems*, Bloodaxe Publishers, UK, 2009.

"Tis Well With Me', Sumangala's Mother, trans. Margaret Macnicol, *Poems of Cloister & Jungle*, ed. Mrs C.A.F. Rhys–David John Murray, London, 1941.

'My Husband's Home', Anon, trans. Madhubhai Patel, *Folksongs of South Gujarat*, Indian Musicological Society, Mumbai and Baroda, 1974.

'The Sceptic Says', Soma, trans. Mrs C.A.F. Rhys-David, *Poems of Cloister and Jungle*, ed. Mrs C.A.F. Rhys-David, John Murray London, 1941.

'Paranomasia', Rukmini Bhaya Nair, *The Yellow Hibiscus*, PBI, Delhi, 2004.

'The Speck', Harinda Dave, trans. Suguna Ramanathan and Rita

Kothari, *Modern Gujarati Poetry*, ed. Suguna Ramanathan and Rita Kothari, Sahitya Akademi, Ahmedabad, 1998.

'Tar and Broom', Kadammanitta Ramakrishna, trans. K. Ayyappa Paniker and Ray King, Sahitya Akademi, Kerala.

'Compulsions', Mamta Kalia, *Tribute to Papa and Other Poems*, Writers Workshop, Kolkata, 1970.

'Where Did It Go Wrong', Tukaram, trans. Dilip Chitre, *Says Tuka*, ed. Dilip Chitre, PBI, Delhi, 1991.

'There Is No Limit to Desire', Anon, trans. Winifred Bryce, *Women's Folksongs from Rajputana*, Publications Department, Ministry of Information and Broadcasting, Delhi, 1961.

'Waiting', Shakunt Mathur, trans. Aruna Sitesh and Arlene Zide, *In Their Own Voice*, PBI, Delhi, 1993.

'Husbands', Shobha Bhagwat, trans. Vinay Dharwadker.

'Dignity', Bilqees Zafirul Hasan, trans. Mehr Afshan Farooqi, *The Oxford India Anthology of Modern Urdu Literature*, OUP, Delhi, 2008.

'Let Faithful Wives', Satavahana Hala, trans. Arvind Krishna Mehrotra, *The Absent Traveller*, Ravi Dayal Publishers, Delhi, 1991.

'Room-Zoom', Anon, trans. Madhubhai Patel, *Folksongs of South Gujarat*, Indian Musicological Society, Mumbai and Baroda, 1974.

'What One of Her Companions Said to Another', Bihari, trans. Krishna P. Bahadur, *The Satasai*, PBI, Delhi, 1990.

'Personal Effects', Manohar Shetty, from *Personal Effects*, Doosra Press, Dona Paula Goa, 2010.

'Cow and Grandmother', Anuradha Mahapatra, trans. Marian Maddern, *When Poetry Comes*, ed. Marian Maddern, Sahitya Akademi, Kolkata, 1999.

From *To the Cuckoo*, Markanda Das, trans. D.B. Pattanaik, *Sahitya Akademi Medieval Indian Literature (Vol. 3)*, ed. K. Ayyappa Paniker, Sahitya Akademi, Delhi, 1999.

'A Memory Comes Back', Shakti Chattopadhyaya, trans. Arvind Krishna Mehrotra, Unpublished.

'Married Love', Srinivas Rayaprol, *Married Love and Other Poems*, Writers Workshop, Kolkata, 1972.

'My Chest Had Been Worn Away', Dhurjati, trans. Hank Heifetz and Velcheru Narayana Rao, *Sahitya Akademi Medieval Indian Literature (Vol. 4)*, ed. K. Ayyappa Paniker, Sahitya Akademi, Delhi, 2000.

'My Pocket', G.S. Sivarudrappa, trans. O.L. Nagabhushana Swamy, *Between You and Me*, ed. O.L. Nagabhushana Swamy, Sahitya Akademi, Delhi, 2003.

'I, My Father', Natwarlal Pandya 'Ushnas', trans. Suguna Ramanathan and Rita Kothari *Modern Gujarati Poetry*, ed. Suguna Ramanathan and Rita Kothari, Sahitya Akademi, Ahmedabad, 1998.

'Marriage Song', Anon, trans. Mohini Mohan Brahma, *Folksongs of the Bodos*, Publications Division, Institute of Tribal Culture and Folklore Research, Gauhati University, 1960.

From *Male Madeshwara*, Madeshwara, trans. C.N. Ramachandran and Padma Sharma, *Strings and Cymbals*, ed. C.N. Ramachandran, Prasaranga Kannada University, Hampi, 2007.

'Son to Mother', Gnanakoothan, trans. Ashokamitran, *Gestures*, ed. K. Satchidanandan, Sahitya Akademi, Delhi, 1996.

'In My Mother's Clothes', Anjum Hassan, *Street on a Hill*, Sahitya Akademi, Delhi, 2006.

'Son-in-law', B.S. Mardhekar, trans. Vinay Dharwadker, *Sahitya Akademi Journal: Indian Literature*, Sahitya Akademi, Delhi, 2008.

'Here Is a Palanquin', Narsinh Mehta, trans. Niranjan Bhagat, *Sahitya Akademi Medieval Indian Literature (Vol. 2)*, ed. K. Ayyappa Paniker, Sahitya Akademi, Delhi, 1997.

'Those Who Have Lost the Nectar', O.N.V. Kurup, trans. S. Velayudhan, *The Ancient Lyre*, Sahitya Akademi, Delhi, 2005.

'In the Smell of Rice Fields in Autumn', Nirmal Prabha Bordoloi, trans. Hiren Gohain, *In Their Own Voice*, ed. Arlene Zide, PBI, Delhi, 1993.

'In a White Town', Daljit Nagra, *Look We Have Coming to Dover*, Faber, London, 2007.

'To Mother', S.A. Usha, trans. A.K. Ramanujan, *In Their Own Voice*, ed. Arlene Zide, PBI, Delhi, 1993.

'One One Side of the Ganga', Anon, trans. Durga Bhagwat, *Folksongs of the Satpura Valleys*, Reprinted from the *Journal of the University of Bombay*, Vol VIII, Part 4, Jan 1940.

'Patalam 8: Jatayu Gives Up His Life', from the Ramayana, Kampan, trans. George L. Harris and Hank Heifetz, *The Forest Book of the Ramayana of Kampan*, University of California Press, Berkeley and Los Angeles, 1988.

'Childhood of Rama' from *The Ramayana*, Tulsidas, trans. Rev. A.G. Atkins, Birla Academy of Art and Culture, Kolkata, 1966.

'A Stalemate', Vinda Karandikar, trans. G.V. Karandikar, *The Sacred Heresy*, Sahitya Akademi, Delhi, 1998.

'Colour Problems in the Family', Adil Jussawalla, *Trying to Say Goodbye*, Almost Island Books, Mumbai, 2011.

'Desperately Seeking India', G.J.V. Prasad *In Delhi Without a Visa*, Har Anand Publishers, Delhi 1996.

'Bombay, Mumbai', Imtiaz Dharker, PBI, Delhi 2007.

'Dhaulagiri', Vinod Shukla, *Sab Kuch Hona Bacha Rahega*, trans. Arvind Krishna Mehrotra, Rajkamal Prakashan, Delhi, 1992.

'In Praise of Guns', Keshav Malik, *India: An Anthology of Contemporary Writing*, ed. David Ray and Amritjit Singh, New Letters (1982), University of Missouri, Kansas City, 1983.

'Really?' Sri Sri, trans. Velcheru Narayana Rao, *Twentieth Century Telugu Poetry*, ed. Velcheru Narayana Rao, OUP, Delhi, 2002.

'The Bedas of Haligali', trans. C.N. Ramachandran and Padma Sharma, *Strings and Cymbals*, ed. C.N. Ramachandran, Prasaranga Kannada University, Hampi, 2007.

'Hiroshima', Ajneya (S.H. Vatsyayan), *Signatures*, ed. trans. by the poet K. Satchidanandan, NBT, Delhi, 2003.

'Ode to Waris Shah', Amrita Pritam, trans. Darshan Singh Maini, Vikas Books, *Studies in Punjabi Poetry*, Delhi, 1979.

From *Unniyarcha* and *Aromal Unni*, Anon, trans. Kamala Das, *Sahitya Akademi Medieval Indian Literature (Vol. 3)*, ed. K. Ayyappa Paniker, Sahitya Akademi, Delhi, 1999.

'Gaddi Aa Gayi', Imtiaz Dharker, Bloodaxe Books, UK.

'The Morning of Freedom', Faiz Ahmed Faiz, trans. Kathleen Grant Jaeger and Baidar Bakht, *Sahitya Akademi Modern Indian Literature*, ed. K.M. George, Sahitya Akademi, Delhi, 1994.

'Flight', Robin Ngangon, trans. by the poet.

'How Do I Know This Is My Son?', Anon, trans. P. Maruthanayagam, *Ancient Indian Literature*, Sahitya Akademi, Delhi, 2000.

'Here Comes God', Tenneti Suri, trans. Velcheru Narayana Rao, *Twentieth Century Telugu Poetry*, ed. Velcheru Narayana Rao, OUP, Delhi, 2002.

'Philistines', K. Ayyappa Paniker, *Signatures*, ed. K. Satchidanandan, NBT, Delhi, 2003.

'Elegy (for Anci),' Auvaiyar, trans. A.K. Ramanujan, *Poems of Love and War*, ed. A.K. Ramanujan, Columbia Universiy, Columbia, 1985.

'A Certain Fiction Bit Me', Khadar Mohinuddin, trans. Velcheru Narayana Rao, *Twentieth Century Telugu Poetry*, ed. Velcheru Narayana Rao, OUP, Delhi, 2002.

'Satirical Verses', Akbar Ilahabadi, trans. Mehr Afshan Farooqi, *The Oxford India Anthology of Modern Urdu Literature*, ed. Mehr Afshan Farooqi, OUP, Delhi, 2008.

'Praises Galore to the Land of Dhat', Rangrelo Bithu, trans. Kesri Singh, *Sahitya Akademi Medieval Indian Literature (Vol. 4)*, ed. K. Ayyappa Paniker, Sahitya Akademi, Delhi, 2000.

'A Woman and Her Dying Warrior', Vanparanar, trans. A.K. Ramanujan, *Poems of Love and War*, ed. A.K. Ramanujan, Columbia University, Columbia, 1985.

From the Mahabharata, Sarala Das, trans. Madhusudhan Pati, *Sahitya Akademi Medieval Indian Literature (Vol. 3)*, ed. K. Ayyappa Paniker, Sahitya Akademi, Delhi, 1999.

From *The State of the Realm*, Mirza Mohammad Rafi Sauda, trans. Shamsur Rahman Faruqi, *Sahitya Akademi Medieval Indian Literature (Vol 4)*, ed. K. Ayyappa Paniker, Sahitya Akademi, Delhi, 2000.

'Kalemegdan', Agyeya, trans. Lucy Rosenstein, *New Poetry in Hindi*, ed. Lucy Rosenstein, Permanent Black, Delhi, 2003.

'Cycle Rickshaw', Raghuvir Sahay, trans. Harish Trivedi and Daniel Weissbort, *Gestures*, ed. K. Satchidanandan, Sahitya Akademi, Delhi, 1996.

'The Secunderabad Club', Jaysinh Birjepatil, *India: An Anthology of Contemporary Writing*, ed. David Ray and Amritjit Singh, University of Missouri, Kansas City, 1982. First appearance in *Critical Quarterly*, Vol. 23, No. 4, Winter 1981.

'Process', Shrikant Varma, trans. Vishnu Khare, *Signatures*, ed. K. Satchidanandan, NBT, Delhi, 2003.

'Remembering Tiananmen', Tabish Khair.

'When That Day Comes', Lakhmi Khilani, trans. Madhu Kewlani, *Sahitya Akademi Journal: Indian Literature*, Sahitya Akademi, Sept.–Oct., 2008.

'Ayodhya', Kunwar Narain, trans. Apurva Narain, *Signatures*, ed. K. Satchidanandan, NBT, Delhi, 2003.

'Bhishma and Parsurama Engage in Combat' from the Mahabharata, Vyasa, trans. P. Lal, Writers Workshop, Kolkata, 1977.

'Gandhari's Lament for the Slain', from the Ramayana & the Mahabharata condeused into English by Romesh C. Dutt, J.M. Dent & Sons, 1910, last reprint 1963.

'The Night is Endless', Anon, *Poems of the Emergency*, Anon publication.

'No, I Am Not Losing My Sleep', Pash, trans. Suresh Sethi, *Signatures*, ed. K. Satchidanandan, NBT, Delhi, 2003.

'Lifetime', Narayan Surve, trans. Vinay Dharwadker, Tri Quarterly Evanston, Illinois.

'Red Bicycle', Sarveshwar Dayal Saxena, trans. Arvind Krishna Mehrotra, *Another India*, PBI, ed. Nissim Ezekiel and Meenakshi Mukherjee, Delhi, 1990.

'Breaking Stones', Nirala, trans. Arvind Krishna Mehrotra, *The Last Bungalow: Writings on Allahabad*, ed. Arvind Krishna Mehrotra, PBI, Delhi, 2007.

'Once Upon a Time', Chandrashekara Patil, trans. by the poet, *10 Years of Kannada Poetry, 1974–83*, ed. Gopalakrishna Adiga, L.S. Seshagiri and Ramchandra Sharma, Sahitya Akademi Karnataka, Bangalore, 1985.

'Where Are the Untouchables', Purandara Dasa, trans. Keshav M. Mutalik, *Songs of Divinity*, ed. Keshav M. Mutalik, Popular Prakashan, Mumbai, 1995.

'Continuum', Gieve Patel, *How Do You Withstand, Body*, Clearing House, Mumbai, 1976.

'An Epic of the Dungri Bhils', trans. Nila Shah, documented & edited by Bhagwandas Patel, Central Institute of Indian Languages & Bhasha Research Centre, Mysore/Vadodara, 2012.

'Bhojpuri Descant', Arvind Krishna Mehrotra, *Middle Earth*, OUP, Delhi, 1984.

'Rama's Last Act', Bhavabhuti, trans. Sheldon I. Pollock, New York University Press and JJC Foundation/Clay Sanskrit Libraty, New York, 2007.

'How to Tame a Pair of New Chappals', Gopal Honnalgere, *60 Indian Poets*, ed. Jeet Thayil, PBI, Delhi 2008.

'The Tradition', Dharmakirti, trans. Octavio Paz, PBI, Delhi.

'I Must Have A Word', Siddalingaiah, trans. Sumatheendra Nadig and David Ray, *India: An Anthology of Contemporary Writing*, ed. David Ray & Amritjit Singh, University of Missouri, Kansas City, 1982.

'The Oblique Invitation', Vallana, trans. Octavio Paz, *A Tale of Two Gardens*, PBI, Delhi, 1977.

'I've Never Known How to Tan or Sew', Ravidas, trans. J.S. Hawley and Mark Juergensmeyer, *Songs of the Saints of India*, OUP, Delhi, 2004.

'A Strange Darkness', Jibananda Das, trans. Joe Winter, *Naked Lonely Hand*, Meteor Books, Kolkata, 2004.

'Let's Go', Kabir, trans. Arvind Krishna Mehrotra, *Songs of Kabir*, Hachette–Permanent Black, Delhi, 2011.

'Why Marry?', Vemana, trans. J.S.R.L. Narayana Moorty and Elliot Roberts, *Selected Verses of Vemana*, Sahitya Akademi, Delhi, 1995.

'Series of Omens', Kanaka Ha. Ma, trans. Kanaka Ha. Ma and Priya D'Souza, Arabi Kadalu, Akshara Prakashan Safar, 2006. First published on the Indian domain of the Poetry International Web.

'From the Art of the Courtesan', Anon, trans. P. Narayana Kurup, *Sahitya Akademi Medieval Indian Literature*, Vol. 3, ed. K. Ayyappa Paniker, Sahitya Akademi, Delhi, 1999.

'That Afternoon', Ravji Patel, trans. Suguna Ramanathan and Rita Kothari, *Modern Gujarati Poetry*, ed. Suguna Ramanathana and Rita Kothari, Sahitya Akademi, Ahmedabad, 1998.

'They Call You Mad', Rabindranath Tagore, *Ancient Indian Literature*, Sahitya Akademi, Delhi.

'What She Told Her Daughter about Unchaste Women' from Jayavallabha's *Vajjalagam*, Anon, trans. H.V. Nagaraja Rao and T.R.S. Sharma, *Sahitya Akademi Medieval Indian Literature*, ed. K. Ayyappa Paniker, Sahitya Akademi, Delhi.

From *The Fool (Ch. V)*, *The Dhammapada* trans. Max Muller, The Clarendon Press, Oxford, 1881.

'Stone Masons, My Father and Me', Namdeo Dhasal trans. Vinay Dharwadker.

'Listen Carefully', Kabir, trans. Arvind Krishna Mehrotra, *Song of Kabir*, Hachette–Permanent Black, Delhi, 2011.

'Do Something Brother', M. Gopalkrishna Adiga, trans. A.K. Ramanujan, *Another India*, ed. Nissim Ezekiel and Meenakshi Mukherjee, PBI, Delhi, 1990.

From *Buddhacarita*, Asvaghosa, trans. A.K. Warder, *Indian Kavya Literature*, Motilal Banarasidas Publications, Delhi, 1974.

'Lines Written to Mothers Who Disagree with Their Sons' Choices of Women', Kynpham Sing Nongkynrih, *SWAG Magazine*, Swansea Writers' and Artists' Group, Swansea, 1991.

'Know How to Tell', Siddaramayya, trans. B.C. Ramchandra Sharma, *Sahitya Akademi Medieval Indian Literature (Vol. 2)*, ed. K. Ayyappa Paniker, Sahitya Akademi, Delhi, 1997.

'Madras Central', Vijay Nambisan, *Gemini*, PBI, Delhi, 1992.

'A Wife's Complaint', Sarangapani, trans. A.K. Ramanujan, Velcheru Narayana Rao and David Shulman, *When God Is a Customer*, University of California Press, Berkeley and Los Angeles, 1994.

'Fire Can Burn', Devara Dasimayya, trans. A.K. Ramanujan, *Speaking of Siva*, PBI, Delhi, 1973.

'Learned Man', Hemacandra Suri, trans. H.V. Nagaraja Rao and T.R.S. Sharma, *Ancient Indian Literature*, Sahitya Akademi, Delhi, 2000.

'Six Shastras, Eight Puranas, and Four Vedas', Sami, trans. Shanti Shahani, *Four Classical Poets of Sind*, ed. G. Allana, Sahitya Akademi, Delhi, 1996.

'What Shall We Sell Next?', Vijayalakshmi, trans. C.P. Sivadasan, *Malayalam Literary Survey*, Sahitya Akademi Kerala, Thrisshur, 2004.

'A Celibate Monk Shouldn't Fall in Love' from *Sutrakritanga*, Anon, trans. A.L. Basham, *The Wonder That Was India*, Picador, London, 1966.

'The Guru', A.K. Ramanujan, *Collected Poems*, OUP, Delhi, 1995.

'A Stone Breaks the Sleeping Water', Mamang Dai.

'A Mound of Earth a Heart', Joy Goswami, trans. Sampurna Chattarji, *Surjo-Poro Chhai*, Ananda Publishers, Kolkata, 1999.

'Man: 1961', Pranabendu Dasgupta, trans. Buddhadeva Bose, *An*

Anthology of Bengali Writing, ed. Buddhadeva Bose, Macmillan, Mumbai, 1971.

'Nostalgia,' Anon, trans. Shafi Shauq, *Sahitya Akademi Medieval Indian Literature*, ed. K. Ayappa Paniker, Sahitya Akademi, Delhi.

'Cemetery', B.B. Borkar, trans. Vrinda Nabar and Nissim Ezekiel, *Goan Literature*, ed. Peter Nazareth, Journal of South Asian Literature, Iowa City, 1983.

'Facts of Life', G.S. Sharat Chandra, *India: An Anthology of Contemporary Writing*, University of Missouri, Kansas City, 1982.

'Vibhishana's Lament for Ravana', Canto 18 from *The Death of Ravana*, Bhatti, trans. Oliver Fallon, New York University Press and JJC Foundation/Clay Sanskrit Libiaty, New York, 2009.

'On Hearing of Pratap's Passing Away', Dursa Adha, trans. Kesri Singh, *Sahitya Akademi Medieval Indian Literature (Vol. 4)*, ed. K. Ayyappa Paniker, Sahitya Akademi, Delhi, 2000.

'Nine Poems on Arrival', Adil Jussawalla, *Missing Person*, Clearing House, Mumbai, 1976.

'Reports of Your Passing', Ramakanta Rath, *Poems*, Grassroots, Bhubhaneshwar, 2004.

'Absence', Indira Sant, trans. Vrinda Nabar and Nissim Ezekiel, *Indira Sant*, Sadanand Publishers, Mumbai, 1975.

'The Colours of the Season's Best Dream', C.P. Surendran.

'Remembering the Year 1947', Kedarnath Singh, trans. Pradeep Gopal Deshpande, *Tree of Tongues*, ed. E.V. Ramakrishnan, Indian Institute of Advanced Study, Shimla, 1999.

'The Year 1979', Nita Ramaiya, trans. by the author, *In Their Own Voice*, ed. Arlene Zide, PBI, Delhi, 1993.

'I Won't Come and Tell You', Gagan Gill, trans. Gagan Gill and Arlene Zide, *In Their Own Voice*, ed. Arlene Zide, PBI, Delhi, 1993.

'Songs of Innocence', Eunice de Souza, *A Necklace of Skulls*, PBI, Delhi, 2010.

'Life in the Desert', Anon, trans. C.F. Usborne, *Panjabi Lyrics and Proverbs*, Civil and Military Gazette Press, Lahore, 1905.

'Looking through Well Water', Meena Alexander, *House of a Thousand Doors*, Three Continents Press, Washington DC, 1988.

From *Old Age*, trans. Max Muller, *Four Classical Poets of Sind*, ed. G Allana, The Calrendon Press Oxford, 1996.

'The Poet's Grave', Henry Derozio, *The Fakeer of Jungheera*, Samuel Smith and Co., Kolkata, 1928.

'Wrong Address', Dom Moraes, *60 Indian Poets*, ed. Jeet Thayil, PBI, Delhi, 2008.

'Moving House', Balmukund Dave, trans. Suguna Ramanathan and Rita Kothari, *Modern Gujarati Poetry*, ed. Suguna Ramanathan and Rita Kothari, Ahmedabad, 1998.

'On the Death of a Friend', B.C. Ramchandra Sharma, trans. by the poet, *The Seven-Walled Fort and Other Poems*, Sahitya Akademi, Delhi.

'Come, O sisters, Let Us Wail for Our Brothers', Anon, trans. Naji Munawar, *Sahitya Akademi Medieval Indian Literature (Vol. 4)*, ed. K. Ayyappa Paniker, Sahitya Akademi, Delhi, 2000.

'Our Casuarina Tree', Toru Dutt, *Ancient Ballads and Legends of Hindustan*, Kegan Paul Trench and Co., London, 2nd edition, 1885.

'Prayers for the Dead', Nida Fazli, trans. Balraj Komal, *Signatures*, ed. K. Satchidanandan, NBT, Delhi, 2003.

'Ranjha Writes to the Bhabis' from *Kissa Heer*, Waris Shah, trans. Gurcharan Singh, *Sahitya Akademi Medieval Indian Literature (Vol. 3)*, ed. K. Ayyappa Paniker, Sahitya Akademi, Delhi, 1999.

'A Time Was When the Wine Cask', Kapilar, trans. Prema Nandkumar, *Ancient Indian Literature*, Sahitya Akademi, Delhi, 2000.

'Can It Be?', Manmohan Ghose, *Songs of Love and Death*, ed. Lawrence Binyon, Basil Blackwell Oxford, 1924.

'Lament of Old Age', Mirza Asadullah Khan Ghalib (1713–80), trans.

Khushwant Singh, *Celebrating the Best of Urdu Poetry*, ed. Khushwant Singh and Kamna Prasad, PBI, Delhi, 2007.

Section titles

'What then shall poetry be about?', Sunil Gangopadhyay, from 'City of Memories'.

'In your gracious garden', Sarojini Naidu, from 'The Bird Sanctuary'.

'Are you looking for a god?', Arun Kolatkar, from 'Yeshwant Rao'.

'I'm ever vigilant', Attoor Ravi Varma, from 'Sitting'.

'My heart's own love', Anon, from 'The Ballad of Laila'.

'The broom's the limit', Cantirakanti, from 'Wanted: A Broom'.

'The sky between us', G.S. Sivarudrappa, from 'My Pocket'.

'River of blood', Sarla Das, from the Mahabharata.

'Sleep on your left side', Arvind Krishna Mehrotra, from 'Bhojpuri Descant'.

'Light like Ash', C.P. Surendran, from 'The Colours of the Season's Best Dream'.